중·고등 영어도 역시 **1위 해커스**다.

해커스북 중·고등

HackersBook.com

기출로 적중 해커스

고등영문법이 특별한 이유!

기출 분석으로 완벽히 적중시키니까!

1 고교 내신·수능·학력평가
기출문제 빅데이터
철저히 분석 및 반영

2 최신 개정 교과서의
핵심 문법 포인트
빠짐없이 반영

어떤 문제에도 적용할 수 있는 **진짜 내 실력**이 되니까!

3 내신형 객관식·서술형 문제와
수능형 문제로
내신 및 수능 완벽 대비

4 서술형 대비 영작 워크시트 및
다양한 부가 학습 자료로
흔들림 없는 실력 완성

이 책을 검토해주신 선생님들

경기
강민정	김진성의 열정어학원
김성재	스윗스터디학원
김성철	코코스영어학원
김주은	김주은어학원
원다혜	IMI영어학원
최지영	다른영어학원
최희정	SJ클쌤영어

서울
양세희	양세희수능영어학원
윤승완	윤승완영어학원
편영우	자이언학원

부산
방주은	마스터잉글리시학원
이지현	7번방의 기적 영어학원

해커스 어학연구소 자문위원단 3기

강원
박정선	잉글리쉬클럽
최현주	최쌤영어

경기
강민정	YLP김진성열정어학원
강상훈	평촌RTS학원
강지인	강지인영어학원
권계미	A&T+ 영어
김미아	김쌤영어학원
김설화	업라이트잉글리쉬
김성재	스윗스터디학원
김세훈	모두의학원
김수아	더스터디(The STUDY)
김영아	백송고등학교
김유경	벨트어학원
김유경	포시즌스어학원
김유동	이스턴영어학원
김지숙	위디벨럽학원
김지현	이지프레임영어학원
김해빈	해빛영어학원
김현지	지앤비영어학원
박가영	한민고등학교
박영서	스윗스터디학원
박은별	더킹영수학원
박재홍	록키어학원
성승민	SDH어학원 불당캠퍼스
신소연	Ashley English
오귀연	루나영어학원
유신애	에듀포커스학원
윤소정	ILP이화학원
이동진	이룸학원
이상미	버밍엄영어교습소
이연경	명품M비욘드수학영어학원
이은수	광주세종학원
이지혜	리케이온
이진희	이엠원영수학원
이충기	영어나무
이효명	갈매리드앤톡영어독서학원
임한글	Apsun앞선영어학원
장광명	엠케이영어학원
전상호	평촌이지어학원
정선영	코어플러스영어학원
정준	고양외국어고등학교
조연아	카이트학원
채기림	고려대학교티에영어학원
최지영	다른영어학원
최한나	석사영수전문
최희정	SJ클쌤영어학원
현지환	모두의학원
홍태경	공감국어영어전문학원

경남
강다훤	더(the)오르다영어학원
라승희	아이작잉글리쉬
박주언	유니크학원
배송현	두잇영어교습소
안윤서	어썸영어학원
임진희	어썸영어학원

경북
권현민	삼성영어석적우방교실
김으뜸	EIE영어학원 옥계캠퍼스
배세왕	비케이영수전문고등관학원
유영선	아이비티어학원

광주
김유희	김유희영어학원
서희연	SDL영어수학학원
송승연	송승연영수학원
오진우	SLT어학원수학원
정영철	정영철영어전문학원
최경옥	봉선중학교

대구
권익재	제이슨영어
김명일	독학인학원
김보곤	베스트영어
김연정	달서고등학교
김혜란	김혜란영어학원
문애주	프렌즈입시학원
박정근	공부의힘pnk학원
박희숙	열공열강영어수학학원
신동기	신통외국어학원
위영선	위영선영어학원
윤창원	공터영어학원 상인센터
이승현	학문당입시학원
이주현	이주현영어학원
이헌욱	이헌욱영어학원
장준현	장쌤독해종결영어학원
최윤정	최강영어학원

대전
곽선영	위드유학원
김지운	더포스둔산학원
박미현	라시움영어대동학원
박세리	EM101학원

부산
김건희	레지나잉글리쉬 영어학원
김미나	위드중고등영어학원
박수진	정모클영어국어학원
박수진	지니잉글리쉬
박인숙	리더스영어전문학원
옥지윤	더센텀영어학원
윤진희	위니드영어전문교습소
이종혁	대동학원
정혜인	엠티엔영어학원
조정래	알파카의영어농장
주태양	솔라영어학원

서울
Erica Sull	하버드브레인영어학원
강고은	케이앤학원
강신아	교우학원
공현미	이은재어학원
권영진	경동고등학교
김나영	프라임클래스영어학원
김달수	대일외국어고등학교
김대니	채움학원
김문영	창문여자고등학교
김정은	강북뉴스터디학원
김혜경	대동세무고등학교
남혜원	함영원입시전문학원
노시은	케이앤학원
박선정	강북세일학원
박수진	이은재어학원
박지수	이플러스영수학원
서승희	함영원입시전문학원
양세희	양세희수능영어학원
우정용	제임스영어앤드학원
이박원	이박원어학원
이승혜	스텔라영어
이정욱	이은재어학원
이지연	중계케이트영어학원
임예찬	학습컨설턴트
장지희	고려대학교사범대학부속고등학교
정미라	미라정영어학원
조민규	조민규영어
채가희	대성세그루영수학원

울산
김기태	그라티아어학원
이민주	로이아카데미
홍영민	더이안영어전문학원

인천
강재민	스터디위드제이쌤
고현순	정상학원
권효진	Genie's English
김솔	전문과외
김정아	밀턴영어학원
서상천	최정서학원
이윤주	트리플워
최예영	영웅아카데미

전남
강희진	강희진영어학원
김두환	해남맨체스터영수학원
송승연	송승연영수학원
윤세광	비상구영어학원

전북
김길자	맨투맨학원
김미영	링크영어학원
김효성	연세입시학원
노빈나	노빈나영어전문학원
라성남	하포드어학원
박재훈	위니드수학지앤비영어학원
박향숙	STA영어전문학원
서종원	서종원영어학원
이상훈	나는학원
장지원	링컨더글라스학원
지근영	한솔영어수학학원
최성령	연세입시학원
최혜영	이든영어수학학원

제주
김랑	KLS어학원
박자은	KLS어학원

충남
김예지	더배움프라임영수학원
김철홍	청경학원
노태겸	최상위학원

충북
라은경	이화윤스영어교습소
신유정	비타민영어클리닉학원

기출에서 찾은 점수 상승의 기적!

기출로 적중 해커스 고등영문법

 해커스 어학연구소

기출로 적중 해커스 고등영문법

목차

목차

구성 미리 보기

◎ 시험에 나온, 또 나올 **기출 적중 POINT**

정답 p.2

기출 적중 POINT

최신 개정 교과서와 내신 및 수능·학력평가 기출문제 빅데이터에서 뽑아낸 문법 포인트를 빠짐없이 학습할 수 있습니다.

기출로적중 POINT 1
1형식과 2형식

1. 1형식 문장은 「주어 + 동사」의 형태이다.

Her birthday party **began** at 6 P.M. on Saturday.
I **went** *to the mall* yesterday to buy a pair of shoes.
　↳ 완전한 문장을 만드는 데 반드시 부사(구)가 필요한 1형식 동사: be, go, live, stay, stand, lie 등

TIP 「There + be동사」는 1형식 문장이며, be동사 뒤에 오는 명사가 주어이다.
There are *many people* in the concert hall.

2. 2형식 문장은 「주어 + 동사 + 주격 보어」의 형태로, 주격 보어 자리에는 명사나 형용사가 올 수 있다. 단, 감각동사의 주격 보어 자리에는 형용사만 온다.

Barack Obama **became** *the president* in 2009.
The beach in front of the hotel **smells** *unpleasant*.

TIP 자주 쓰이는 2형식 동사

상태(~이다, ~하다)	be, stay, keep, remain 등
변화(~이 되다, ~하게 되다)	become, get, turn, grow, go 등
판단(~인 것 같다)	seem, appear 등
감각	look, sound, smell, taste, feel

핵심 문법 사항

명쾌한 설명과 예문을 통해 내신 및 수능 대비에 꼭 필요한 문법 사항을 정확하게 이해할 수 있습니다.

연습문제

다양한 유형의 연습문제를 통해 문법 내용을 암기하지 않고도 자연스럽게 이해할 수 있습니다.

[1-4] 다음 문장의 동사에는 동그라미를 치고, 주격 보어가 있는 경우 주격 보어에는 밑줄을 치시오.

1 A blue whale is the biggest animal in the world.

2 The rich man once lived in a luxurious mansion.

3 Cindy could not stay calm when she watched the scary movie. <수능 응용>

4 There are a few possible theories about the origin of the universe. <학평 응용>

[5-8] 괄호 안에서 알맞은 것을 고르시오.

5 You can train your brain to become (confident / confidently). <학평 응용>

6 Because the situation turned (badly / bad), we had to minimize the living expenses.

7 The restaurant's customers said that the soup tasted (bitterly / bitter).

8 The athlete appeared (hopeful / hopefully) about winning a gold medal.

9 다음 글에서 어법상 틀린 부분을 찾아 쓰고 바르게 고쳐 쓰시오.

> Some people feel comfortably when they socialize online, not face to face. They seem active in the virtual world but are rather shy in the real world.

_____ → _____

체계적으로 시작하는
기초 문법

고등영문법을 학습하기 위해 꼭 알아야 하는 기초 문법이 정리되어 있어, 문법 실력이 부족한 학생들도 기초를 탄탄히 다지고 체계적으로 학습할 수 있습니다.

기초 문법

1. 품사

영어 단어는 기능과 성격에 따라 명사, 대명사, 동사, 형용사, 부사, 전치사, 접속사, 감탄사로 분류할 수 있으며, 이를 품사라고 한다.

1 명사

사람, 사물, 장소, 개념 등의 이름을 나타내는 말로, 문장에서 주어, 목적어, 보어 역할을 한다.

Thomas Newcomen invented the first steam engine. <주어>
She usually has **bread** in the morning. <목적어>
The church became a **shelter** for the refugees. <보어>

2 대명사

명사를 대신해서 쓰는 말로, 문장에서 주어, 목적어, 보어 역할을 한다.

Michael is very diligent. **He** always gets up early. <주어>
The box is too small to use. Do you have **another**? <목적어>
There was a pen on the table. It was **mine**. <보어>

빈출 포인트가 한눈에 보이는
최근 7개년 출제 경향

철저히 분석한 고등학교 내신 및 수능·학력평가의 출제 경향이 모든 챕터에 정리되어 있어, 각 문법 포인트 별 시험 출제 경향과 중요도를 한눈에 확인할 수 있습니다.

2	3형식과 4형식
3	5형식: 명사/형용사/to부정사를 목적격 보어로 쓰는 동사
4	5형식: 사역동사와 지각동사

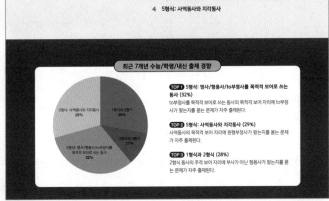

최근 7개년 수능/학평/내신 출제 경향

TOP 1 5형식: 명사/형용사/to부정사를 목적격 보어로 쓰는 동사 (32%)
to부정사를 목적격 보어로 쓰는 동사의 목적격 보어 자리에 to부정사가 오는지를 묻는 문제가 자주 출제된다.

TOP 2 5형식: 사역동사와 지각동사 (29%)
사역동사의 목적격 보어 자리에 원형부정사가 오는지를 묻는 문제가 자주 출제된다.

TOP 3 1형식과 2형식 (28%)
2형식 동사의 주격 보어 자리에 부사가 아닌 형용사가 오는지를 묻는 문제가 자주 출제된다.

정답 적중률을 높이는
Review Test

내신·수능·학력평가 기출문제의 빈출 유형과 출제 포인트가 반영된 객관식 및 주관식 문제를 풀어보며 실제 시험에서의 정답 적중률을 높일 수 있습니다.

Review Test

[1-4] 다음 빈칸에 들어갈 말이 순서대로 짝지어진 것을 고르시오. (X는 필요 없음을 의미함)

1

· Jenna kept _____ about her final grade.
· Signing a contract makes the purchase of a property _____.

① quiet – official
② quietly – official
③ quiet – officially
④ quietly – officially
⑤ to be quiet – officially

2

· A Siberian Husky is a type of dog that closely resembles _____ a wolf.
· The bank will lend money _____ Mr. Lewis.

[5-6] 다음 중 어법상 틀린 것을 고르시오.

5

① A cup of coffee helps me stay awake. <학평 응용>
② The mountain climbers could feel the air temperature to drop.
③ They got the soccer match postponed because of the bad weather.
④ Some people have their pets sleep on the bed.
⑤ The taxi driver asked Jenny to fasten the seatbelt.

6

① All of the planets in the solar system travel around the Sun.
② David's watch looks very expensive.

기초 문법

1. 품사

영어 단어는 기능과 성격에 따라 명사, 대명사, 동사, 형용사, 부사, 전치사, 접속사, 감탄사로 분류할 수 있으며, 이를 품사라고 한다.

1 명사

사람, 사물, 장소, 개념 등의 이름을 나타내는 말로, 문장에서 주어, 목적어, 보어 역할을 한다.

Thomas Newcomen invented the first steam engine. <주어>

She usually has **bread** in the morning. <목적어>

The church became a **shelter** for the refugees. <보어>

2 대명사

명사를 대신해서 쓰는 말로, 문장에서 주어, 목적어, 보어 역할을 한다.

Michael is very diligent. **He** always gets up early. <주어>

The box is too small to use. Do you have **another**? <목적어>

There was a pen on the table. It was **mine**. <보어>

3 동사

사람, 동물, 사물 등의 상태를 서술하거나 행위나 동작을 나타내는 말로, be동사, 일반동사, 조동사가 있다.

My house **is** close to my workplace.

The teacher **explained** the mathematical equation.

A giraffe **can reach** the leaves at the top of trees.

※ 동사의 형태가 변하여 동사가 아닌 명사, 형용사, 부사 등의 역할을 하는 것을 준동사라고 하며, 준동사에는 to부정사, 동명사, 분사가 있다.

Thank you for **inviting** me to your party.

We heard the **surprising** news yesterday.

He goes to the library **to borrow** some books.

4 형용사

명사의 형태, 성질, 상태 등을 나타내는 말로, 문장에서 명사를 꾸미는 수식어 또는 주어나 목적어를 보충 설명하는 보어 역할을 한다.

She delivered an **excellent** *performance*. <명사 수식>

The sky turned **dark** before the storm. <주격 보어>

Technology makes *our lives* **convenient**. <목적격 보어>

5 부사

동사, 형용사, 다른 부사, 또는 문장 전체를 꾸미는 말로, 문장에서 수식어 역할을 한다.

The plane *landed* **safely** in spite of the heavy fog. <동사 수식>

Fresh vegetables are **easily** *available* at the local market. <형용사 수식>

The man returned home **very** *late* at night. <부사 수식>

Luckily, *he could buy the last product*. <문장 전체 수식>

6 전치사

명사(구) 앞에서 시간, 장소, 방법 등을 나타내는 말로, 명사(구)와 함께 형용사나 부사 역할을 한다.

I turned on *the lamp* **beside** my bed.

My brother always *plays soccer* **on** Saturday.

7 접속사

어떤 것을 다른 것에 연결하는 말로, 단어와 단어, 구와 구, 절과 절을 대등하게 연결하는 **등위접속사**와 하나의 절을 다른 절에 종속시키는 **종속접속사**가 있다.

Most plants need *water* **and** *sunlight* to grow properly.

We saw many works of art **when** *we visited the National Gallery*.

8 감탄사

기쁨, 놀람, 슬픔과 같은 다양한 감정을 표현하는 말이다.

Bravo! Our team finally won the game.

Oops, I left my umbrella on the bus.

2. 구와 절

두 개 이상의 단어가 모여 하나의 품사 역할을 하는 덩어리를 **구**나 **절**이라고 한다.

1 구

「주어 + 동사」를 포함하지 않은 덩어리로, **명사구**, **형용사구**, **부사구**가 있다.

ⓐ **명사구**: 명사처럼 주어, 목적어, 보어 역할을 한다. to부정사구, 동명사구, 「의문사 + to부정사」 등이 명사구에 속한다.

To keep a diary every day is not an easy habit.

The policymakers consider **reducing the use of plastic**.

ⓑ **형용사구**: 형용사처럼 명사를 꾸미는 수식어 또는 주어나 목적어를 보충 설명하는 보어 역할을 한다. 「전치사 + 명사(구)」, to부정사구, 분사구 등이 형용사구에 속한다.

The main purpose **of our foundation** is to prevent poverty.

This TV show seems **more interesting** than the one we watched yesterday.

ⓒ **부사구**: 부사처럼 명사 이외의 것을 꾸미면서 '언제/어디에서/왜' 등의 부가적인 정보를 제공하는 수식어 역할을 한다. 「전치사 + 명사(구)」, to부정사구, 분사구문 등이 부사구에 속한다.

The baby *made a mess* **in the living room**.

Watching scary movies, *he always sweats a lot*.

2 절

「주어 + 동사」를 포함한 덩어리로 **등위절**과 **종속절**이 있으며, 종속절은 **명사절**, **형용사절**, **부사절**로 나뉜다.

ⓐ **등위절**: 등위접속사로 대등하게 연결된 절을 가리킨다.

I bought some ingredients, and **my mom cooked dinner**.

ⓑ **종속절**: 종속접속사나 관계사로 연결되어, 다른 절의 주어/목적어/보어/수식어 등의 역할을 하는 절을 가리킨다.

· **명사절**: 명사처럼 주어, 목적어, 보어 역할을 하는 절로, that/what 등의 명사절 접속사가 이끄는 절을 가리킨다.

They knew **that the rumor was not true**.

· **형용사절**: 형용사처럼 앞에 있는 명사인 선행사를 꾸미는 절로, who/which/that/where 등의 관계사가 이끌기 때문에 관계절이라고도 불린다.

Lisa really hates to wear *perfumes* **that smell flowery**.

Tell me *the reason* **why he was absent yesterday**.

· **부사절**: 부사처럼 명사 이외의 것을 꾸미면서 '언제/왜' 등의 부가적인 정보를 제공하는 절로, when/while/because/if 등의 부사절 접속사가 이끄는 절을 가리킨다.

If you are afraid of heights, *you shouldn't look down now*.

3. 문장 성분

하나의 문장을 구성하는 요소들을 **문장 성분**이라고 한다. 문장 성분에는 필수 성분인 주어, 동사, 목적어, 보어와, 필수 성분은 아니지만 내용이 더 풍부해지도록 부가적인 정보를 제공하는 수식어가 있다.

1 주어

문장의 주체를 가리키며, 명사 역할을 하는 것들이 주어 자리에 올 수 있다.

The doctor was concerned because **his patient** showed little improvement.

Taking a vacation can provide relief from everyday stresses.

2 동사

주어의 상태나 행위를 나타내는 말이다.

The company's sales **have declined** since 2018.

Jeremy **speaks** Korean as fluently as native speakers.

3 목적어

동사가 나타내는 상태나 행위의 대상을 가리키며, 명사 역할을 하는 것들이 목적어 자리에 올 수 있다.

Studies showed **that yogurt is good for health**.

You must take off **your shoes** before you enter **someone's home**.

4 보어

동사만으로는 주어나 목적어에 대한 설명이 불완전할 때 주어나 목적어를 보충 설명하는 말이다. 명사나 형용사 역할을 하는 것들이 보어 자리에 올 수 있다.

My dream was **to become a pianist**.

She found *the dog* **sleeping under the tree**.

5 수식어

문장에 부가적인 정보를 제공하는 말이다. 형용사나 부사 역할을 하는 것들이 수식어 자리에 올 수 있다.

Dishes **which taste spicy** have peppers in them.

Online classes helped me to *learn Spanish* **quickly**.

해커스북 중·고등

www.HackersBook.com

CHAPTER 1
문장의 형식

기출로 적중 POINT

최근 7개년 수능/학평/내신 출제 경향

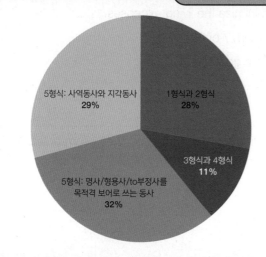

5형식: 사역동사와 지각동사
29%

1형식과 2형식
28%

3형식과 4형식
11%

5형식: 명사/형용사/to부정사를
목적격 보어로 쓰는 동사
32%

TOP 1 5형식: 명사/형용사/to부정사를 목적격 보어로 쓰는 동사 (32%)

to부정사를 목적격 보어로 쓰는 동사의 목적격 보어 자리에 to부정사가 왔는지를 묻는 문제가 자주 출제된다.

TOP 2 5형식: 사역동사와 지각동사 (29%)

사역동사의 목적격 보어 자리에 원형부정사가 왔는지를 묻는 문제가 자주 출제된다.

TOP 3 1형식과 2형식 (28%)

2형식 동사의 주격 보어 자리에 부사가 아닌 형용사가 왔는지를 묻는 문제가 자주 출제된다.

1. 1형식 문장은 「주어 + 동사」의 형태이다.

Her birthday party **began** at 6 P.M. on Saturday.

I **went** *to the mall* yesterday to buy a pair of shoes.
> 완전한 문장을 만드는 데 반드시 부사(구)가 필요한 1형식 동사: be, go, live, stay, stand, lie 등

TIP 「There + be동사」는 1형식 문장이며, be동사 뒤에 오는 명사가 주어이다.
There are *many people* in the concert hall.

2. 2형식 문장은 「주어 + 동사 + 주격 보어」의 형태로, 주격 보어 자리에는 명사나 형용사가 올 수 있다. 단, 감각동사의 주격 보어 자리에는 형용사만 온다.

Barack Obama **became** *the president* in 2009.

The beach in front of the hotel **smells** *unpleasant*.

TIP 자주 쓰이는 2형식 동사

상태(~이다, ~하다)	be, stay, keep, remain 등
변화(~이 되다, ~하게 되다)	become, get, turn, grow, go 등
판단(~인 것 같다)	seem, appear 등
감각	look, sound, smell, taste, feel

[1-4] 다음 문장의 동사에는 동그라미를 치고, 주격 보어가 있는 경우 주격 보어에는 밑줄을 치시오.

1 A blue whale is the biggest animal in the world.

2 The rich man once lived in a luxurious mansion.

3 Cindy could not stay calm when she watched the scary movie. <수능 응용>

4 There are a few possible theories about the origin of the universe. <학평 응용>

[5-8] 괄호 안에서 알맞은 것을 고르시오.

5 You can train your brain to become (confident / confidently). <학평 응용>

6 Because the situation turned (badly / bad), we had to minimize the living expenses.

7 The restaurant's customers said that the soup tasted (bitterly / bitter).

8 The athlete appeared (hopeful / hopefully) about winning a gold medal.

9 다음 글에서 어법상 틀린 부분을 찾아 쓰고 바르게 고쳐 쓰시오.

> Some people feel comfortably when they socialize online, not face to face. They seem active in the virtual world but are rather shy in the real world.

_____ → _____

POINT 2 3형식과 4형식

정답 p.2

1. 3형식 문장은 「주어 + 동사 + 목적어」의 형태로, 목적어 자리에는 명사가 올 수 있다.

The explorer **found** *an ancient temple* in the Amazon Rainforest.

> TIP 전치사 없이 바로 목적어를 가지는 동사: explain, discuss, mention, marry, resemble, reach, enter, attend, approach, answer 등
> We will (~~approach to~~, **approach**) *offline advertising* differently. <학평 응용>

2. 4형식 문장은 「주어 + 동사 + 간접 목적어(…에게) + 직접 목적어(~을)」의 형태이며, 4형식 문장의 동사를 수여동사라고 한다.

He **bought** *his staff members pizza* on Friday afternoon.

> TIP 4형식 문장은 「주어 + 동사 + 직접 목적어 + to/for/of + 간접 목적어」 형태의 3형식 문장으로 바꿔 쓸 수 있다.
> He **bought** *pizza* **for** *his staff members* on Friday afternoon.

[1-4] 우리말과 같도록 괄호 안의 말을 알맞게 배열하시오.

1 Jake는 다음 일요일에 교회에서 Rhonda와 결혼할 것이다. (Rhonda, will marry)

= Jake _____ at a church next Sunday.

2 그 여자는 버스에 탑승하면서 기사에게 그녀의 표를 줬다. (gave, her ticket, the driver)

= The woman _____ as she boarded the bus.

3 그 자선 단체는 여러 나라에서 어려움에 처한 가족들에게 집을 지어준다. (homes, families in need, builds)

= The charity _____ in several countries.

4 인간은 1969년에 처음으로 달의 표면에 도달했다. (the surface of the moon, reached)

= Humans first _____ in 1969.

[5-9] 괄호 안의 말을 활용하여 다음 4형식 문장을 3형식 문장으로 바꿔 쓰시오.

5 The real estate agent found me an affordable apartment. (for)

→ The real estate agent _____.

6 She brought the prince a bunch of grapes. (to)

→ She _____. <학평 응용>

7 Flight attendants offered the passengers cold beverages. (to)

→ Flight attendants _____.

8 The manager asked the applicant many questions during the interview. (of)

→ The manager _____ during the interview.

9 Healthy foods give us more energy and prevent us from getting sick. (to)

→ Healthy foods _____ and prevent us from getting sick.

<학평 응용>

1. 5형식 문장은 「주어 + 동사 + 목적어 + 목적격 보어」의 형태로, 동사에 따라 목적격 보어 자리에 오는 것이 달라진다. 다음 동사의 목적격 보어 자리에는 명사나 형용사가 온다.

call	make	keep	find	think	consider	leave	name	elect

The company **made** me *a marketing manager* last week.
Some students **found** the history assignment so *difficult*.

2. 다음 동사의 목적격 보어 자리에는 to부정사가 온다.

want	ask	tell	cause	order	persuade
allow	force	advise	encourage	expect	enable

The security guard **asked** the man *to open* his briefcase.
Sign language **enables** deaf individuals *to communicate* easily.

[1-3] 괄호 안에서 알맞은 것을 고르시오.

1 They told him (to keep / keep) his eyes closed. <수능 응용>

2 What makes our modern society so (competitively / competitive)? <학평>

3 We expect snow (falling / to fall) heavily throughout the area this afternoon.

[4-8] 우리말과 같도록 괄호 안의 말을 활용하여 문장을 완성하시오.

4 그는 학생들이 도서관에 있는 오래된 신문을 읽는 것을 허락했다. (read, the students, allowed)
= He _____ old newspapers in the library. <학평 응용>

5 생물학자들은 북극곰이 사람들에게 극도로 위험하다고 생각한다. (polar bears, consider, extremely dangerous)
= Biologists _____ to people.

6 의사는 그 환자가 증상의 어떤 변화라도 보고하기를 원한다. (wants, report, the patient)
= The doctor _____ any change in the symptoms.

7 Sam과 Anne은 한 달이 넘는 동안 그들의 관계를 비밀로 유지했다. (their relationship, kept, a secret)
= Sam and Anne _____ for over a month.

8 온실 가스의 방출은 지구의 온도가 올라가게 한다. (causes, rise, global temperatures)
= The release of greenhouse gases _____ .

9 다음 글에서 어법상 틀린 부분을 찾아 쓰고 바르게 고쳐 쓰시오.

> Kyle found his old neighbors very inconsiderate. He asked them to stop making noise late at night, but they continued to do this. The situation forced him look for a new apartment.

_____ → _____

5형식: 사역동사와 지각동사

1. 사역동사 make, have, let의 목적격 보어 자리에는 원형부정사가 온다.

My brother **made** me *wash* the dishes on Wednesday.

2. 준사역동사 help의 목적격 보어 자리에는 to부정사와 원형부정사가 모두 올 수 있고, get의 목적격 보어 자리에는 to부정사만 온다.

The program will **help** the teachers (*to*) *conduct* successful classes. <수능 응용>
The lady **got** the technician *to repair* her computer.

3. 지각동사의 목적격 보어 자리에는 원형부정사나 V-ing형이 오며, V-ing형이 오면 동작이 진행 중인 것이 강조된다.

see	watch	look at	observe	notice	hear	listen to	smell	feel

I'm so eager to **see** him *sing*[*singing*] in person. <수능>

> TIP (준)사역동사와 지각동사의 목적어와 목적격 보어의 관계가 수동이면 목적격 보어 자리에 과거분사가 온다.
> The scientist **got** his experiment results *confirmed* by a colleague.

[1-10] 괄호 안에서 알맞은 것을 <u>모두</u> 고르시오.

1 Why don't you help me (pick / to pick) up the trash? <수능 응용>

2 The lawyer had the client (to sign / sign) the lease agreement.

3 This essay is interesting and gets people (to think / think). <학평 응용>

4 Let me (to take / take) care of your tomatoes while you're away. <수능>

5 I could hear the rain (fall / falling) through my bedroom window.

6 An owl's excellent night vision helps it (locate / locating) prey.

7 It is not always easy to get work (to finish / finished) on time. <수능 응용>

8 The basketball team's coach made the players (practice / practicing) for five hours.

9 Marie noticed Nina (to fix / fixing) her eyes on the last piece of the cake. <수능 응용>

10 Some children were watching the clown (making / make) balloon animals.

11 다음 글에서 어법상 <u>틀린</u> 부분을 찾아 쓰고 바르게 고쳐 쓰시오.

> Derek's mother let him adopting a lizard. She thought that owning a pet would help him to become more responsible. For the first few weeks, she observed him caring for the lizard to make sure that he didn't make any mistakes.

_____ → _____

Review Test

[1-4] 다음 빈칸에 들어갈 말이 순서대로 짝지어진 것을 고르시오. (X는 필요 없음을 의미함)

1

· Jenna kept _____ about her final grade.
· Signing a contract makes the purchase of a property _____.

① quiet – official
② quietly – official
③ quiet – officially
④ quietly – officially
⑤ to be quiet – officially

2

· A Siberian Husky is a type of dog that closely resembles _____ a wolf.
· The bank will lend money _____ Mr. Lewis.

① X – X
② X – to
③ with – X
④ with – to
⑤ to – to

3

· The general ordered the army _____.
· Some fast-food restaurants have their workers _____ a uniform.

① advance – wear
② advance – to wear
③ advance – wearing
④ to advance – to wear
⑤ to advance – wear

4

· Michael got Sarah _____ him the picture.
· Customers find the atmosphere of the Coastal Resort _____.

① show – comfortably
② to show – comfortably
③ show – comfortable
④ to show – comfortable
⑤ showing – comfortable

[5-6] 다음 중 어법상 틀린 것을 고르시오.

5

① A cup of coffee helps me stay awake. <학평 응용>
② The mountain climbers could feel the air temperature to drop.
③ They got the soccer match postponed because of the bad weather.
④ Some people have their pets sleep on the bed.
⑤ The taxi driver asked Jenny to fasten the seatbelt.

6

① All of the planets in the solar system travel around the Sun.
② David's watch looks very expensive.
③ The serious traffic accident left Mr. Connor gloomily.
④ Her classmates called Crystal a genius when she solved the problem.
⑤ There is enough time to see the art exhibits.

7 다음 중 어법상 바른 것끼리 묶인 것은?

ⓐ Many parents let their kids to own a cell phone.
ⓑ A long vacation helped us to relax after a stressful year.
ⓒ We observed deer running through the forest.
ⓓ My father advised me save a portion of my monthly allowance.
ⓔ The speaker kept the conference attendees interested by telling jokes.

① ⓐ, ⓑ
② ⓐ, ⓒ
③ ⓑ, ⓓ
④ ⓑ, ⓒ, ⓔ
⑤ ⓒ, ⓓ, ⓔ

[8-9] 다음 문장에서 어법상 <u>틀린</u> 부분을 찾아 쓰고 바르게 고쳐 쓰시오.

8

> Preparing every meal helped me developed my cooking skills.

_____ → _____

9

> My grandfather told me keeping my mouth closed while chewing food.

_____ → _____

10 다음 문장에서 어법상 <u>틀린</u> 부분을 바르게 고쳐 완전한 문장을 쓰시오.

> The tour guide got Carl for a dance performance ticket.

→ _____ .

→ _____ .

11 다음 글에서 어법상 <u>틀린</u> 부분을 찾아 쓰고 바르게 고쳐 쓰시오.

> The lion silently approached to the zebra near the river. However, the zebra heard something moving around it.

_____ → _____

[12-14] 우리말과 같도록 괄호 안의 말을 알맞게 배열하시오.

12

> 그 회계 소프트웨어에 많은 문제들이 있었다. (were, there, many problems)

= _____ with the accounting software.

13

> Luke는 Brenda에게 그의 오래된 자전거를 팔았다. (Brenda, Luke, his old bicycle, sold)

= _____ .

14

> Warren은 저녁 식사로 프라이드 치킨이 배달되게 했다. (a fried chicken, had, delivered, Warren)

= _____ for dinner.

[15-16] 우리말과 같도록 괄호 안의 말을 활용하여 문장을 완성하시오.

15

> 그녀는 내가 그녀의 노트북 컴퓨터를 빌리게 했다. (borrow, let, her laptop computer)

= _____ .

16

> 그 호텔은 투숙객들이 방에서 흡연하는 것을 허용하지 않는다. (smoke, the hotel, guests, allow)

= _____ in the rooms.

17 우리말과 같도록 주어진 <조건>에 맞게 문장을 완성하시오.

> 밤하늘은 과거 세대가 시간을 기록하고 달력을 만드는 것을 도왔다.

> <조건>
> 1. help, the night sky, keep, past generations를 활용하시오.
> 2. 8단어로 쓰시오.

= _____ track of time and create calendars. <학평>

[18-19] 다음 대화를 읽고 주어진 질문에 답하시오.

> A: Wade, you sound very ⓐ sadly. What's the matter?
> B: I can't go to the concert tonight because my father wants me ⓑ being home.
> A: But why? He must have ⓒ mentioned the reason.
> B: (A) 그는 어제 내가 차고를 청소하게 하셨어. (make, clean, the garage) However, he noticed boxes and other things ⓓ lying on the floor today.
> A: I don't want to see you ⓔ miss the concert. Let's clean up the garage together. Then he may change his mind.

18 위 대화의 밑줄 친 우리말 (A)와 같도록 괄호 안의 말을 활용하여 문장을 완성하시오.

= _____ yesterday.

19 위 대화의 밑줄 친 ⓐ~ⓔ 중 어법상 틀린 것의 기호를 쓰고 바르게 고쳐 쓰시오.

(1) _____ → _____
(2) _____ → _____

20 (A), (B), (C)의 각 네모 안에서 어법에 맞는 표현으로 가장 적절한 것은?

> One way to make a pursuer (A) work / working harder is to zigzag. For example, a rabbit running from a coyote moves quickly back and forth and forces the coyote (B) change / to change direction. Zigzagging is easier for the rabbit than for the larger coyote. The coyote also cannot tell whether the rabbit will run this way or that way, so it cannot plan its next move. As a result, the rabbit makes the chase more (C) difficult / difficultly for the coyote. Though a coyote may still succeed in catching its prey, there is a chance that it may tire out and go look for an easier meal. <학평 응용>
>
> *pursuer: 추적자, 추격자   **zigzag: 지그재그로 나아가다

	(A)	(B)	(C)
①	working	to change	difficultly
②	work	to change	difficult
③	work	to change	difficultly
④	work	change	difficult
⑤	working	change	difficultly

21 다음 글의 밑줄 친 부분 중, 어법상 틀린 것은?

> I was working at a nursing home. It was late in the evening when I finished, so I ran down the street to the bus stop. I enjoyed the ride home and watched my fellow passengers ① exit the bus at their stops. After a while, I was the only one left on the bus. As the bus ② reached my stop, the driver called out to me, "Where do you live?" I explained that I ③ lived just up the next street. Then, he let me ④ get off in front of my house. I felt so ⑤ gratefully for his kindness.
>
> <학평 응용>

CHAPTER 2

시제

기출로 적중 POINT

최근 7개년 수능/학평/내신 출제 경향

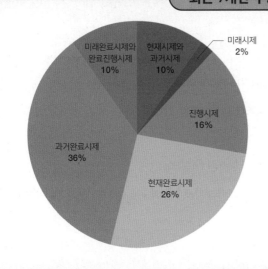

TOP 1 **과거완료시제 (36%)**
사건의 전후 관계를 파악하여 과거완료시제가 올바르게 쓰였는지를 묻는 문제가 자주 출제된다.

TOP 2 **현재완료시제 (26%)**
현재완료시제의 형태와 쓰임을 묻는 문제가 자주 출제된다.

TOP 3 **진행시제 (16%)**
진행시제의 형태와 쓰임을 묻는 문제가 자주 출제된다.

1. 현재시제는 현재의 사실이나 상태, 현재의 습관이나 반복되는 일, 일반적·과학적 사실을 나타낸다.

He **delivers** newspapers in the morning these days.
Penguins **live** in large groups for protection and warmth.

2. 과거시제는 과거의 동작이나 상태, 역사적 사실을 나타낸다.

She **moved** to a new city earlier this year.
Alexander Fleming **discovered** penicillin in 1928.

[1-7] 괄호 안에서 가장 알맞은 것을 고르시오.

1 Nowadays, he (rides / rode) the bus from home to work.

2 Beth (drinks / drank) coffee in the café with her dad two days ago.

3 The last King of France (rules / ruled) the country for around 18 years.

4 Salt water in the oceans (covers / covered) a majority of the earth's surface.

5 Coco Chanel (opens / opened) her first clothing store in Paris in 1910.

6 Your body (feels / felt) pain when it is in danger and is being overworked. <학평 응용>

7 The basketball team (wins / won) second place in the national competition last week.

[8-12] 괄호 안의 동사를 활용하여 빈칸에 쓰시오.

8 South Korea _____ the Winter Olympics in 2018. (host)

9 Asia _____ the continent with the largest population in the world. (be)

10 Tim _____ his lunch in the office at noon these days. (eat)

11 Chinese workers _____ the Great Wall after about 20 years of building. (complete)

12 Cheetahs _____ up to 70 miles per hour during a hunt. (run)

[13-17] <보기>의 동사를 한 번씩만 활용하여 빈칸에 쓰시오.

<보기>	elect	watch	play	become	paint

13 Currently, Ray _____ soccer with his friends on the weekends.

14 Leonardo da Vinci _____ the *Mona Lisa* between 1503 and 1519.

15 Jules _____ television before bed yesterday.

16 Voters _____ a president every four years in the United States.

17 East and West Germany _____ one country again after the fall of the Berlin Wall in 1989.

POINT 2 미래시제

정답 p.3

1. 미래시제는 미래의 일을 예측할 때 쓰며, 「will + 동사원형」이나 「be going to + 동사원형」의 형태이다.

I **will spend** time with my dog at the park.

Megan and her sister **are going to see** their relatives in Busan.

> TIP 주어의 의지나 말하는 시점에 결정된 미래의 일을 나타낼 때는 「will + 동사원형」을 쓰고, 예정된 미래의 일을 나타낼 때는 「be going to + 동사원형」을 쓴다.

2. 미래의 일을 나타내는 현재시제와 현재진행시제

❶ 현재시제는 확실히 정해진 시간표나 일정표 상의 일을 나타낼 수 있으며, 이때 가까운 미래를 나타내는 부사(구)가 주로 함께 쓰인다.

His flight from Los Angeles **lands** *at 3 P.M. today*.

❷ 시간이나 조건을 나타내는 부사절에서는 미래의 일을 나타낼 때 미래시제가 아닌 현재시제를 쓴다.

The criminal will stay in jail *until* his trial (~~will end~~, **ends**).

❸ 현재진행시제는 실현 가능성이 높은 가까운 미래의 일을 나타낼 수 있다.

The Prime Minister **is speaking** at the event later this week.

[1-4] 괄호 안의 말을 활용하여 다음 문장을 미래시제로 바꿔 쓰시오.

1 The weather is cold and rainy. (will)

→ _____ tomorrow.

2 Fans wait in line to purchase the new album. (be going to)

→ _____ tonight.

3 My family members gather for the holiday. (will)

→ _____ for the upcoming holiday.

4 She works as a swimming coach. (be going to)

→ _____ from next month. <학평 응용>

[5-11] 밑줄 친 부분이 어법상 맞으면 O를 쓰고, 틀리면 바르게 고쳐 쓰시오.

5 The play <u>begins</u> early tomorrow evening in the auditorium downtown. → _____

6 They will go to London after they <u>will receive</u> their new passports. → _____

7 Jessica <u>is taking</u> a math test this afternoon. → _____

8 The restaurant <u>will serve</u> the dish until their menu changes in spring. → _____

9 We <u>going to</u> see a parade at the theme park tomorrow. → _____

10 The customer <u>will ask</u> the manager for help with her laptop. → _____

11 I'll teach you how to ride a bike if you <u>will get</u> on the bike first. <학평 응용> → _____

1. 진행시제는 특정 시점에 진행되고 있는 동작을 나타낸다.

현재진행시제 am/is/are + V-ing	My sister **is shopping** at the mall now.
과거진행시제 was/were + V-ing	I **was exercising** at the gym yesterday afternoon.
미래진행시제 will be + V-ing	The performers **will be dancing** on the stage tonight.

2. 소유(have 등), 인식(think, know 등), 감정(love, hate 등), 감각(smell, taste 등) 등의 상태를 나타내는 동사는 진행형으로 쓸 수 없다.

They (~~are having~~, **have**) a beautiful garden at home.
Your drink (~~is smelling~~, **smells**) like vanilla and cinnamon.

[1-4] 우리말과 같도록 괄호 안의 동사를 활용하여 문장을 완성하시오.

1 그 의사는 병원에서 아픈 환자들을 치료하고 있다. (treat)

= The doctor _____ the sick patients at the hospital.

2 그 정치인들은 다음 달에 새로운 법안을 논의하고 있을 것이다. (discuss)

= The politicians _____ the new law next month.

3 우리는 비닐봉지와 같은 쓰레기로 바다를 오염시키고 있다. (pollute)

= We _____ the sea with trash such as plastic bags.

4 나는 교통 카메라의 플래시를 봤을 때 천천히 운전하고 있었다. (drive)

= I _____ slowly when I saw the flash of a traffic camera. <학평>

[5-8] 밑줄 친 부분이 어법상 맞으면 O를 쓰고, 틀리면 바르게 고쳐 쓰시오.

5 Joseph is hating crowded places like the mall. → _____

6 Linda is working on the second floor with her team now. → _____

7 The zookeepers are knowing lots of facts about animals. → _____

8 Michael was teaching science at high school last year. → _____

9 다음 글에서 어법상 틀린 부분을 찾아 쓰고 바르게 고쳐 쓰시오.

> Our family is packing for a trip to Australia. We will be traveling around the country next week. We are liking exploring new countries together during our vacation time.

_____ → _____

현재완료시제(have/has + p.p.)는 과거에 발생하여 현재까지 영향을 미치는 일을 나타내며, 완료, 경험, 계속, 결과의 의미로 쓰인다.

완료	Julie **has** *already* **arrived** at the hotel. TIP 함께 자주 쓰이는 표현: already, yet, just, lately, recently 등
경험	**Have** you *ever* **played** a sport for a school team? TIP 함께 자주 쓰이는 표현: before, once, ~ times, ever, never 등
계속	Marketers **have known** *for decades* that you buy what you see first. <학평> TIP 함께 자주 쓰이는 표현: for ~, since ~, how long ~? 등
결과	He **has forgotten** the password for his bank account.

TIP 현재완료시제는 특정 과거 시점을 나타내는 표현과 함께 쓸 수 없다.
The actor (~~has won~~, **won**) an award for his part in a popular movie *last year*.

[1-5] 괄호 안에서 알맞은 것을 고르시오.

1 Lisa (cared / has cared) for the animals in the shelter so far.

2 We (slept / have slept) in the tent at the campground two days ago.

3 The government (hasn't / didn't) announced a new rule about recycling yet.

4 She (gave up / has given up) music in the 1970s because she couldn't make a living. <학평 응용>

5 The tree planting event (took / has taken) place every year since 2002. <학평 응용>

[6-9] 우리말과 같도록 괄호 안의 말을 활용하여 빈칸에 쓰시오.

6 그 도시의 관광객 수는 겨울 이후로 증가해왔다. (increase)

= The number of tourists to the city _____ _____ since the winter.

7 쇼핑은 이미 여가 활동이 되었다. (already, become)

= Shopping _____ _____ _____ a leisure activity. <학평>

8 우리는 오늘 일찍 약간의 아이스크림을 사러 가게로 걸어갔다. (walk)

= We _____ to the store for some ice cream earlier today.

9 너는 이 방법으로 수학 문제를 풀어본 적이 있니? (ever, try)

= _____ _____ _____ _____ solving a math problem this way?

10 다음 글의 밑줄 친 ⓐ~ⓒ 중 어법상 틀린 것의 기호를 쓰고 바르게 고쳐 쓰시오.

> Some historians believe that Marco Polo ⓐ<u>brought</u> pasta to Italy after a trip to China in the 13th century. Italians ⓑ<u>used</u> pasta in many of their famous dishes since then. In addition, the popularity of the food ⓒ<u>has grown</u> in many other countries with globalization.

_____ → _____

과거완료시제(had + p.p.)는 특정 과거 시점 이전에 발생하여 그 과거 시점까지 영향을 미치는 일을 나타낸다.

The Second World War **had** already **started** when America joined. <완료>
The tourists **had tried** only a few tacos before they visited Mexico. <경험>
I **had surfed** for three hours until the weather became cloudy. <계속>
We couldn't drive any further because our car **had stopped** running. <결과>

TIP 「had + p.p.」는 과거에 발생한 두 개의 일 중 먼저 발생한 일을 나타내기 위해 쓰기도 하며, 이때 먼저 발생한 일을 대과거라고 한다.
Before we *went* to the swimming pool, we **had put** on sunscreen.

[1-5] 괄호 안에서 알맞은 것을 고르시오.

1 My dog (has / had) escaped from the yard when I got home.

2 John (uses / had used) his bike for over ten years until he sold it.

3 (Have / Had) you ever read the book before you met the author?

4 At present, the employees (have / had) worked from home for one year.

5 The CEO agreed that success (hasn't / hadn't) just happened to her by luck. <학평 응용>

[6-10] 우리말과 같도록 괄호 안의 말을 활용하여 완료시제 문장을 완성하시오.

6 그 커플은 결혼하기 전에 유치원 때부터 서로를 알아왔었다. (know)
= Before they got married, the couple ＿＿＿＿＿＿＿＿＿＿＿ each other since kindergarten.

7 나는 유람선 여행을 가기 전까지 고래를 본 적이 없었다. (see, never)
= I ＿＿＿＿＿＿＿＿＿＿＿ a whale until I went on the cruise.

8 우리는 사전에 표를 샀기 때문에 지금 그 콘서트에 갈 수 있다. (buy)
= We can go to the concert now because we ＿＿＿＿＿＿＿＿＿＿＿ tickets in advance.

9 그 등산객은 길을 찾기 전까지 몇 시간 동안 헤매왔었다. (wander)
= The hiker ＿＿＿＿＿＿＿＿＿＿＿ for hours until he found the path.

10 오늘 아침에 그녀의 알람이 울리기 전에 Kate는 이미 깼었다. (already, wake)
= Kate ＿＿＿＿＿＿＿＿＿＿＿ up before her alarm went off this morning.

---

11 (A), (B)의 각 네모 안에서 어법에 맞는 표현으로 가장 적절한 것을 고르시오.

The first human in space was Soviet cosmonaut Yuri Gagarin who was launched on April 12, 1961. However, Gagarin was not the first living thing that (A) has / had been in space. The United States and the Soviet Union (B) have / had sent many different species of animals prior to this.

*cosmonaut: (과거 러시아의) 우주 비행사

---

1. 미래완료시제(will have + p.p.)는 특정 미래 시점까지 완료되거나 계속될 일을 나타낸다.

By 8 o'clock tomorrow morning, the postal worker **will have delivered** the package.

Mike **will have lived** in Chicago for over three months this December.

2. 완료진행시제는 완료시제의 계속의 의미와 쓰임이 비슷하지만, 동작이 진행 중임을 강조한다.

현재완료진행시제 have/has been + V-ing	Why **has** he **been crying** in his room all day?
과거완료진행시제 had been + V-ing	Amy **had been painting** the wall before I called her.
미래완료진행시제 will have been + V-ing	When he turns 40, he **will have been working** as a firefighter for 15 years.

[1-4] 괄호 안에서 알맞은 것을 고르시오.

1 He (had recovered / will have recovered) from his illness next week.

2 I (have been / will have been) recording a video for three hours by 9 P.M.

3 The scientists (have been / had been) talking about their theories for over 30 minutes now.

4 She (has been / had been) practicing very hard, but she didn't seem to improve. <학평 응용>

[5-8] 다음 문장을 완료진행시제 문장으로 바꿔 쓰시오.

5 Rick began writing his paper four days ago. At this moment, he is still writing it.

→ Rick _____ his paper for four days.

6 I bought her a snack an hour after she had started crying.

→ She _____ for an hour when I bought her a snack.

7 The photographer started taking pictures five years ago. Next year will be his sixth year.

→ The photographer _____ pictures for six years next year.

8 They called him three days after he had started feeling nervous about the results.

→ He _____ nervous about the results for three days when they called him.

[9-12] 밑줄 친 부분이 어법상 맞으면 O를 쓰고, 틀리면 바르게 고쳐 쓰시오.

9 Until he found his job, he <u>has been</u> volunteering at the child care center. → _____

10 Helen <u>hasn't been</u> going to classes because she is sick with the flu. → _____

11 People <u>have invented</u> flying cars by the start of the next century. → _____

12 It <u>will have been</u> raining for four days in the city by tomorrow morning. → _____

Review Test

[1-4] 다음 빈칸에 들어갈 알맞은 것을 고르시오.

1

Google _____ its search engine in 2004.

① introduces
② introduced
③ will introduce
④ has introduced
⑤ had introduced

2

People _____ religions since the beginning of society.

① follow
② will follow
③ have followed
④ will have followed
⑤ was following

3

I _____ cleaning the house by the time you get back from the store.

① finish
② finished
③ was finishing
④ had finished
⑤ will have finished

4

The kids _____ holes at the beach for two hours when their parents called them over.

① are digging
② will be digging
③ have been digging
④ had been digging
⑤ will have been digging

5 다음 중 밑줄 친 부분이 어법상 바른 것은?

① At a younger age, the celebrity will be working at a convenience store.
② The artist painted that picture since 2018.
③ A person's ears and nose grow throughout their entire life.
④ My mom has baked cookies when I got home.
⑤ She had been serving food at the same restaurant for ten years next month.

6 다음 중 어법상 틀린 것은?

① The tennis competition ends on March 5.
② She will remain queen until she will give up her crown.
③ They will have moved all the furniture by tomorrow evening.
④ Karen hasn't replaced her old helmet with a new one yet.
⑤ The employees hadn't been using their printer correctly before it eventually broke.

7 다음 중 어법상 틀린 것끼리 묶인 것은?

ⓐ When she heard the news, Emily has been driving her car.
ⓑ I hadn't known about coding until I took the course.
ⓒ Andy is loving skiing during the winter every year.
ⓓ We have been learning new words since childhood. <학평 응용>
ⓔ They stayed in the mountains since summer.

① ⓐ, ⓑ, ⓒ
② ⓐ, ⓑ, ⓔ
③ ⓐ, ⓒ, ⓔ
④ ⓑ, ⓒ, ⓓ
⑤ ⓒ, ⓓ, ⓔ

[8-12] 다음 문장에서 어법상 **틀린** 부분을 찾아 쓰고 바르게 고쳐 쓰시오.

8

> The parents attended the school performances since the day their child entered school.

_____ → _____

9

> The possibility of us becoming happy will increase by 15 percent if someone we know will become happy. <학평 응용>

_____ → _____

10

> Selene has never met a person from Japan until she went on a business trip there.

_____ → _____

11

> The new dessert for this season is tasting like strawberries and cheese.

_____ → _____

12

> By the end of this year, we have been living with our cat for over ten years.

_____ → _____

[13-14] 우리말과 같도록 괄호 안의 말을 활용하여 완료시제 문장을 완성하시오.

13

> 영어 수업을 듣기 전에 그 학생은 이미 알파벳을 외웠었다. (memorize, already, the alphabet)

= The student _____
before taking English classes.

14

> 이야기하는 것을 마칠 때쯤이면 그들은 그 문제들을 해결했을 것이다. (the issues, resolve)

= They _____ by the time
they are done talking.

[15-16] 우리말과 같도록 괄호 안의 말을 활용하여 완료진행시제 문장을 완성하시오.

15

> 그는 1월 이후로 그 여행을 위해 돈을 모으고 있다. (money, save)

= He _____ for the trip
since January.

16

> Doris가 나의 집에 왔을 때 나는 두 시간 동안 책을 읽고 있었다. (read, a book)

= I _____ for two hours
when Doris came to my home.

17 우리말과 같도록 주어진 <조건>에 맞게 문장을 완성하시오.

> 그들이 그들의 첫 번째 앨범을 발매했을 때 Karl은 6년 동안 그 밴드를 이끌어왔었다.

> <조건>
> 1. the band, for, lead, six years를 활용하시오.
> 2. 8단어로 쓰시오.

= _____ when they released their first album.

[18-19] 다음 글을 읽고 주어진 질문에 답하시오.

> People ⓐ carried cell phones since the 1980s. Before they became a hit, (A) <u>모토로라의 엔지니어 Martin Cooper는 그 휴대폰을 개발했었다.</u> (the mobile phone, develop) He ⓑ had been inspired by a device used in *Star Trek* and made the first public cell phone call. Nowadays, people ⓒ depend on cell phones for much more than making phone calls. People ⓓ have been using them for text messaging, listening to music, and playing games. The technology ⓔ has advanced even more by the time 6G technology becomes available to the public in the future.

18 위 글의 밑줄 친 우리말 (A)와 같도록 괄호 안의 말을 활용하여 빈칸에 쓰시오.

= Motorola engineer Martin Cooper _____
_____ _____ _____ _____

19 위 글의 밑줄 친 ⓐ~ⓔ 중 어법상 틀린 것의 기호를 쓰고 바르게 고쳐 쓰시오.

(1) _____ → _____
(2) _____ → _____

20 (A), (B), (C)의 각 네모 안에서 어법에 맞는 표현으로 가장 적절한 것은?

> I (A) have / had just finished writing an essay when my computer stopped. In a panic, I called my friend Neil, a computer consultant. It turned out that I had a bad spyware, which had made my computer slower. I (B) became / have become better at taking care of my computer since then. We take our cars to the mechanic for regular checkups. But why do we expect our computers (C) run / to run normally without the same care?
> <학평 응용>
>
> *spyware: 스파이웨어(사용자 몰래 개인 정보를 수집하는 악성 소프트웨어)

	(A)	(B)	(C)
①	had	became	run
②	have	became	to run
③	had	have become	to run
④	have	have become	to run
⑤	had	have become	run

21 다음 글의 밑줄 친 부분 중, 어법상 틀린 것은?

> Last year, Green County Library ① decided to stay open until 8 P.M. every day. This was to make library services ② available to people for whom evening was the only convenient time to visit. However, visitor numbers ③ didn't show a strong demand for the later hours since the change. So I have to inform you that the hours of operation will return to normal, from 9 A.M. to 6 P.M. All normal library services will still be open if you ④ visit during those hours. Additionally, the shift will let Green County Library ⑤ improve services to the community. <학평 응용>

CHAPTER 3
조동사

기출로 적중 POINT

1 can, may

2 must, have to

3 should, ought to

4 used to, would

5 조동사 관용 표현

6 조동사 + have + p.p.

최근 7개년 수능/학평/내신 출제 경향

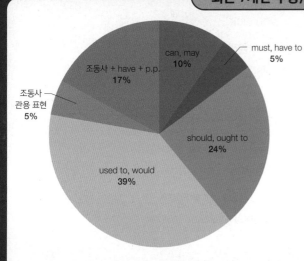

TOP 1 used to, would (39%)
조동사 used to, would의 의미와 쓰임 및 used to를 이용한 표현을 묻는 문제가 자주 출제된다.

TOP 2 should, ought to (24%)
제안, 주장 등을 나타내는 동사 뒤 that절의 동사 자리에 should가 생략되고 동사원형이 왔는지를 묻는 문제가 자주 출제된다.

TOP 3 조동사 + have + p.p. (17%)
「조동사 + have + p.p.」의 형태와 쓰임을 묻는 문제가 자주 출제된다.

can, may

1. can은 능력(~할 수 있다), 허가(~해도 된다), 요청(~해주겠니?), 가능성(~할 가능성이 있다)을 나타내며, 능력을 나타낼 때는 be able to로 바꿔 쓸 수 있다.

Cats **can**(= **are able to**) see well in the dark.
Eating too much junk food **can** cause health issues.

TIP ① 조동사는 두 개를 연속해서 쓸 수 없으므로, 다른 조동사 뒤에는 can 대신 be able to를 쓴다.
Everyone (~~will can~~, *will* **be able to**) participate in the event.

② could는 can의 과거형으로 쓰이거나, 더 정중한 허가나 요청 또는 약한 추측을 나타낸다.
Could you help me move some furniture tomorrow?
George **could** be in his room now.

2. may는 허가(~해도 된다)나 약한 추측(~일지도 모른다)을 나타낸다.

Students **may** use a calculator for this test.

TIP might는 may보다 더 불확실한 추측을 나타낸다.
Robots **might** completely replace human labor in many industries.

[1-5] 괄호 안에서 가장 알맞은 것을 고르시오.

1 The team may (can / be able to) play in the final.

2 (Can / May) you recommend me a way to relieve my stress?

3 I (can / could) experience new things during my overseas trip last year.

4 The restaurant (might / was able to) improve when they hired Lucy as a head chef.

5 Don't bring any perishable food because it (may / is able to) spoil in the hot weather. <학평 응용>

[6-11] 우리말과 같도록 괄호 안의 말을 활용하여 문장을 완성하시오.

6 오늘 밤 저녁 식사 후에 설거지를 해주겠니? (wash)
= _____ the dishes after dinner tonight?

7 겨울에 오래 밖에 있는 것은 너를 아프게 할 가능성이 있다. (make)
= Being out long in winter _____ you sick.

8 외로운 누군가는 다른 사람들을 도와주는 것으로부터 이익을 얻을지도 모른다. (benefit)
= Someone lonely _____ from helping others. <학평 응용>

9 누구나 인터넷에 이 사진들을 공유해도 된다. (share)
= Anybody _____ these photos on the Internet.

10 몇몇 물고기들은 소리를 냄으로써 의사소통할 수 있다. (communicate)
= Some fish _____ by making sounds.

11 만약 네가 규칙적인 휴식을 취한다면 너는 더 잘 집중할 수 있을 것이다. (will, concentrate)
= You _____ better if you take regular breaks. <학평 응용>

must, have to

1. must는 의무(~해야 한다)를 나타내며, 이때 have to로 바꿔 쓸 수 있다.

A scientist **must**(= **has to**) wear safety equipment in the laboratory.

> TIP ① 의무를 나타내는 must의 과거형은 had to를 쓰고, 미래형은 will have to를 쓴다.
> Passengers **had to** return to their seats due to turbulence.
> The factory **will have to** employ more workers soon.
>
> ② must not은 강한 금지(~하면 안 된다)를 나타내며, don't have to[don't need to/need not]은 불필요(~할 필요가 없다)를 나타낸다.
> The sign says that pedestrians **must not** cross here.
> You **don't have to**[**don't need to/need not**] get me a present for my birthday.

2. must는 강한 추측(~임이 틀림없다)도 나타낸다.

My sister **must** be tired because she stayed up all night.

> TIP 강한 추측을 나타내는 must의 부정은 can't(~일 리가 없다)를 쓴다.
> Evan **can't** win the marathon. He has never trained for it.

[1-5] 괄호 안에서 가장 알맞은 것을 고르시오.

1 Lighthouse lamps (must not / don't have to) go out because sailors rely on them.

2 Mark was busy yesterday as he (has to / had to) adjust to his new work schedule.

3 If you haven't called your mother back, she (must / has to) be worried now.

4 I don't know who is at the door, but it (need not / can't) be Sarah.

5 You (have to / don't need to) do the assignment right now. You can do it tomorrow.

[6-8] 다음 빈칸에 알맞은 말을 <보기>에서 한 번씩만 골라 쓰시오.

<보기>   must   must not   doesn't have to

6 The man _____ pay the late fee. He's on time. <수능 응용>

7 The meal _____ contain meat because the diner is a vegetarian.

8 Maria _____ know every lyric of the song. She is not looking at the screen.

[9-11] 우리말과 같도록 괄호 안의 말을 활용하여 문장을 완성하시오.

9 Jason은 그의 오래된 냉장고를 교체해야 할 것이다. (replace)

= Jason _____ his old refrigerator.

10 온라인 뱅킹 덕분에, 고객들은 지점을 방문할 필요가 없다. (visit)

= Thanks to online banking, customers _____ a branch.

11 자원봉사하기를 원하는 누구나 사전에 등록해야 한다. (sign up)

= Anyone who wants to volunteer _____ beforehand. <학평 응용>

1. **should는 충고·의무(~해야 한다)를 나타내며, 이때 ought to로 바꿔 쓸 수 있다.**

   You **should**(= **ought to**) go to the hospital for a checkup once a year.

   > TIP should의 부정형은 shouldn't이고, ought to의 부정형은 ought not to이다.
   > Dogs **shouldn't[ought not to]** eat chocolate because it is toxic for them.

2. **제안, 주장, 요구, 명령을 나타내는 동사 뒤 that절의 내용이 '~해야 한다'인 경우 동사 자리에 「should + 동사원형」 이 오며, 이때 should는 생략할 수 있다.**

suggest	recommend	insist	request	require	demand	order

   He *requested* that Katherine (**should**) **repay** the money she borrowed from him.

   > TIP ① 제안, 주장, 요구, 명령을 나타내는 동사 뒤 that절의 내용이 '~해야 한다'가 아니라 단순한 사실인 경우, 동사 자리에 should를 쓰지 않고 동사를 인칭·수·시제에 맞게 쓴다.
   > She *insisted* that she **saw** something shiny in the garage.
   >
   > ② 필요나 주장을 나타내는 형용사(necessary, important, essential 등) 뒤 that절의 동사 자리에도 「(should) + 동사원형」이 온다.
   > It is *necessary* that every citizen (**should**) **vote** in the election.

[1-4] 괄호 안에서 가장 알맞은 것을 고르시오.

1 There is only a little rice left. We (should / shouldn't) buy some soon.

2 We (should / ought to) not fear making mistakes because they help us learn.

3 The travel agency recommended that people (purchased / purchase) travel insurance.

4 You (should / ought not to) use your phone right before bed. It is bad for your eyes.

[5-8] 우리말과 같도록 괄호 안의 말을 활용하여 빈칸에 쓰시오.

5 그 여자는 Laura가 전문가를 만나야 한다고 제안했다. (see)

   = The woman suggested that Laura _____ _____ a specialist.

6 성공적이기 위해서, 투자자들은 그들의 일시적인 손실에 초점을 맞추면 안 된다. (focus)

   = To be successful, investors _____ _____ on their temporary losses. <학평 응용>

7 어린 아이들과 아기들은 아동용 안전석에 타야 한다. (ride)

   = Young children and babies _____ _____ _____ in child safety seats. <학평>

8 모든 스쿠버 다이버들이 바다에 들어가기 전에 훈련을 받아야 하는 것은 필수적이다. (get)

   = It is essential that all scuba divers _____ training before going into the ocean.

9 다음 글에서 어법상 틀린 부분을 찾아 쓰고 바르게 고쳐 쓰시오.

   > A wildfire spread in Colorado earlier this week. Authorities ordered that everyone evacuates the area. Residents shouldn't return to their homes until the blaze is under control. *blaze: 불길

   _____ → _____

used to, would

1. used to는 과거의 반복적인 습관(~하곤 했다)이나 과거의 상태(전에는 ~이었다)를 나타낸다.

I **used to** watch TV a lot, but I prefer reading now.
This library **used to** be a church before it was renovated.

TIP used to를 이용한 표현

① 「be used to + 동사원형」: ~하는 데 사용되다
Antibiotics **are used to** *treat* infections caused by bacteria.

② 「be used to + V-ing」: ~하는 데 익숙하다
As a nurse, my aunt **is used to** *helping* people.

2. would는 과거의 반복적인 습관(~하곤 했다)을 나타낸다.

My family **would** decorate our house each Christmas.

TIP would는 과거의 상태를 나타낼 수 없다.
There (~~would~~, **used to**) be lots of blue whales before the 19th century.

[1-4] 괄호 안에서 가장 알맞은 것을 고르시오.

1 James (would / used to) be short, but he is tall now.

2 Water from the lake is used to (cultivate / cultivating) agricultural crops.

3 Ms. Ashely (would / was used to) encourage her students to drink milk. <학평 응용>

4 Celebrities are used to (sign / signing) autographs for fans.

[5-8] 우리말과 같도록 used to와 괄호 안의 말을 활용하여 문장을 완성하시오.

5 전에는 제국주의 국가들이 세계 각국에 식민지를 가지고 있었다. (have)
= Imperialist nations _____ colonies in countries around the world.

6 현재, 휴대폰은 환자들을 의사들과 연결하는 데 사용된다. (connect)
= Now, mobile phones _____ patients to doctors. <학평>

7 그 영화감독은 비평가들로부터 좋지 않은 평가를 받는 데 익숙했다. (receive)
= The film director _____ bad reviews from critics.

8 부유한 사람들이 죽었을 때, 고대 이집트인들은 그들을 무덤에 묻곤 했다. (bury)
= When wealthy people died, ancient Egyptians _____ them in tombs.

9 다음 글에서 어법상 틀린 부분을 찾아 쓰고 바르게 고쳐 쓰시오.

In the past, Native Americans would make everything, from clothes to weapons, themselves. The kinds of things that each tribe used to make depended upon what they found in nature. Their skills were used to helping them survive in the wilderness. <학평 응용>

_____ → _____

조동사 관용 표현

다음은 조동사를 사용한 관용 표현이다.

would['d] like to ~하고 싶다	We **would[We'd] like to** reserve a table for four people.
would['d] rather (차라리) ~하겠다	I **would[I'd] rather** pay with a credit card. I should keep some cash. TIP 「would rather A than B」: B하느니 차라리 A하겠다 I **would[I'd] rather** *clean* my room **than** *do* the homework.
may well (~하는 것도) 당연하다	She likes that band. She **may well** go to their concert.
may as well ~하는 편이 좋다	Since it's midnight already, we **may as well** leave for home.
had['d] better ~하는 것이 낫다	The wind is strong, so you **had[you'd] better** close the windows.

[1-6] 괄호 안에서 가장 알맞은 것을 고르시오.

1 I (would rather / may well) send a text message than make a phone call.

2 I'll find out the truth anyway, so you (may as well / would like to) tell me now.

3 This is going to be on the test, so you (would like to / had better) take notes.

4 I (would like to / may well) remind you of the new healthcare program. <학평 응용>

5 You exercised too hard yesterday. You (may well / may as well) have an ache in your ankle.

6 Tom (would rather / had better) apologize to Sophie. He spread a rumor about her.

[7-12] 우리말과 같도록 괄호 안의 말을 활용하여 문장을 완성하시오.

7 나는 나의 이전의 구매에 대해 환불을 받고 싶다. (get)

= I _____ a refund for my previous purchase.

8 나는 하루 종일 해변에 누워있느니 차라리 관광하러 가겠다. (go)

= I _____ sightseeing than lie on the beach all day.

9 그 범인은 그가 유죄라는 사실을 인정하는 것이 낫다. (admit)

= The criminal _____ the fact that he is guilty.

10 너는 너의 건강을 향상하기 위해 학교에 걸어가는 것이 낫겠다. (walk)

= You _____ to school to enhance your health. <학평 응용>

11 그는 초과근무를 했기 때문에 돈을 더 받는 것도 당연하다. (earn)

= He _____ more money because he worked overtime.

12 오늘 밤에, 너는 네가 이번 학기 동안 배운 것을 복습하는 편이 좋다. (review)

= Tonight, you _____ what you learned through this semester. <수능 응용>

POINT 6 · 조동사 + have + p.p.

정답 p.5

「조동사 + have + p.p.」는 과거 사실에 대한 추측이나 후회·유감을 나타낸다.

추측	may[might] + have + p.p. ~했을지도 모른다	The lecture **may[might] have inspired** Jane. She studies very hard these days.
	must + have + p.p. ~했음이 틀림없다	He **must have painted** his house recently. It looks new.
	can't + have + p.p. ~했을 리가 없다	They **can't have gone** shopping. The mall doesn't open today.
후회·유감	should + have + p.p. ~했어야 했다(하지만 하지 않았다)	I **should have brought** my umbrella. It is raining now.
	could + have + p.p. ~했을 수도 있었다 (하지만 하지 않았다)	You **could have done** your work better. However, you spent too much time on other things. <학평 응용> TIP 「could + have + p.p.」는 과거 사실에 대한 가능성을 나타낼 수도 있다. I **could have said** something bad to Max. He was upset with me.

[1-5] 괄호 안에서 가장 알맞은 것을 고르시오.

1 His new car is beautiful. It (must / should) have cost a lot of money.

2 I (may / could) have made a mistake on my math test. The score is below my expectation.

3 You (must / can't) have finished the movie already. You started watching it 20 minutes ago.

4 The librarian told me that I (might / should) have returned this book last week.

5 You were over the speed limit. The police (can't / could) have written you a ticket.

[6-11] 우리말과 같도록 괄호 안의 말을 활용하여 문장을 완성하시오.

6 나는 오늘 아침에 나의 약속을 취소했어야 했다. (cancel)

= I _____ my appointment this morning. <학평 응용>

7 그의 기사는 십대들에게 부정적으로 영향을 미쳤을 수도 있었다. (influence)

= His article _____ the teenagers negatively.

8 Paula는 바깥의 공사 때문에 잘 잤을 리가 없다. (sleep)

= Paula _____ well because of the construction outside.

9 우리는 전에 서로를 만났을지도 모르지만, 나는 기억하지 못한다. (meet)

= We _____ each other before, but I don't remember.

10 그 선생님은 학생들에게 현장 학습에 대해 안내할 것을 잊었음이 틀림없다. (forget)

= The teacher _____ to inform the students about the field trip. <학평 응용>

11 너는 너의 여행 가방에 이름표를 붙였어야 했다. (attach)

= You _____ a name tag to your suitcase.

Review Test

[1-4] 다음 두 문장의 의미가 같도록 빈칸에 들어갈 알맞은 것을 고르시오.

1

> At the festival, we can show our musical talents.
> → At the festival, we _____ show our musical talents. <학평 응용>

① might ② have to ③ should
④ are able to ⑤ may as well

2

> Your new password must contain both numbers and alphabets.
> → Your new password _____ contain both numbers and alphabets.

① might ② can ③ has to
④ may well ⑤ would rather

3

> A big statue was in the park before. But I can't find it now.
> → A big statue _____ be in the park.

① can ② must ③ would
④ should ⑤ used to

4

> I'm not sure, but I think Scott solved the puzzle before lunch.
> → Scott _____ have solved the puzzle before lunch.

① may ② must ③ can't
④ should ⑤ would like to

[5-7] 다음 중 어법상 틀린 것을 고르시오.

5

① Employees don't need to wear a suit.
② You may begin whenever you are ready.
③ Charlie would listen to the radio at night.
④ We had better leave now before sunset.
⑤ You ought to not make important decisions without thinking carefully.

6

① This toy can't be that expensive.
② You should sign your name on the paper.
③ A ruler is used to measuring short distances.
④ The actor may well receive an award.
⑤ Some bamboo can grow well in cold climates.

7

① The weather might be better tomorrow.
② Amy should have requested a raise of her salary.
③ I will must go to the gym regularly to lose weight.
④ A Spartan soldier would rather die than lose in battle.
⑤ You must not speak loudly in the library.

8 다음 중 어법상 바른 것끼리 묶인 것은?

> ⓐ You should submit your essay by March 1.
> ⓑ May you tell me the way to the subway station?
> ⓒ The guest would like to see the menu.
> ⓓ It is important that every adult sets a good example for children.
> ⓔ They had to have a small wedding due to the insufficient budget.

① ⓐ, ⓑ, ⓒ ② ⓐ, ⓑ, ⓓ ③ ⓐ, ⓒ, ⓔ
④ ⓑ, ⓒ, ⓔ ⑤ ⓒ, ⓓ, ⓔ

[9-10] 다음 문장에서 어법상 틀린 부분을 찾아 쓰고 바르게 고쳐 쓰시오.

9

People were used to believe that Earth was the center of the solar system.

_____ → _____

10

The doctor insisted that the patient taking the medication twice a day.

_____ → _____

11 다음 글에서 어법상 틀린 부분을 찾아 쓰고 바르게 고쳐 쓰시오.

I noticed an injured cat on the street. I thought I had to save its life, I took it to the animal hospital. Thankfully, the veterinarian told me that it might can survive after the surgery.

_____ → _____

[12-13] 우리말과 같도록 괄호 안의 말을 알맞게 배열하시오.

12

너는 한국인으로서 애국가를 알아야 한다. (know, to, the national anthem, ought, you)

= _____ as a Korean.

13

풍차는 재생 가능한 에너지를 생산하는 데 사용된다. (used, produce, are, renewable energy, windmills, to)

= _____.

[14-17] 우리말과 같도록 괄호 안의 말을 활용하여 문장을 완성하시오.

14

너는 우리가 지난번에 만났을 때보다 훨씬 더 키가 커졌음이 틀림없다. (become)

= _____ a lot taller than when we met last time.

15

직원들은 두 시간마다 잠시 휴식을 취해도 된다. (staff members, a break, have)

= _____ every two hours.

16

나는 이번 주말에 밖에 나가느니 차라리 집에 머무르겠다. (go out, stay home)

= _____ this weekend.

17

그 승무원은 내가 머리 위의 짐칸에 휴대용 수하물을 보관해야 한다고 요구했다. (that, the flight attendant, hand luggage, store, require)

= _____ in overhead compartments.

18 우리말과 같도록 주어진 <조건>에 맞게 문장을 완성하시오.

> 내가 약 2분 전에 그를 봤기 때문에 그 낯선 사람은 멀리 갔을 리가 없다.

> <조건>
> 1. the stranger, go를 활용하시오.
> 2. 5단어로 쓰시오.

= _____ far because I saw him about two minutes ago.

[19-20] 다음 글을 읽고 주어진 질문에 답하시오.

> I ⓐ used to asking my parents for a pet when I was an elementary school student. Then my mother ⓑ would say I wasn't ready to handle the responsibility, and she was right. I ⓒ might have forgotten to feed a pet. I am ready now, though, and my parents said I can adopt one. I thought I ⓓ would rather have a dog than a cat. (A) 나의 아버지는 우선 내가 동물들을 어떻게 돌봐야 하는지 배워야 한다고 권하셨다. (that, recommend, my father, learn) So, I ⓔ ought not to read a book on the subject.

19 위 글의 밑줄 친 우리말 (A)와 같도록 괄호 안의 말을 활용하여 문장을 완성하시오.

= _____ how to take care of animals first.

20 위 글의 밑줄 친 ⓐ~ⓔ 중 어법상 **틀린** 것의 기호를 쓰고 바르게 고쳐 쓰시오.

(1) _____ → _____
(2) _____ → _____

수능형

21 (A), (B), (C)의 각 네모 안에서 어법에 맞는 표현으로 가장 적절한 것은?

> Many people enjoy hunting for wild mushrooms. However, some wild mushrooms cause people (A) die / to die because they are poisonous. To be safe, a person must (B) can / be able to tell the difference between an edible mushroom and a poisonous one. Most poisonous mushrooms are colorful, so you (C) must not / don't have to consume mushrooms with bright red caps, for example. <학평 응용>   *edible: 먹을 수 있는

	(A)	(B)	(C)
①	die	can	must not
②	die	be able to	don't have to
③	to die	can	must not
④	to die	be able to	must not
⑤	to die	be able to	don't have to

수능형

22 다음 글의 밑줄 친 부분 중, 어법상 **틀린** 것은?

> An employee ① need not be always rewarded for his or her achievements with money or other material items. A company I once worked for had a great way of recognizing sales success. The sales director ② was used to blow an air horn every time a salesperson settled a deal. Even though the noise ③ could interrupt others' work, it had a positive impact on everyone. Sometimes, rewarding success ④ might be as easy as that, especially when peer recognition is important. You ⑤ should have seen the way the rest of the sales team wanted the air horn blown for them. <학평 응용>   *air horn: (압축 공기로 작동하는) 경적

CHAPTER 4
수동태

기출로 적중 POINT

최근 7개년 수능/학평/내신 출제 경향

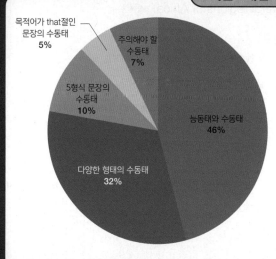

목적어가 that절인 문장의 수동태 5%

주의해야 할 수동태 7%

5형식 문장의 수동태 10%

다양한 형태의 수동태 32%

능동태와 수동태 46%

TOP 1 능동태와 수동태 (46%)
주어와 동사의 관계에 따라 능동태와 수동태를 구분하는 문제가 자주 출제된다.

TOP 2 다양한 형태의 수동태 (32%)
시제에 따른 수동태와 조동사가 있는 수동태의 형태를 묻는 문제가 자주 출제된다.

TOP 3 5형식 문장의 수동태 (10%)
5형식 문장에서의 수동태의 형태를 묻는 문제가 자주 출제된다.

1. 능동태는 주어가 행위의 주체가 되는 것을 나타내고, 수동태는 「be동사 + p.p. + by + 행위자」의 형태로 주어가 행위의 대상이 되는 것을 나타낸다.

John Wilkes Booth **shot** Abraham Lincoln in 1865. <능동태>

→ Abraham Lincoln **was shot** by *John Wilkes Booth* in 1865. <수동태>

TIP ① 행위자가 일반인이거나 중요하지 않을 때는 「by + 행위자」를 생략할 수 있다.
Grains **are eaten** (*by people*) in countries across the globe.

② 수동태는 「get + p.p.」의 형태로도 쓸 수 있다.
My friends and I **got wounded** during the exercise.

2. 목적어를 가지지 않는 동사(appear, happen, occur 등)나, 목적어를 가지는 동사 중 소유나 상태를 나타내는 동사(have, resemble, lack 등)는 수동태로 쓸 수 없다.

A serious car accident (~~was happened~~, **happened**) on a snowy day.

[1-4] 다음 능동태 문장을 수동태 문장으로 바꿔 쓰시오.

1 The students' behavior hurt the teacher.

→ _____ by the students' behavior. <학평 응용>

2 My favorite boxer defeated the champion at the latest game.

→ _____ by my favorite boxer at the latest game.

3 Bites from snakes kill many hikers annually.

→ _____ by bites from snakes annually. <수능 응용>

4 Sarah invented a hair care product when she worked as a maid.

→ _____ by Sarah when she worked as a maid. <학평 응용>

[5-7] 우리말과 같도록 괄호 안의 말을 활용하여 문장을 완성하시오.

5 다이아몬드의 많은 매장량이 아프리카의 여러 지역에서 발견되었다. (discover)

= Large deposits of diamonds _____ in several regions of Africa. <학평 응용>

6 갑자기, 이상한 물체가 불쾌한 소리와 함께 하늘에 나타났다. (appear)

= Suddenly, a strange object _____ in the sky with an unpleasant sound.

7 그 군인은 적에 의해 붙잡혔고 감옥에서 6년을 보냈다. (capture, spend)

= The soldier _____ by the enemy and _____ six years in the prison. <학평 응용>

8 다음 글에서 어법상 틀린 부분을 찾아 쓰고 바르게 고쳐 쓰시오.

> Two attacks occurred on September 11 in New York City. Terrorists flew planes into the twin towers of the World Trade Center. A huge part of the city destroyed due to the attacks.

_____ → _____

1. **미래시제 수동태:** 「will be + p.p.」

   T-shirts and calendars **will be provided** as souvenirs. <학평 응용>

2. **진행시제 수동태:** 「be동사 + being + p.p.」

   My bike **is being repaired** by Joseph in the garage.

3. **완료시제 수동태:** 「have/had been + p.p.」

   These items **have been left** in the lost and found box for months.

4. **조동사가 있는 수동태:** 「조동사 + be + p.p.」

   The flight **might be delayed** because of the storm.

5. **명령문의 수동태:** 「Let + 목적어 + be +p.p.」

   Let the plan be set by this weekend. (← Set the plan by this weekend.)

[1-3] 다음 능동태 문장을 수동태 문장으로 바꿔 쓰시오.

1 The detective is recording the suspect's voice.

→ _____ by the detective.

2 Release the innocent people from jail.

→ _____ from jail.

3 They have made promising advances in the area of human genetics.

→ _____ by them in the area of human genetics. <학평>

[4-7] 우리말과 같도록 괄호 안의 말을 활용하여 문장을 완성하시오.

4 너의 주문은 가장 가까운 가게에서 배송되고 있다. (deliver)

= Your order _____ from the nearest store.

5 그 책의 주인공은 그의 팀 동료에 의해 배신당할 것이다. (will, betray)

= The main character of the book _____ by his teammate.

6 모든 직원은 추가 공장을 위한 계획에 포함되어야 한다. (should, include)

= All staff _____ in the planning for additional factories. <학평 응용>

7 외적 동기 부여의 부정적인 효과는 몇 년 동안 입증되어왔다. (document)

= The negative effects of extrinsic motivation _____ for several years. <수능 응용>

8 다음 글에서 어법상 틀린 부분을 찾아 쓰고 바르게 고쳐 쓰시오.

> The votes will be counted tonight. By tomorrow morning, a new president may elect. Supporters of each party have been worried about the results all day because they wish for their candidate to win.

_____ → _____

1. 4형식 문장은 목적어가 두 개이므로 각 목적어를 주어로 하는 두 가지 형태의 수동태 문장을 만들 수 있다. 이때 직접 목적어가 주어인 수동태 문장은 간접 목적어 앞에 주로 to/for/of 중 하나를 쓴다.

Lisa **gave** *her friend advice.* → *Her friend* **was given** *advice* by Lisa. <간접 목적어가 주어>
→ *Advice* **was given to** *her friend* by Lisa. <직접 목적어가 주어>

TIP buy, cook, make, get 등의 동사가 쓰인 4형식 문장을 수동태 문장으로 바꿀 때는 주로 직접 목적어를 주어로 쓴다.
My dad **bought** *me a scarf.* → *A scarf* **was bought for** *me* by my dad. (O)
→ I was bought a scarf by my dad. (X)

2. 직접 목적어가 주어인 수동태 문장에서 간접 목적어 앞에 쓰는 전치사는 동사에 따라 다르다.

❶ to를 쓰는 동사: give, send, bring, show, teach, tell, write, lend, sell, offer 등
❷ for를 쓰는 동사: buy, cook, find, make, get, choose, order, build 등
❸ of를 쓰는 동사: ask, inquire 등

The invitation cards **were sent to** the guests by the event organizer.
The soup **was made for** homeless children by the charity.

[1-4] 다음 능동태 문장을 수동태 문장으로 바꿔 쓰시오.

1 The chef cooked the customers an amazing local dish.

→ An amazing local dish _____ by the chef.

2 A Canadian friend taught us some English proverbs.

→ We _____ by a Canadian friend.

→ Some English proverbs _____ by a Canadian friend.

3 Although my budget was tight, I bought my brother a graduation gift.

→ Although my budget was tight, a graduation gift _____ by me. <수능 응용>

4 The project manager showed the team members a sales performance.

→ The team members _____ by the project manager.

→ A sales performance _____ by the project manager.

[5-7] 우리말과 같도록 괄호 안의 말을 활용하여 문장을 완성하시오.

5 어려운 질문들이 그 선생님에 의해 학생들에게 물어졌다. (ask, students)

= Difficult questions _____ by the teacher. <학평 응용>

6 그 퀴즈 쇼의 우승자는 수십억 달러를 제공받았다. (offer, billions of dollars)

= The winner of the quiz show _____. <학평 응용>

7 이 노래는 그 작곡가에 의해 그가 가장 좋아하는 배우에게 만들어졌다. (make, his favorite actor)

= This song _____ by the composer.

POINT 4 5형식 문장의 수동태

정답 p.6

1. 목적격 보어가 명사, 형용사, to부정사, 분사인 5형식 문장을 수동태 문장으로 바꿀 때는 목적격 보어를 「be동사 + p.p.」 뒤에 그대로 쓴다.

He **told** me **to wash** my hands before dinner.
→ I **was told to wash** my hands before dinner by him.

2. 사역동사나 지각동사가 쓰인 5형식 문장을 수동태 문장으로 바꿀 때는 목적격 보어로 쓰인 원형부정사를 to부정사로 바꾼다.

The coach **made** the athletes **train** in the horrible heat.
→ The athletes **were made to train** in the horrible heat by the coach.

TIP 지각동사의 목적격 보어로 쓰인 원형부정사는 수동태 문장에서 V-ing형으로도 바꿀 수 있다.
The crowd **heard** the performer **sing** her new song.
→ The performer **was heard singing[to sing]** her new song by the crowd.

[1-8] 다음 능동태 문장을 수동태 문장으로 바꿔 쓰시오.

1 The climber found the air scarce at the top of the mountain.
→ _____ by the climber.

2 Politicians expect the law to benefit education in the country.
→ _____ by politicians.

3 The guard saw a stranger enter a building sneakily.
→ _____ by the guard.

4 Theresa persuaded citizens to donate money for the poor.
→ _____ by Theresa.

5 Someone considers rats pests in much of Europe and North America.
→ _____ by someone. <학평 응용>

6 The professor made some participants think positively about themselves.
→ _____ by the professor. <학평 응용>

7 The tiger saw an antelope run through the trees.
→ _____ by the tiger.

8 People in many countries consider chocolate a tasty treat.
→ _____ by people in many countries.

9 다음 글에서 어법상 틀린 부분을 찾아 쓰고 바르게 고쳐 쓰시오.

> Yesterday, motorists were made going another way due to a multi-vehicle collision. None of the injuries were life-threatening, and those who were involved are expected to recover soon.   *collision: 충돌

_____ → _____

목적어가 that절인 문장의 수동태

정답 p.6

목적어가 that절인 문장은 두 가지 형태의 수동태 문장을 만들 수 있다.

❶ 수동태 문장의 주어가 that절 전체인 문장: 「It + be동사 + p.p. + that ~」

Experts **say** that depression increases during the winter.

→ **It is said that** depression increases during the winter.

❷ 수동태 문장의 주어가 that절의 주어인 문장: 「that절의 주어 + be동사 + p.p. + to부정사 ~」

They **thought** that *the news on the radio* **was** real.

→ *The news on the radio* **was thought to be** real.

TIP 수동태 문장의 주어가 that절의 주어인 경우 that절의 시제가 주절의 시제보다 앞서면 to부정사를 「to have + p.p.」의 형태로 쓴다.

People **believe** that *humans* **migrated** from Africa to the rest of the world.

→ *Humans* **are believed to have migrated** from Africa to the rest of the world.

[1-5] 다음 능동태 문장을 수동태 문장으로 바꿔 쓰시오. (단, 행위자를 드러내지 마시오.)

1 Some say that wild animals ruined the agricultural land.

→ It _____.

2 They expect that emergency workers undergo a counseling process after traumatic events.

→ Emergency workers _____. <학평 응용>

3 We know that big gifts are not necessarily the nicest ones.

→ It _____. <학평 응용>

4 They consider that the research paper includes unreliable information.

→ The research paper _____.

5 The weather forecast reports that yesterday was the coldest day of the year.

→ Yesterday _____.

[6-10] 우리말과 같도록 괄호 안의 말을 활용하여 문장을 완성하시오.

6 그 도시는 내년에 새로운 기차역을 지을 것이라고 추정된다. (suppose, build, the city)

= It _____ a new train station next year.

7 그 백신은 바이러스로부터 사람들을 보호한다고 보고된다. (protect, report)

= The vaccine _____ people from the virus.

8 그 회사는 의도적으로 시장을 조작했다고 알려져 있다. (know, manipulate, the company)

= It _____ the market intentionally.

9 셰익스피어는 그의 모든 희곡들을 혼자 쓰지 않았다고 믿어진다. (write, believe, Shakespeare)

= It _____ all of his plays alone. <학평 응용>

10 우리의 직계 조상의 인구는 약 2,000명이었다고 추정된다. (estimate, be)

= The population of our direct ancestors _____ around 2,000 individuals. <학평 응용>

주의해야 할 수동태

1. 두 개 이상의 단어로 이루어진 구동사를 수동태로 쓸 때, 동사만 「be동사 + p.p.」의 형태로 쓰고 나머지 부분은 그 뒤에 그대로 쓴다.

laugh at ~를 보고 비웃다	**look after** ~를 돌보다	**call off** ~을 취소하다
look up to ~를 존경하다	**take care of** ~를 돌보다	**catch up with** ~을 따라잡다
look down on ~를 무시하다	**deal with** ~을 다루다	**pay attention to** ~에 주의를 기울이다

I **looked after** my cousin for a few days.
→ My cousin **was looked after** by me for a few days.

2. 다음은 수동태를 쓰는 관용 표현이다.

be satisfied with ~에 만족하다	**be worried about** ~에 대해 걱정하다	**be covered with** ~으로 덮여 있다
be pleased with ~에 기뻐하다	**be known as** ~으로서 알려져 있다	**be filled with** ~으로 가득 차 있다
be interested in ~에 흥미가 있다	**be known for** ~으로 유명하다	**be made of** ~으로 만들어지다
be surprised at ~에 놀라다	**be known to** ~에게 알려져 있다	(재료 성질이 변하지 않음)
be disappointed at ~에 실망하다	**be composed of** ~으로 구성되다	**be made from** ~으로 만들어지다
		(재료 성질이 변함)

Many doctors **are worried about** young adults' health.
King Sejong **is known for** the creation of Hangeul.

[1-5] 괄호 안에서 알맞은 것을 고르시오.

1 The issue was (paid attention to / paying attention to) by media all over the world.

2 Most of the mountains were covered (with / from) snow last week.

3 Peasants were (looked down / looked down on) by aristocrats in the past.

4 The United Kingdom is (composed / made) of England, Scotland, Wales, and Northern Ireland.

5 The berries which disturbed sleeping would later be known (as / to) coffee berries. <학평 응용>

[6-9] 우리말과 같도록 괄호 안의 말을 활용하여 문장을 완성하시오.

6 그녀는 온라인 수업을 위한 프로그램을 개발하는 것에 흥미가 있다. (interest)
= She _____ developing programs for online classes. <수능 응용>

7 그 소풍은 예기치 않은 폭우 때문에 취소되었다. (call)
= The excursion _____ because of the unexpected heavy rain.

8 그 왕자가 그의 첫 번째 사슴을 죽였을 때, 그 왕은 자부심으로 가득 차 있었다. (fill)
= When the prince killed his first deer, the king _____ pride. <학평 응용>

9 우리의 매출이 우리의 경쟁자들에 의해 따라잡히면 안 된다. (catch)
= Our sales should not _____ by our competitors.

Review Test

[1-4] 다음 빈칸에 들어갈 알맞은 것을 고르시오.

1

> Three months ago, Amy got _____ because of her laziness at work.

① be fired   ② fires   ③ fired
④ to fire   ⑤ be firing

2

> Let your report _____ by Friday night.

① did   ② be done   ③ be doing
④ to do   ⑤ to be done

3

> The audience was made _____ by the movie's dramatic ending.

① cry   ② cried   ③ crying
④ to cry   ⑤ to crying

4

> The reason for the old man's death _____ to be cancer.

① believes   ② believed   ③ believing
④ was believing   ⑤ was believed

5 다음 빈칸에 들어갈 말이 순서대로 짝지어진 것은?

> · High-level skills were taught _____ me by my teacher.
> · Tourists in Korea are surprised _____ how fast the Internet is.

① for – to   ② to – to   ③ for – at
④ to – at   ⑤ of – at

[6-8] 다음 중 어법상 틀린 것을 고르시오.

6

① Jessica was advised to call the service center as soon as possible.
② Bookings will be accepted up to two hours before the event starts. <학평>
③ A fancy suit was bought for Matt by his mother.
④ The class should be reviewed until the next chapter is covered.
⑤ This place is resembled a famous beach in Southeast Asia.

7

① Celebrations were held around the world on New Year's Eve last year.
② It is expected that the IT department collects individuals' data.
③ I was heard say goodbye on the phone by John.
④ The new hospital is being built across the street.
⑤ The presentation had been completed already when I arrived at the office.

8

① *The Lord of the Rings* was made into a movie series in 1999.
② The meeting was called off by the CEO after the demands were met.
③ Wine is made from grapes or some wild berries.
④ The tsunami was caused to occur by the earthquake.
⑤ The form must be fill out before you get off the plane.

[9-11] 다음 문장에서 어법상 틀린 부분을 찾아 쓰고 바르게 고쳐 쓰시오.

9

> The Australian Prime Minister Harold Holt was disappeared during a swim in 1967.

_____ → _____

10

> The cruise ship was seen leave the port.

_____ → _____

11

> All the decorations in the living room had been preparing by my friends.

_____ → _____

[12-15] 다음 능동태 문장을 수동태 문장으로 바꿔 쓰시오. (단, 행위자를 드러내지 마시오.)

12

> The orchestra is playing Christmas carols to make citizens happy.

→ _____ to make citizens happy.

13

> She told us the truth about the rumor.

→ _____.

→ _____.

14

> The executives dealt with the sensitive issue at the annual conference.

→ _____ at the annual conference.

15

> Hindus believe that the god Brahma created the universe.

→ The god Brahma _____

_____.

[16-18] 우리말과 같도록 괄호 안의 말을 활용하여 문장을 완성하시오.

16

> 사치품의 가격은 최근의 경제 위기 동안 인상되었다. (the price of luxury items, raise)

= _____ during the recent economic crisis.

17

> 음식은 그 파티의 시작 전에 제공될 것이다. (the food, serve)

= _____ before the start of the party.

18

> 그 판매자는 구매자로부터의 제안에 만족했다. (the seller, satisfy)

= _____ the offer from the buyer.

19 우리말과 같도록 주어진 <조건>에 맞게 문장을 완성하시오.

> 그 토지 소유자는 부동산에 의해 돈을 받았다.

> <조건>
> 1. the landowner, give, the real estate, money를 활용하시오.
> 2. 9단어로 쓰시오.

= _____ .

[20-21] 다음 글을 읽고 주어진 질문에 답하시오.

> Located on Salisbury Plain, Stonehenge ⓐ is composed in a circle of massive stones. Stonehenge ⓑ is considered mysterious as both its purpose and how it was built are uncertain. (A) People think that Stonehenge was a burial site of early humans. This theory ⓒ might prove by the researchers one day, but for now, it is simply the most plausible conclusion. As for how it was constructed, the people who built it ⓓ lacked sophisticated technology, so what did they use? Some think that the stones ⓔ were moved by workers using sledges from long distances away.

20 위 글의 밑줄 친 (A)를 수동태 문장으로 바꿔 쓰시오. (단, 행위자를 드러내지 마시오.)

= Stonehenge _____
of early humans.

21 위 글의 밑줄 친 ⓐ~ⓔ 중 어법상 틀린 것의 기호를 쓰고 바르게 고쳐 쓰시오.

(1) _____ → _____

(2) _____ → _____

수능형
22 (A), (B), (C)의 각 네모 안에서 어법에 맞는 표현으로 가장 적절한 것은?

> Our perception of food can (A) influence / be influenced by what it looks like, even more than what it tastes and smells like. The same is true of wine. One study of Bordeaux University students of wine and winemaking revealed that they chose tasting notes appropriate for red wines, such as "prune and chocolate," when they (B) gave / were given white wine colored with a red dye. Experienced New Zealand wine experts were similarly tricked into thinking that the white wine Chardonnay was in fact a red wine when it (C) had / had been colored with a red dye. <학평 응용>
>
> *prune: 자두 **dye: 염료

	(A)	(B)	(C)
①	influence	gave	had
②	influence	were given	had been
③	be influenced	gave	had been
④	be influenced	were given	had
⑤	be influenced	were given	had been

수능형
23 다음 글의 밑줄 친 부분 중, 어법상 틀린 것은?

> It ① is known that tempers are easily lost in many arguments. It's easy to say one should keep ② calm, but how? Sometimes, the person you're arguing with is trying to make you angry. They may say things that ③ are designed to annoy you. They know that if you ④ lose your cool and say something foolish, you will not win the argument. So, don't fall for it. You may be made ⑤ get angry with some remarks, but responding calmly while focusing on the issue at hand is more effective than getting upset. <학평 응용>

CHAPTER 5
명사/관사/대명사

기출로 적중 POINT

최근 7개년 수능/학평/내신 출제 경향

부정대명사: both, either, neither 4%

셀 수 있는 명사와 셀 수 없는 명사 5%

부정대명사: all, each, none 11%

지시대명사 11%

부정대명사: one, another, other 12%

재귀대명사 25%

it의 다양한 쓰임 32%

TOP 1 it의 다양한 쓰임 (32%)
it의 가주어와 가목적어로서의 쓰임을 묻는 문제가 자주 출제된다.

TOP 2 재귀대명사 (25%)
재귀대명사의 재귀 용법과 강조 용법을 묻는 문제가 자주 출제된다.

TOP 3 부정대명사: one, another, other (12%)
부정대명사 one, another, other의 쓰임을 묻는 문제가 자주 출제된다.

1. 셀 수 있는 명사가 단수일 때는 명사 앞에 a(n)을 붙이고, 복수일 때는 복수형으로 쓴다.

보통명사	일반적인 사람·동물·사물을 나타내는 명사 (baby, monkey, umbrella 등)
집합명사	사람·동물·사물이 모인 집합을 나타내는 명사 (family, audience, committee 등)

The **girls** were looking at **an ant** in the **garden**.

My **family** goes to the **park** when the **weather** is warm.

TIP 집합명사는 의미에 따라 단수 취급하거나 복수 취급한다. 단, people, police, cattle 등은 항상 복수 취급한다.

The **audience** *is* waiting for the show. <하나의 덩어리로서의 집단>

The **audience** *were* invited to ask questions. <집단에 속한 구성원 모두>

2. 셀 수 없는 명사는 명사 앞에 a(n)을 붙일 수 없고, 복수형으로도 쓸 수 없다.

고유명사	사람이나 장소 등의 고유한 이름을 나타내는 명사 (Jake, Rome, Sunday 등)
추상명사	추상적인 개념을 나타내는 명사 (love, information, news 등)
물질명사	일정한 형태가 없는 물질을 나타내는 명사 (water, air, money 등)

Chris needs some **information** about **Vietnam**.

She is carrying *two bowls of* **salad**.

↳ 셀 수 없는 명사는 그것을 담는 그릇이나 단위를 나타내는 말을 활용하여 수량을 나타낸다.

[1-6] 괄호 안에서 알맞은 것을 고르시오.

1 (Lady / A lady) stopped me to ask for directions.

2 The recipe says to add three spoons of (salt / salts).

3 People (is / are) attracted to things they cannot readily obtain. <학평 응용>

4 Could you please blow (air / an air) into the balloons?

5 Several studies found that pet (owner / owners) have lower levels of stress. <학평 응용>

6 (A Canada / Canada) has more than 8,500 (rivers / river) and two million lakes.

[7-10] 우리말과 같도록 괄호 안의 말과 be동사를 활용하여 문장을 완성하시오.

7 많은 용기가 전장에 있는 군인들에게 요구된다. (courage)

= A lot of _____ required of soldiers on the battlefield.

8 몇몇 유명한 역사학자들이 그 대학교에서 강의에 참석하고 있었다. (well-known historian)

= Some _____ attending the lecture at the university.

9 그 위원회는 7명의 이사진들로 구성된다. (committee)

= The _____ made up of seven board members.

10 빨간 불은 경찰이 항상 감시하고 있다는 것을 의미한다. (police)

= The red lights imply that the _____ always watching. <학평 응용>

정답 p.8

1. 부정관사 a(n)은 셀 수 있는 명사의 단수형 앞에 쓴다.

He works as **a** *lawyer* in Seoul. <막연한 하나>　　　There was **an** *accident* last night. <하나의(one)>

The staff is paid twice **a** *month*. <~마다(per)>　　**A** *man* called you right before. <어떤(certain)>

2. 정관사 the는 셀 수 있는 명사와 셀 수 없는 명사 앞에 모두 쓸 수 있다.

I met *an author* last week. **The** *author* is really famous. <앞에서 언급된 명사>

Can you hand me **the** *remote control*? <정황상 서로 알고 있는 것>

The *customer who complained yesterday* wants an apology. <구나 절의 수식을 받는 명사>

They ran home after they saw black clouds in **the** *sky*. <유일한 것>

Chris plays **the** *violin* in the orchestra. <악기 이름>

The *first* person to cross the finish line wins the race. <서수, 최상급, only, same>

3. 다음과 같은 경우에는 명사 앞에 관사를 쓰지 않는다.

Nancy's favorite subject is *science*. <운동·식사·과목 이름 앞에>

You can only get to the island *by boat*. <by + 교통·통신수단>

My family goes to *church* at 9 A.M. on Sundays. <장소나 건물이 본래의 목적으로 쓰일 때>

[1-9] 괄호 안에서 가장 알맞은 것을 고르시오.

1 This is (an / the) only grocery store in the neighborhood.

2 Everyone has probably lost (the / a) key at least once in their lives.

3 Lots of media reports claim that (breakfast / the breakfast) is the most important meal.

4 Please make sure (news / the news) that you provided is correct.

5 My friend has a parrot. (A / The) parrot is unique because it can speak. <학평 응용>

6 Can you recommend (a / the) fastest way to the airport?

7 He went to (school / a school) early because he had to prepare for the test.

8 The origin of (universe / the universe) is frequently a subject of debate.

9 During the Industrial Revolution, factory workers labored for around 80 hours (a / the) week. <학평 응용>

[10-14] 밑줄 친 부분이 어법상 맞으면 O를 쓰고, 틀리면 바르게 고쳐 쓰시오.

10 You should submit your application form by an e-mail.　　→ ＿＿＿＿＿＿＿＿

11 A survey shows that the majority of Americans believe in aliens.　　→ ＿＿＿＿＿＿＿＿

12 People say that lightning never strikes twice in same place.　　→ ＿＿＿＿＿＿＿＿

13 I need to borrow some books. Library is still open, right?　　→ ＿＿＿＿＿＿＿＿

14 Dorothy likes to sing a song while she is playing the guitar.　　→ ＿＿＿＿＿＿＿＿

1. this/these는 가까이 있는 사람이나 사물을 가리킬 때, that/those는 멀리 있는 사람이나 사물을 가리킬 때 쓴다.

   This is the most popular restaurant in my town.
   Look at **those** birds sitting on the tree branches.

2. that/those는 명사(구)의 반복을 피하기 위해서도 쓴다.

   The quality of our clothes is better than **that** of others.
   His *movements* were graceful like **those** of dancers.

3. those는 '~한 사람들'이라는 의미로도 쓴다.

   Those who spend time wisely are likely to reach the goal.
   I admire **those** who do volunteer work without being paid.

[1-5] 괄호 안에서 알맞은 것을 고르시오.

1   (This / That) woman over there is my store manager.

2   The temperature here is not as low as (that / those) in Iceland.

3   (That / Those) who have high self-monitoring want their behavior to be socially acceptable. <수능>

4   Most of the children's habits are copies of (these / those) of their parents. <학평 응용>

5   *A*: (These / Those) are my classmates, David and John.

    B: Glad to meet you guys. I'm Samantha.

[6-8] 우리말과 같도록 괄호 안의 말을 알맞게 배열하시오.

6   이 향수의 냄새는 나의 샴푸의 그것과 같다. (of, my, that, shampoo)

    = The smell of this perfume is the same as _____.

7   내가 너의 정원에서 이 꽃들 중 하나를 가져가도 되니? (these, of, one, flowers)

    = Can I take _____ from your garden?

8   건강관리가 필요한 사람들은 정부의 서비스를 신청해야 한다. (who, medical care, need, those)

    = _____ should apply for the government's service.

9   다음 대화에서 어법상 틀린 부분을 찾아 쓰고 바르게 고쳐 쓰시오.

   > *A*: Wendy, have you found a bike you like among these models?
   > *B*: Yes. I think the one with the brown seat is the best. Its wheels are larger than that of the others.
   > *A*: Do you mean the one right next to the checkout? Isn't it too big for you?

   _____   →   _____

POINT 4 재귀대명사

정답 p.8

재귀대명사는 '~ 자신, 직접, 스스로'의 의미로, 인칭대명사의 소유격이나 목적격에 -self/-selves를 붙인 형태이다.

❶ 재귀 용법: 동사나 전치사의 목적어가 주어와 같은 대상인 경우 목적어로 재귀대명사를 쓴다. 이때 재귀대명사는 생략할 수 없다.
   A panther protects **itself** with its sharp claws and teeth.

❷ 강조 용법: 문장의 주어나 목적어를 강조하기 위해 강조하는 말 바로 뒤나 문장 맨 뒤에 재귀대명사를 쓴다. 이때 재귀대명사는 생략할 수 있다.
   Tony (**himself**) realized his mistake.
   = *Tony* realized his mistake (**himself**).

TIP 명령문에는 주어 You가 생략되어 있으므로, 재귀대명사로 yourself/yourselves를 쓴다.
   (*You*) Believe in **yourself** and your ability.

[1-5] 괄호 안에서 알맞은 것을 고르시오.

1 The architect approved the new building plan (him / himself).

2 The pen that my classmate was holding seemed similar to (mine / myself).

3 After reading books, keep asking (you / yourself) what the author's main idea is. <학평 응용>

4 Many of us reflect on (us / ourselves) to make our lives better. <학평 응용>

5 He left a note on Allison's desk to remind (her / herself) about the meeting.

[6-10] 우리말과 같도록 빈칸에 알맞은 말을 쓰시오.

6 나는 실수를 할 때 나 자신에게 화가 난다.

   = I am angry with _____ when I make a mistake.

7 Nicole은 그녀의 집을 떠나기 전에 거울에 비친 그녀 자신을 확인한다.

   = Before Nicole leaves her house, she checks _____ in the mirror.

8 그 용의자는 어제 체포되었고, 경찰이 지금 그를 심문하고 있다.

   = The suspect was arrested yesterday, and the police are questioning _____ now.

9 그 사업가들은 그들의 사업이 성공하기 전에 스스로 열심히 노력했었다.

   = The entrepreneurs had tried hard _____ before their business succeeded. <학평 응용>

10 만약 너의 주변에 가까운 친구들이 있다면 너 자신을 운이 좋다고 여겨라.

   = Consider _____ fortunate if you have close friends around you.

11 다음 글에서 어법상 틀린 부분을 찾아 쓰고 바르게 고쳐 쓰시오.

   Kittens usually start grooming them by the time they are about four weeks old. They learn to do this by imitating their mother. Namely, the mother cat herself teaches her offspring the necessary skills.

   *groom: (동물이 털을) 다듬다

   _____ → _____

it의 다양한 쓰임

정답 p.8

1. 문장의 주어나 목적어 자리에 to부정사(구)나 명사절 등이 와서 길어질 때는 주로 해당 자리에 가주어/가목적어 it을 쓰고 원래 주어/목적어를 뒤로 보낸다.

It is dangerous *to ride a bicycle without a helmet.*

I thought **it** surprising *that he attended the meeting on time.*

2. 날씨, 온도, 계절, 시간, 요일, 날짜, 명암, 거리 등을 나타낼 때 비인칭 주어 it을 쓰며, 이때 it은 해석하지 않는다.

It is sunny and warm today. **It's** already April.

I don't know why **it** is still bright outside even though **it's** 8:30 P.M.

[1-6] 밑줄 친 it의 쓰임을 <보기>에서 골라 그 기호를 쓰시오.

<보기> ⓐ 가주어   ⓑ 가목적어   ⓒ 비인칭 주어

1 It was lucky that no one was injured in the fire.   [   ]

2 I believed it certain that she cheated during the exam.   [   ]

3 It is about 130 miles from Las Vegas to the Grand Canyon.   [   ]

4 Sailing ships made it possible to exchange products with other countries. <학평 응용> [   ]

5 It is necessary to recognize your pet's particular needs. <학평 응용>   [   ]

6 It will be autumn in a few days, and the weather will get cool.   [   ]

[7-10] 우리말과 같도록 괄호 안의 말을 알맞게 배열하시오.

7 그 코치는 선수들이 연습을 빠지면 안 된다는 것을 분명히 했다. (made, clear, the coach, it)

= _____ that players must not miss practice.

8 내가 마지막으로 영화를 보러 간 이후로 세 달이 됐다. (has, three months, it, been)

= _____ since I last went to watch a movie.

9 가난한 나라들을 도와주는 것은 중요하지만, 간단하지 않다. (important, to help, is, it, poor countries)

= _____, but it's not simple. <학평>

10 그가 사무실을 떠났을 때는 이미 어두웠다. (dark, it, was)

= _____ already when he left the office.

11 다음 글에서 어법상 틀린 부분을 찾아 쓰고 바르게 고쳐 쓰시오.

Gossip is harmful because it can hurt people's feelings. Most people know that it isn't polite to gossip. Yet, some find this hard to resist telling their friends stories that they have heard about others.

*gossip: 소문, 험담; 험담을 하다

_____ → _____

POINT 6 부정대명사: one, another, other

1. one은 앞에서 언급된 명사와 같은 종류의 불특정한 대상을 가리킬 때 쓰며, 복수형은 ones이다. one은 일반적인 사람을 가리킬 때도 쓴다.

The new *television* has a bigger screen than my old **one**.
One never knows what the future may be.

TIP 앞에서 언급된 특정한 대상을 가리킬 때는 it이나 they/them을 쓴다.
This bag is heavy. Can you carry **it** for a while?

2. another는 '하나 더, 또 다른 (하나)'라는 의미이다.

I dropped my fork on the floor, so the waiter got me **another**.

3. other는 '(불특정한) 다른 (사람들/것들)'이라는 의미이며, 대명사로 쓸 때는 주로 복수형인 others로 쓴다. 「the + other(s)」는 '나머지 (전부)'라는 의미이다.

Making **others** laugh makes my life more meaningful.
There are two backpacks. One is mine, and **the other** belongs to my friend.

4. 여럿 중 일부를 나타내는 표현

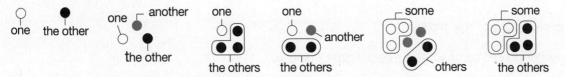

[1-7] 괄호 안에서 알맞은 것을 고르시오.

1 I went to the store to change my sneakers to bigger (one / ones).

2 The chess club has five members. One is a girl, and (others / the others) are boys.

3 This math problem is difficult. I can't figure out how to solve (it / one).

4 Most people have one foot that is slightly larger than (another / the other). <학평>

5 I have four plates. One is green, (another / the other) is black, and the others are blue.

6 I will use this software until I find a more efficient (one / it).

7 Some insects don't live through the winter, but (the other / others) have clever ways to survive. <학평 응용>

8 다음 글에서 어법상 <u>틀린</u> 부분을 찾아 쓰고 바르게 고쳐 쓰시오.

> There are two major political parties in the United States: the Democratic Party and the Republican Party. One is represented by a donkey, and another is represented by an elephant. The origins of these mascots can be traced to the 19th century.

_____ → _____

부정대명사: all, each, none

정답 p.8

1. all은 '모두, 모든 (것)'이라는 의미로, 대명사로 쓰여 사람을 나타낼 때는 복수 취급하고 사물이나 상황을 나타낼 때는 단수 취급한다. 「all (of) + 명사」의 형태로 쓸 때는 all (of) 뒤의 명사에 동사를 수일치시킨다.

All *were* enchanted by the singer's beautiful voice.
All (of) his money *is* kept in the bank account.

2. each는 '각각(의)'이라는 의미로 단수 취급하고, 「each of + 복수명사」나 「each + 단수명사」의 형태로도 쓴다.

Our team has excellent members. **Each** *performs* his or her tasks with great skill.
Each of the passengers *needs* to take their boarding pass with them.

> TIP every는 '모든'이라는 의미의 형용사로 단수 취급하고, 「every + 단수명사」의 형태로만 쓴다.
> **Every house** on this street *has* a big fence and yard.

3. none은 '아무(것)도 ~않다'라는 의미로, 셀 수 있는 명사와 함께 쓸 때는 단수 취급하거나 복수 취급하고 셀 수 없는 명사와 함께 쓸 때는 단수 취급한다.

None of the doctors *was*[*were*] sure about the patient's symptoms.
None of the oil *has* leaked into the ocean from the tank yet.

[1-5] 괄호 안에서 알맞은 것을 고르시오.

1 The waiter poured some wine into each (glass / glasses).

2 All university students (is / are) able to get a discount. <학평 응용>

3 After spending two days in the desert, none of the water (was / were) left in the bottle.

4 In 2004, every medal winner (was / were) given an olive wreath along with their medal. <학평 응용>

5 (All / None) of her books arouses readers with a sense of curiosity. <학평 응용>

[6-10] 우리말과 같도록 괄호 안의 말을 활용하여 빈칸에 쓰시오.(단, 명사의 형태는 바꾸지 마시오.)

6 각각의 귀는 올빼미가 소리를 구별하는 것을 돕는다. (ear, help)
= _____ _____ _____ the owl distinguish between sounds. <학평 응용>

7 모든 방문객이 그 새로운 롤러코스터를 타기 위해 줄을 서서 기다리고 있다. (be, visitor)
= _____ _____ _____ waiting in line to ride the new roller coaster.

8 그 설명에 따르면 각각의 정답들은 맞다. (be, the answers)
= _____ _____ _____ _____ _____ correct according to the explanation.

9 그 가구 중 아무것도 아직 나의 아파트에 도착하지 않았다. (the furniture, have)
= _____ _____ _____ _____ _____ arrived at my apartment yet.

10 비록 모든 우리의 뇌들은 같은 구조를 가지지만, 우리의 신경망은 유일무이하다. (contain, our brains)
= Even though _____ _____ _____ _____ _____ the same structures, our neural networks are unique. <학평>

부정대명사: both, either, neither

정답 p.8

1. both는 '둘 다 (모두)'라는 의미로 복수 취급하고, 「both (of) + 복수명사」의 형태로도 쓴다.

The hotel has a pool and a gym. **Both** *were* renovated recently.
Adam and Rachel are watching a sad movie, and **both of them** *are* crying.

2. either는 '둘 중 어느 것이든, 누구든'이라는 의미로 주로 단수 취급하고, 「either of + 복수명사」나 「either + 단수명사」의 형태로도 쓴다.

Between the two plans, we think that **either** *is* acceptable.
Either day *is* fine with me, but I prefer the weekend more. <학평 응용>

3. neither는 '둘 중 어느 것도, 누구도 ~않다'라는 의미로 주로 단수 취급하고, 「neither of + 복수명사」나 「neither + 단수명사」의 형태로도 쓴다.

Neither of my parents *has*[*have*] ever tried Greek food.
↳ 구어체에서는 「either/neither of + 복수명사」를 복수 취급하기도 한다.

Neither theater *is* open after 10 P.M.

[1-6] 괄호 안에서 알맞은 것을 고르시오.

1 I saw both of your (sister / sisters) at the mall last night.

2 Neither company (have / has) commented on the issue.

3 If you don't want to use milk, you can substitute it for water in either (recipe / recipes).

4 Trade will not occur unless both parties (want / wants) what the other party offers. <학평 응용>

5 (Either / Both) of these TV programs is suitable for a child under the age of 13.

6 We were disappointed at the restaurant because (either / neither) of the meals was good.

[7-10] 우리말과 같도록 괄호 안의 말을 활용하여 빈칸에 쓰시오.

7 두 기자들 중 누구도 그 소문을 퍼뜨린 것에 대해 사과하지 않았다. (the journalist, apologize)
= _____ _____ _____ _____ _____ for spreading the rumor.

8 두 자동차 중 어느 것이든 지금 시승이 가능하다. (car, be)
= _____ _____ _____ available for the test drive now.

9 두 호수 모두 공장으로부터의 화학물질 때문에 오염되었다. (lake, be pollute)
= _____ _____ _____ _____ because of the chemicals from factories.

10 나는 두 외국인 친구가 있지만, 둘 중 누구도 한국어를 잘하지 않는다. (be)
= I have two foreign friends, but _____ _____ good at Korean.

Review Test

[1-2] 다음 빈칸에 공통으로 들어갈 알맞은 것을 고르시오.

1

> · Children's opinions sometimes do not agree with _____ of adults.
> · This memorial is a reminder of _____ who sacrificed for our country.

① it   ② this   ③ these
④ that   ⑤ those

2

> · _____ seems impossible that we could lose the football game tonight.
> · _____ is October 31 tomorrow.

① It   ② One   ③ Another
④ This   ⑤ That

[3-4] 다음 빈칸에 들어갈 말이 순서대로 짝지어진 것을 고르시오.

3

> · The bus leaves once _____ hour.
> · Mercury is _____ only metal that is liquid at room temperature.

① a – a   ② an – an   ③ an – the
④ the – an   ⑤ the – the

4

> · Jerry caught several small fish, but he had wanted to catch a big _____.
> · He grabbed the bow with one hand and pulled back the arrow with _____.

① one – another
③ one – the other
⑤ ones – the other
② one – other
④ ones – another

[5-6] 다음 중 밑줄 친 부분이 어법상 **틀린** 것을 <u>모두</u> 고르시오.

5

① She read <u>a magazine</u> while she was waiting.
② Astronomers hope the new telescope will increase our <u>knowledges</u> of space.
③ I usually go to the local restaurant to eat <u>lunch</u>.
④ There is a beach not far from here. We can get to <u>the beach</u> on foot.
⑤ Quit comparing <u>you</u> to your friends.

6

① The computer is not working, so I have to fix <u>one</u>.
② Nelson thought <u>it</u> strange that his roommate didn't come back yet.
③ In this village, all the houses <u>have</u> central heating.   <학평 응용>
④ The sportscaster believes that either of the <u>team</u> could win.
⑤ <u>It</u> began to grow chilly as the sun set.

7 다음 중 어법상 바른 것끼리 묶인 것은?

> ⓐ Both of the drivers was at fault.
> ⓑ These engines are used in many vehicles such as trains or buses.
> ⓒ Every rooms are fully booked because the vacation season comes.
> ⓓ Some passengers on the flight stayed awake, while the others slept.
> ⓔ Students themselves should decide what topic they want to write about.

① ⓐ, ⓑ, ⓒ   ② ⓐ, ⓒ, ⓓ   ③ ⓑ, ⓒ, ⓔ
④ ⓑ, ⓓ, ⓔ   ⑤ ⓒ, ⓓ, ⓔ

[8-11] 다음 문장에서 어법상 <u>틀린</u> 부분을 찾아 쓰고 바르게 고쳐 쓰시오.

8

Most students typically encounter same issue when they graduate from college.

_____ → _____

9

An advance reservation is required for these who wish to taste the special menu.

_____ → _____

10

She considered that challenging to put her thoughts into words.

_____ → _____

11

None of the evidence were missing at the crime scene.

_____ → _____

12 다음 글에서 어법상 <u>틀린</u> 부분을 찾아 쓰고 바르게 고쳐 쓰시오.

On my way back home, I felt something wrong with my car and checked the tires. One was flat, but others were fine.

_____ → _____

[13-14] 우리말과 같도록 괄호 안의 말을 알맞게 배열하시오.

13

각각의 부품들은 이 기계를 작동시키는 데 대단히 중요하다. (of, critical, the components, each, is)

= _____ to operating this machine.

14

두 운동선수 중 누구도 결승전에 진출하지 못한 것은 실망스러웠다. (disappointing, went, athlete, it, neither, that, was)

= _____
to the final.

[15-17] 우리말과 같도록 괄호 안의 말을 활용하여 문장을 완성하시오.

15

이 편의점은 문을 닫았어. 가까운 곳에 또 다른 가게가 있니? (convenience store, store)

= _____ is closed. Is there _____ nearby?

16

비록 그녀는 초보자이지만, 그녀의 능력들은 전문가의 그것들에 필적한다. (her abilities, rival)

= Even though she is a beginner, _____
_____ of an expert.

17

나는 운전면허증을 취득한 것에 대해 나 자신을 자랑스러워했다. (be proud of)

= _____ for acquiring the driver's license.

18 우리말과 같도록 주어진 <조건>에 맞게 문장을 완성하시오.

> 두 사진들 모두 알려지지 않은 사진작가에 의해 찍혔다.

> <조건>
> 1. picture, take, an unknown photographer를 활용하시오.
> 2. 수동태를 활용하시오.
> 3. 8단어로 쓰시오.

= _____ .

[19-20] 다음 글을 읽고 주어진 질문에 답하시오.

> Deaf people communicate with sign language. (A) <u>이것은 그들이 손동작들과 얼굴 표정들로 그들 자신을 표현한다는 것을 의미한다.</u> (express) Namely, the only communicative method to receive ⓐ<u>an</u> <u>information</u> is such visual interaction. However, the collection of symbols used by deaf people in North America is different from ⓑ<u>those</u> used in other countries. Therefore, deaf travelers may ⓒ<u>be confused</u> by unfamiliar types of sign language. Worse still, they may be unable to communicate in ⓓ<u>other</u> countries. All ⓔ<u>nations</u> and each politician should try to solve the issue mentioned above.

19 위 글의 밑줄 친 우리말 (A)와 같도록 괄호 안의 말을 활용하여 문장을 완성하시오.

= This means that _____
with hand movements and facial expressions.

20 위 글의 밑줄 친 ⓐ~ⓔ 중 어법상 틀린 것의 기호를 쓰고 바르게 고쳐 쓰시오.

(1) _____ → _____

(2) _____ → _____

21 (A), (B), (C)의 각 네모 안에서 어법에 맞는 표현으로 가장 적절한 것은?

> If you have a problem with a neighbor, don't avoid the neighbor, and don't call the police. (A) This / It is unlikely that either of those ways will work well. Try handling the problem by using these strategies: Don't criticize your neighbor's behavior; instead, explain how the behavior is affecting you. Rather than react emotionally, ask (B) you / yourself what you want to say and then say it calmly. Be ready to compromise. If these strategies are not effective, the ideal solution may be to ask (C) another / the other neighbor to help you solve the problem. <학평 응용>

	(A)	(B)	(C)
①	This	you	another
②	This	yourself	another
③	It	you	the other
④	It	yourself	the other
⑤	It	yourself	another

22 다음 글의 밑줄 친 부분 중, 어법상 틀린 것은?

> Accepting ①<u>a job</u> means that you accept the responsibility that goes with it. Even if every task you are expected to perform ②<u>is</u> not in the job description, you should always do anything that needs to be done. For example, if you use the last piece of paper in the tray of a copy machine, what should you do? You should refill it because you were ③<u>the one</u> who emptied the paper in the machine. This way, you can make ④<u>that</u> easier for the next person to use the machine. Having paper in the tray made your work easier, so why not refill it for ⑤<u>others</u>? <학평 응용>

CHAPTER 6
형용사와 부사

기출로 적중 POINT

1 형용사의 용법

2 수량형용사

3 부사의 역할

4 주의해야 할 부사의 위치

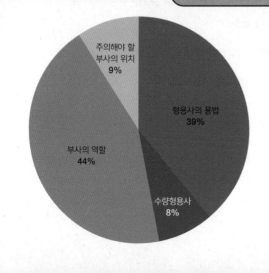

주의해야 할
부사의 위치
9%

형용사의 용법
39%

부사의 역할
44%

수량형용사
8%

TOP 1 **부사의 역할 (44%)**
동사나 형용사를 수식하는 자리에 형용사가 아닌 부사가 왔는지를
묻는 문제가 자주 출제된다.

TOP 2 **형용사의 용법 (39%)**
주격 보어 자리에 부사가 아닌 형용사가 왔는지를 묻는 문제가 자
주 출제된다.

TOP 3 **주의해야 할 부사의 위치 (9%)**
특정 부사의 알맞은 위치를 묻는 문제가 자주 출제된다.

1. 한정적 용법: (대)명사를 수식하여 범위를 한정한다. 대부분의 명사는 형용사를 앞에 쓰고, -thing/-body/ -one으로 끝나는 대명사는 형용사를 뒤에 쓴다.

Famous *actors* attended the award ceremony.

Try *something* **new** once a day. It doesn't have to be *anything* **major**. <학평 응용>

2. 서술적 용법: 보어로 쓰여 주어나 목적어를 보충 설명한다.

Although *these earrings* look **valuable**, they only cost $10.

Art does not solve problems, but it makes *us* **aware** of their existence. <학평>

TIP 서술적 용법으로만 사용되는 형용사: afraid(무서워하는), alike(비슷한), alive(살아있는), alone(혼자인), ashamed(부끄러운), asleep (잠든), awake(깨어 있는), aware(알고 있는), worth(~의 가치가 있는), content(만족하는)

[1-7] 괄호 안에서 알맞은 것을 고르시오.

1 A frog must stay (moistly / moist) to breathe through its skin. <학평 응용>

2 (Brave someone / Someone brave) rescued the kids from the burning building.

3 The lawyer suggested several revisions because she found the contract (unfairly / unfair).

4 The zookeepers were silently watching (asleep / sleeping) koalas.

5 Companies can remain (competitive / competitively) by reducing manufacturing costs. <수능 응용>

6 The (frightened / afraid) child couldn't enter the dental clinic.

7 The (brutality / brutal) storm caused (extensive / extensively) flooding throughout the region.

[8-14] 밑줄 친 부분이 어법상 맞으면 O를 쓰고, 틀리면 바르게 고쳐 쓰시오.

8 Luckily, there was <u>nobody hurt</u> during the earthquake.　　　→ ＿＿＿＿＿＿＿＿

9 The map seemed <u>accurately</u>, but it contained a lot of errors.　　　→ ＿＿＿＿＿＿＿＿

10 Some shoppers considered customer reviews <u>importantly</u>. <학평 응용>　　→ ＿＿＿＿＿＿＿＿

11 The ancient Celts built homes from <u>natural</u> materials.　　　→ ＿＿＿＿＿＿＿＿

12 The milk that I accidently left on the counter has turned <u>badly</u>.　→ ＿＿＿＿＿＿＿＿

13 Some drivers think it <u>unreasonably</u> that parking fees have increased.　→ ＿＿＿＿＿＿＿＿

14 The support I received shows that kindness is still <u>alive</u>. <학평 응용>　→ ＿＿＿＿＿＿＿＿

15 다음 글에서 어법상 **틀린** 부분을 찾아 쓰고 바르게 고쳐 쓰시오.

> A stingray has something dangerous in its tail. The spines at the end are harmfully because they can inject venom into other creatures. Stingray venom makes people sick and may even cause death.
>
> *stingray: 노랑가오리　**spine: 가시

＿＿＿＿＿＿＿＿　→ ＿＿＿＿＿＿＿＿

수량형용사

정답 p.9

1. 셀 수 있는 명사와 함께 쓰는 수량형용사: many(많은), a few(약간의), few(거의 없는)

Many *chimpanzees* live in the forested areas of central Africa.

There have been **a few** *studies* on the health benefits of kimchi. <학평 응용>

2. 셀 수 없는 명사와 함께 쓰는 수량형용사: much(많은), a little(약간의), little(거의 없는)

Sophie does not have **much** *time*, so she cannot meet us for coffee.

Certain plants can grow well in sandy soil with **little** *water*. <학평 응용>

3. 셀 수 있는 명사, 셀 수 없는 명사와 모두 함께 쓰는 수량형용사: a lot of/lots of/plenty of(많은), some/any(약간의)

The man showed **a lot of[lots of/plenty of]** *interest* in learning how to play chess.

I made **some** *chocolate-chip cookies* to share with my classmates.

Did you see **any** *parcels* by the front door when you came in?

TIP some은 주로 긍정문과 권유·요청을 나타내는 의문문에 쓰고, any는 주로 부정문과 의문문, '어떤 ~이라도'를 의미하는 긍정문에 쓴다.

[1-7] 괄호 안에서 알맞은 것을 고르시오.

1 There is too (much / many) noise coming from the air conditioner.

2 Some people spent their (little / few) free hours reading books. <학평 응용>

3 The team came up with (much / plenty of) ideas to promote the new product.

4 (A little / A few) encouragement can help a student perform better in school.

5 He offered me (some / any) dessert after I finished my meal.

6 Denise invited (few / many) friends to the party, so the room was crowded.

7 I couldn't find (some / any) information about updating the software. <수능 응용>

[8-11] 우리말과 같도록 <보기>와 괄호 안의 말을 한 번씩만 활용하여 문장을 완성하시오.

> <보기> a few   little   lots of   some

8 Zack은 부엌 바닥에 약간의 페인트를 쏟아서 곤경에 처했다. (paint)

= Zack got into trouble for spilling _____ on the kitchen floor.

9 네스호 괴물이 진짜라는 증거는 거의 없다. (evidence)

= There is _____ that the Loch Ness Monster is real.

10 그 사냥꾼은 약간의 사나운 사냥개들을 소유했다. (fierce hunting dogs)

= The hunter owned _____. <학평 응용>

11 Sarah Breedlove는 많은 여자들을 판매 대리인으로 교육시켰다. (women)

= Sarah Breedlove trained _____ as sales agents. <학평 응용>

부사의 역할

부사는 동사, 형용사, 다른 부사, 문장 전체를 수식한다.

Teenagers **frequently** *communicate* using social networks. <학평 응용>

His **exceptionally** *large* donation to the charity was appreciated.

TIP ① -ly로 끝나지만 부사가 아닌 형용사인 단어: friendly(친절한), lovely(사랑스러운), lonely(외로운), costly(값비싼), likely(그럴듯한), orderly(정돈된) 등

Working from home for several months made *me* **lonely**.

② 주의해야 할 부사

형용사와 형태가 같은 부사	late(늦은 / 늦게)	early(이른 / 일찍)	close(가까운 / 가까이)
	near(가까운 / 가까이)	fast(빠른 / 빠르게)	high(높은 / 높이, 높게)
	enough(충분한 / 충분히)	most(가장 많은 / 가장 많이)	hard(열심인, 어려운 / 열심히)
-ly가 붙으면 의미가 달라지는 부사	late(늦게) – lately(최근에)		close(가까이) – closely(면밀히)
	near(가까이) – nearly(거의)		high(높이, 높게) – highly(매우, 대단히)
	most(가장 많이) – mostly(주로, 대부분)		hard(열심히) – hardly(거의 ~않다)

[1-6] 괄호 안에서 알맞은 것을 고르시오.

1 The politicians argued about the national budget (endless / endlessly). <수능 응용>

2 As she woke up (late / lately), she could not arrive at the train station on time.

3 Dr. Anderson examined the wounds of the (severely / severe) injured soldier.

4 The luxury department store sells many (cost / costly) items.

5 (Unfortunately / Unfortunate), the tornado destroyed several homes in the town.

6 Robots are good at (high / highly) repetitive tasks that involve (simple / simply) motions. <수능 응용>

[7-12] 밑줄 친 부분이 어법상 맞으면 O를 쓰고, 틀리면 바르게 고쳐 쓰시오.

7 The cat approached the ducks very <u>cautious</u>. → _____

8 My neighbor is a <u>friendly</u> person who always wants to chat. → _____

9 The accounting team must work <u>fast</u> to meet its project deadline. → _____

10 The figure skater practiced <u>hardly</u> to win the international competition. → _____

11 I'm <u>absolute</u> thrilled because I'll soon get a new cell phone. <학평 응용> → _____

12 The effects of climate change are being studied <u>close</u> by scientists. → _____

13 다음 문장에서 어법상 틀린 부분을 찾아 쓰고 바르게 고쳐 쓰시오.

> Gina had trained hard for six months to prepare for the Westport Marathon. Although she knew finishing the race would be hard, she felt extreme confident.

_____ → _____

POINT 4 주의해야 할 부사의 위치

정답 p.10

1. 부사는 일반적으로 형용사나 다른 부사를 앞에서 수식하지만, 부사로 쓰인 enough는 형용사나 다른 부사를 뒤에서 수식한다.

   The soup wasn't *spicy* **enough**, so I added more seasonings.

2. 빈도부사는 일반동사의 앞 또는 be동사나 조동사의 뒤에 위치한다.

   Killer whales **often** *hunt* seals and other marine mammals for food.
   Even during the winter, it *is* **rarely** cold in Honolulu.
   People *must* **always** wear seatbelts when driving.

3. 「타동사 + 부사」의 목적어가 명사인 경우 「타동사 + 부사 + 명사」나 「타동사 + 명사 + 부사」의 형태로 쓰고, 목적어가 대명사인 경우 「타동사 + 대명사 + 부사」의 형태로 쓴다.

   I **turn off** *the TV* [**turn** *the TV* **off**] when I do my homework. <학평 응용>
   He finished the sales report and **turned** *it* **in** to his manager.

[1-7] 괄호 안에서 알맞은 것을 <u>모두</u> 고르시오.

1 I (eat seldom / seldom eat) out because I enjoy cooking.

2 The pillow wasn't (soft enough / enough soft) for me to feel comfortable.

3 Please (turn off the lights / turn the lights off) in the office when you leave.

4 There (usually is / is usually) a correct way of holding musical instruments. <학평 응용>

5 I (can hardly / hardly can) wait to visit my grandparents next week.

6 Seeing a wallet lying on the ground, Samuel (picked it up / picked up it).

7 Ms. Polson went into the room to (wake up her son / wake him up).

[8-12] 우리말과 같도록 괄호 안의 말을 알맞게 배열하시오.

8 만약 네가 그것을 결코 사용하지 않는다면, 정보는 쓸모없다. (use, you, it, never)
   = Information is worthless if _____. <학평>

9 코미디를 보는 것은 내가 우울할 때 나를 기운 나게 한다. (me, watching a comedy, up, cheers)
   = _____ when I'm depressed.

10 Chad는 충분히 오래 자지 않아서 매우 피곤하게 느꼈다. (enough, didn't, long, Chad, sleep)
   = _____, so he felt very tired.

11 Irene은 퇴근 후에 때때로 슈퍼마켓에 들를 것이다. (stop, will, Irene, sometimes)
   = _____ at the supermarket after work.

12 그 학생은 망설임 없이 정답들을 적었다. (down, wrote, the student, the answers)
   = _____ without hesitation.

Review Test

[1-4] 다음 빈칸에 들어갈 말이 순서대로 짝지어진 것을 고르시오.

1

- _____ doesn't need to ride this roller coaster.
- His goal is to become _____ to retire at 50.

① Scared anyone – rich enough
② Scared anyone – enough rich
③ Scared anything – rich enough
④ Anyone scared – enough rich
⑤ Anyone scared – rich enough

2

- The muffins that she is baking smell _____.
- The obesity rate is increasing _____.

① wonderful – rapidity   ② wonderful – rapid
③ wonderful – rapidly   ④ wonderfully – rapid
⑤ wonderfully – rapidly

3

- The sound of thunder made the babies _____.
- _____ people truly understand the theory.

① nervously – Little   ② nervous – A little
③ nervously – A little   ④ nervous – Few
⑤ nervously – Few

4

- In 2021, an asteroid _____ hit our planet.
- Lara _____ take the subway after she buys a car.

① nearly – will rarely   ② nearly – rarely will
③ nearness – will rarely   ④ near – rarely will
⑤ near – will rarely

[5-7] 다음 중 밑줄 친 부분이 어법상 바른 것을 모두 고르시오.

5

① Much effort was put into making the Christmas party a success.
② I don't have some desire to start playing golf.
③ I spent a little days solving the crossword puzzle.
④ Would you like to add some sugar to your tea?
⑤ My father has a few information about investing.

6

① The national economy remained stably despite the global financial crisis.
② The scarlet macaw is a type of parrot with brightly colored feathers.
③ The concert started late due to an error in the sound system.
④ Mr. Reynolds keeps himself busily with hobbies.
⑤ Mom said she had important something to tell me.

7

① The falcon flew highly over the forest searching for prey.
② It is likely that the weather will be rainy tomorrow.
③ Snow fell heavy throughout the night, blocking many roads in the city.
④ She never is late for an appointment with a client.
⑤ I am uncertain about the best smartphone model to buy.

[8-10] 다음 문장에서 어법상 <u>틀린</u> 부분을 찾아 쓰고 바르게 고쳐 쓰시오.

8

Kate and Mindy look similar, so people frequent confuse them.

_____ → _____

9

A little exercise each day can have a significantly positively impact on one's health.

_____ → _____

10

Cameron felt so ashamedly when he completely forgot his older sister's birthday.

_____ → _____

11 다음 글에서 어법상 <u>틀린</u> 부분을 찾아 쓰고 바르게 고쳐 쓰시오.

Eating lots of fruits and vegetables is necessary to keep your body healthily. They make us take enough vitamins.

_____ → _____

[12-13] 우리말과 같도록 괄호 안의 말을 알맞게 배열하시오.

12

그 일자리 제의가 낮은 급여를 포함했기 때문에, Miller씨는 그것을 거절했다. (it, Ms. Miller, down, turned)

= As the job offer included a low salary, _____
_____.

13

그 개는 안내견이 될 만큼 충분히 똑똑하다. (the dog, enough, smart, is)

= _____ to be a guide dog.
<학평 응용>

[14-16] 우리말과 같도록 괄호 안의 말을 활용하여 문장을 완성하시오.

14

그 다큐멘터리는 내가 대기 오염 문제를 알고 있게 했다. (make, the documentary, aware)

= _____ of the air pollution issue.

15

조지 오웰은 매우 높이 평가되는 영국 작가들 중 한 명이다. (British writers, respected, high)

= George Orwell is one of the _____
_____.

16

그녀의 영화는 보통 의미 있는 교훈들을 포함한다. (meaningful, usually, her movie, contain, lessons)

= _____.

17 우리말과 같도록 주어진 <조건>에 맞게 문장을 완성하시오.

> 분명히, 아이들은 너무 많은 정크 푸드를 먹으면 안 된다.

> <조건>
> 1. obvious, should, children, eat, junk food, too를 활용하시오.
> 2. 8단어로 쓰시오.

= _____, _____.

[18-19] 다음 대화를 읽고 주어진 질문에 답하시오.

> A: Our office is freezing. Is the heater turned on?
> B: Yes. I checked the thermostat, and there was ⓐ nothing wrong with the settings.
> A: Did you reset it? Doing that ⓑ sometimes solves the problem.
> B: I tried that ⓒ a little times. Maybe we should call a technician.
> A: Good idea. Hopefully, someone can come ⓓ immediate.
> B: In the meantime, why don't you ⓔ put my jacket on? (A) 그것은 너를 따뜻하게 해줄 거야. (warm, make)
> A: Thanks. I appreciate that.
>
> *thermostat: 온도 조절 장치

18 위 대화의 밑줄 친 우리말 (A)와 같도록 괄호 안의 말을 활용하여 문장을 완성하시오.

= It _____.

19 위 대화의 밑줄 친 ⓐ~ⓔ 중 어법상 틀린 것의 기호를 쓰고 바르게 고쳐 쓰시오.

(1) _____ → _____
(2) _____ → _____

20 (A), (B), (C)의 각 네모 안에서 어법에 맞는 표현으로 가장 적절한 것은?

> Impressionist paintings do not ask the viewer to work (A) ⟦hard / hardly⟧ to understand the imagery. Impressionism is comfortable to look at, with its summer scenes and bright colors. It is important to remember, however, that this new way of painting was challenging to its public not only in the way that it (B) ⟦made / was made⟧ but also in what was shown. They had never seen such informal paintings before. The edge of the canvas cut off the scene in an arbitrary way. The subject matter included modern landscape feature such as railways and factories. Never before had these subjects been considered (C) ⟦appropriate / appropriately⟧ for artists. <학평 응용>
>
> *arbitrary: 임의적인

	(A)	(B)	(C)
①	hard	made	appropriate
②	hardly	made	appropriate
③	hard	was made	appropriate
④	hardly	was made	appropriately
⑤	hard	was made	appropriately

21 다음 글의 밑줄 친 부분 중, 어법상 틀린 것은?

> Nancy's 16-year-old daughter had a negative perspective on her life and abilities. So, Nancy intentionally noted one positive accomplishment of her daughter. "I know you've not felt positive about your life ① lately. But you did a great job cleaning up your room today, and I know that must ② have been a big effort for you." The next day, the girl seemed somewhat ③ cheerfully. She said, "Mom, thanks for saying the positive thing about me yesterday. I couldn't think of ④ anything good about myself. You helped me ⑤ see one good quality in myself." <수능 응용>

CHAPTER 7
전치사

기출로 적중 POINT

최근 7개년 수능/학평/내신 출제 경향

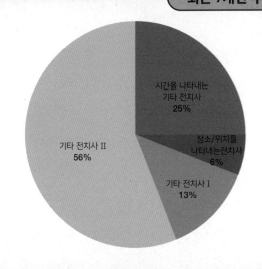

TOP 1 **기타 전치사 II (56%)**
다양한 의미를 나타내는 전치사의 쓰임을 묻는 문제가 자주 출제된다.

TOP 2 **시간을 나타내는 기타 전치사 (25%)**
시간을 나타내는 전치사의 쓰임을 묻는 문제가 자주 출제된다.

TOP 3 **기타 전치사 I (13%)**
원인이나 이유를 나타내는 전치사의 쓰임을 묻는 문제가 자주 출제된다.

전치사 at, on, in은 '~에'라는 의미로, 시간을 나타낸다.

at	시각, 시점	**at** 2 o'clock **at** 5:30 P.M. **at** noon **at** night
on	요일, 날짜, 기념일	**on** Monday **on** November 11, 2021 **on** New Year's Day TIP 「on + 요일s」: (요일)마다 **on** Thursdays
in	월, 계절, 연도, 세기, 아침·오후·저녁	**in** June **in** spring **in** 2002 **in** the 16th century **in** the morning/afternoon/evening TIP ① 특정한 날의 아침·오후·저녁을 나타낼 때는 on을 쓴다. 　　　**on** Sunday morning **on** Halloween evening ② in 뒤에 기간을 나타내는 말이 오면 '~ 후에'라는 의미이다. 　　　The train will arrive **in** *a few minutes*.

TIP 시간을 나타내는 표현이 last, this, next, every 등으로 시작할 때는 at, on, in을 쓰지 않는다.
I have to give a speech in class (~~on next~~, **next**) Friday.

[1-10] 괄호 안에서 알맞은 것을 고르시오.

1 She had to work overtime (at / on / in) her birthday.

2 Antonio Vivaldi was born in Italy (at / on / in) 1678. <학평 응용>

3 My dad and brother will play basketball (at / on / in) 7 o'clock today.

4 Gary said that he would call me again (at / on / in) an hour.

5 Sleep clinicians treat patients who can't sleep (at / on / in) night. <학평 응용>

6 They are planning to move to a new apartment (at / on / in) May.

7 I often go swimming at a lake near my home (at / on / in) summer.

8 We drove from New York City to Princeton (at / on / in) Saturday afternoon. <수능 응용>

9 The bakery will give away free samples (at / on / in) its 10th anniversary.

10 The names of the winners will be posted on the website (at / on / in) September 3. <학평 응용>

[11-14] 우리말과 같도록 괄호 안의 말을 활용하여 문장을 완성하시오.

11 Mary는 아침에 그 버스에 탑승하는 세 번째 학생이다. (the morning)
= Mary is the third student to board the bus _____. <수능 응용>

12 우리는 크리스마스이브에 우리의 선물 중 하나를 개봉한다. (Christmas Eve)
= We open one of our presents _____.

13 제가 그 숙제를 이번 수요일에 끝내도 되나요? (Wednesday)
= Could I finish the homework _____? <학평 응용>

14 아프리카 아이들을 위한 신발은 화요일마다 수거될 것이다. (Tuesdays)
= Shoes for the African children will be picked up _____. <학평 응용>

다음은 시간을 나타내는 다양한 전치사이다.

before ~ 전에	The boys always do their homework **before** dinner.
after ~ 후에	She returned to Norway **after** World War II. <학평 응용>
from ~부터	Employees have to attend the monthly meeting **from** next year. TIP 「from ~ to …」는 '~부터 …까지'라는 의미로, 기간을 나타낸다. Taking photos is not allowed **from** 10 P.M. **to** 7 A.M. <수능>
since ~ 이후로	주로 완료시제와 함께 쓰여 어떤 행동이나 상황이 특정 시점부터 계속되는 것을 나타낸다. My mother has been knitting a sweater **since** last month.
for/during ~ 동안	for 뒤에는 숫자를 포함한 기간 표현이 오고, during 뒤에는 특정 기간을 나타내는 명사가 온다. Cover the pot and boil the stew on low heat **for** an hour. **During** the long holidays, I'm going to visit my friend in Paris.
by/until ~까지	by는 어떤 행동이나 상황이 특정 시점까지 완료되는 것을 나타내고, until은 계속되는 것을 나타낸다. Your essay has to be submitted **by** the end of the week. The artworks will be on display **until** October 8.

[1-6] 괄호 안에서 알맞은 것을 고르시오.

1 The library will be closed (from / since) tomorrow.

2 He taught mathematics at Queen's College (by / until) his death. <학평 응용>

3 The ship has been docked there (from / since) Friday.

4 The package from my grandparents is going to arrive (by / until) 3 P.M. today.

5 (For / During) summer, many of the small ponds in this area dry up.

6 Jim will not be in the office (for / during) two weeks.

[7-11] 우리말과 같도록 괄호 안의 말을 활용하여 문장을 완성하시오.

7 나는 그 일이 기한 전에 완료되게 할 수 있다. (the deadline)

= I can get the job done _____. <수능>

8 그 가게는 내일까지 모든 제품에 대해 15% 할인을 제공할 것이다. (tomorrow)

= The store will offer a 15% discount on all items _____.

9 그 화가는 그녀의 삶 중 말년 동안 그림을 그릴 수 없었다. (the later years)

= The painter was not able to paint _____ of her life. <학평 응용>

10 Michael은 중학교 이후로 과학자가 되기를 원해왔다. (middle school)

= Michael has wanted to be a scientist _____.

11 그는 경기 후에 상대 선수들과 악수했다. (the game)

= He shook hands with the opposing players _____.

장소/위치를 나타내는 전치사

다음 전치사는 장소나 위치를 나타낸다.

at ~에(서)	비교적 좁은 장소나 하나의 지점을 나타낸다. I watched the planes taking off **at** the airport.
on ~ (위)에	표면에 접촉한 상태를 나타낸다. The shattered glass lay **on** the floor.
in ~ (안)에	비교적 넓은 장소나 공간의 내부를 나타낸다. She went for a swim **in** the ocean.
in front of ~ 앞에	He spoke **in front of** a hundred people to raise money. <학평 응용>
behind ~ 뒤에	All the skaters gathered **behind** the starting line. <학평 응용>
over ~ (덮여 있듯이 바로) 위에	I turned on the air conditioner **over** my desk.
under ~ (덮여 있듯이 바로) 아래에	Christina likes to rest in the shade **under** a tree.
above ~(보다) 위에	Please hang the wall clock **above** the couch.
below ~(보다) 아래에	Andy has a small scar just **below** his left eye.
next to/by/beside ~ 옆에	Our office is located right **next to[by/beside]** a flower shop.
near ~ 근처에	She parked her car **near** the entrance of the concert hall.
between ~ (둘) 사이에	There are significant differences **between** the two groups.
among ~ (셋 이상) 사이에	They found a caterpillar hidden **among** the leaves.

[1-9] 다음 빈칸에 가장 알맞은 전치사를 <보기>에서 한 번씩만 골라 쓰시오.

<보기> at   behind   below

1 The miners discovered some gold _____ the ground.

2 It is important for me to relax _____ home after a busy day.

3 The moon slowly disappeared _____ a cloud.

<보기> in   next to   between

4 Animals including dogs are not permitted _____ this restaurant.

5 We traveled across the border _____ Canada and the United States.

6 Cindy happened to sit _____ a famous singer in a café. <학평>

<보기> in front of   under   among

7 In order to pass _____ the bridge, ships can't be higher than 50 meters.

8 A lot of people had already lined up _____ the bakery.

9 The teacher let the students discuss the problem _____ themselves. <학평 응용>

방향을 나타내는 전치사

다음 전치사는 방향을 나타낸다.

up ~ 위로	Dad climbed **up** the ladder to repair the ceiling.
down ~ 아래로	They hiked **down** the mountain because of the unexpected rain.
into ~ 안으로	He heard someone come **into** his house. <학평 응용>
out of ~ 밖으로	Impressively, the magician pulled a rabbit **out of** his hat.
off ~에서 떨어져	Sophie fell **off** a horse and broke her shoulder.
across ~을 가로질러	I walk **across** a field to get to my school each day.
along ~을 따라서	Jacob is riding his bicycle on the path **along** the highway.
around ~ 주위에	She put her arms **around** me and gave me a hug.
through ~을 통해서	The doctor told him to take a deep breath **through** his nose.
from ~에서, ~으로부터	What is the distance **from** Seoul to Beijing?
to ~에, ~으로	The injured man went **to** the hospital right away.
for ~으로, ~을 향해	By the time we departed **for** home, it was already dark outside.
toward(s) ~ 쪽으로, ~을 향해	A stray cat came **toward(s)** them when they offered it some food.

[1-9] 다음 빈칸에 가장 알맞은 전치사를 <보기>에서 한 번씩만 골라 쓰시오.

> **<보기>** along   around   for

1 The students fastened the seatbelts ＿＿＿＿＿＿＿ their waists.

2 When the fire alarm rang, everyone headed ＿＿＿＿＿＿＿ the nearest exit.

3 Some men were running ＿＿＿＿＿＿＿ the beach. <수능 응용>

> **<보기>** into   across   from

4 As soon as she went ＿＿＿＿＿＿＿ the room, everyone turned to look at her.

5 My mom came home ＿＿＿＿＿＿＿ the shop with a present for me. <학평 응용>

6 Amelia Earhart was the first woman to fly ＿＿＿＿＿＿＿ the Atlantic Ocean.

> **<보기>** out of   to   toward

7 Good songs can inspire emotions ranging from happiness ＿＿＿＿＿＿＿ grief.

8 The police officer pulled over a driver who threw trash ＿＿＿＿＿＿＿ his car window.

9 An old man with a cane was walking ＿＿＿＿＿＿＿ the bench. <학평 응용>

1. 다음 전치사는 원인이나 이유를 나타낸다.

because of/due to ~ 때문에	The school is closed **because of[due to]** the snowstorm. <일반적인 원인>
at ~에	Audiences were amazed **at** the artist's creativity. <감정의 원인>
for ~ 때문에	The band became famous **for** their new song. <일반적인 원인> Everyone looked impatient **for** some reason. <감정의 원인>
from ~으로	A lot of people suffer **from** insomnia these days. <신체상의 이유>
with ~으로, ~ 때문에	The spectators were shouting **with** joy. <감정의 원인> The kids were trembling **with** extreme cold. <신체상의 이유>

2. 다음 전치사는 목적을 나타낸다.

| for ~을 위해 | Exercising and dieting can be effective tools **for** weight loss. |
| on ~의 용건으로 | I was away **on** business for five days. |

3. 다음 전치사는 도구나 수단을 나타낸다.

with ~(도구)를 이용해서	The nurse wrapped the patient's ankle **with** a bandage.
without ~ 없이	We cannot visit foreign countries **without** a passport.
by ~(교통·통신수단)을 타고/으로, ~(도구/수단)으로	I often go to work **by** taxi. Will you pay **by** cash or credit card?
in ~(언어)로	The students are practicing speaking **in** English.

[1-5] 우리말과 같도록 <보기>와 괄호 안의 말을 한 번씩만 활용하여 문장을 완성하시오.

| <보기> | for | due to | without | with | by |

1 그들은 페리를 타고 홍콩에서 마카오로 이동했다. (ferry)

= They moved from Hong Kong to Macau _____.

2 우주에서의 대부분의 임무는 승선한 승무원들 없이 완수된다. (crews)

= Most missions in space are accomplished _____ aboard. <학평 응용>

3 그녀는 베이킹 수업을 위해 돈을 모으려고 식당에서 일했다. (baking lessons)

= She worked at a restaurant to save money _____. <학평 응용>

4 Tony는 바닥에 있는 우유를 대걸레를 이용해서 닦았다. (a mop)

= Tony cleaned the milk on the floor _____.

5 그 회사는 오염 때문에 그것의 식료품 중 일부를 회수했다. (contamination)

= The company recalled some of its food products _____.

기타 전치사 II

정답 p.11

다음은 그 외 의미를 나타내는 다양한 전치사이다.

despite/in spite of ~에도 불구하고	**Despite[In spite of]** her age, she still looks like a teenager.
about/of/on ~에 대해	He won a Nobel Prize for his research **about[of/on]** black holes.
except ~을 제외하고	Every student submitted their papers **except** Anna. <학평 응용>
instead of ~ 대신	I asked the waiter for a fork **instead of** chopsticks.
as ~(자격)으로	We nominated Carl **as** our class president.
for ~에 찬성하는	Only a few people are **for** the new health insurance plan.
against ~에 반대하여, 맞서	Many nations around the world have joined the fight **against** terrorism.
with ~을 가진	There is a house **with** a large swimming pool in this town.
like ~처럼, ~ 같이	The roof of that building is shaped **like** a triangle.
such as ~과 같은	Animals **such as** mice, birds, and monkeys eat fruit.
according to ~에 따라	We should not live **according to** others' expectations. <학평>

[1-14] 괄호 안에서 가장 알맞은 것을 고르시오.

1 I dislike cheese (with / as) a strong flavor and aroma.

2 We assembled the chair (except / according to) the instructions.

3 The study is (despite / about) the hidden dangers of obesity.

4 All of my family members are (with / for) throwing out the old sofa.

5 They'll use public transportation (of / instead of) their own cars. <학평 응용>

6 There is nothing left in the refrigerator (except / against) a bottle of juice.

7 We watched a video (on / in spite of) the history of Yugoslavia today.

8 To make extra money during university, I worked (according to / as) a part-time cashier.

9 Lauren studied music (in spite of / on) her parents' wish that she become a lawyer.

10 The shelter couldn't care for more people (about / despite) its efforts. <학평 응용>

11 The filmmakers are creating a documentary (of / such as) reefs in the Caribbean.

12 He has dedicated his entire life to speaking out (against / like) injustice and intolerance.

13 Some think that carob, a type of flour extracted from the carob bean, tastes (for / like) chocolate.

14 Doctors (such as / despite) John Snow and Rudolf Virchow saw the connection between poor living conditions and disease. <학평 응용>

Review Test

[1-3] 다음 빈칸에 공통으로 들어갈 알맞은 것을 고르시오.

1

- Deer in tundra environments eat moss that grows _____ rocks.
- He usually drinks hot chocolate _____ Friday afternoon.

① at ② since ③ on ④ in ⑤ next to

2

- If we take the night train, we'll arrive in Gwangju _____ 7 o'clock.
- Goods such as cars and oil are transported _____ ship.

① until ② at ③ before ④ by ⑤ with

3

- They have to buy those books _____ their lectures. <학평 응용>
- The Cold War between the United States and Soviet Union lasted _____ over four decades.

① with ② since ③ during ④ to ⑤ for

[4-5] 다음 빈칸에 들어갈 말이 순서대로 짝지어진 것을 고르시오.

4

- You must send in your completed application _____ next Thursday.
- _____ my stay in Tokyo, I visited the biggest fish market in the world.

① by – during ② by – for ③ after – for
④ until – during ⑤ until – for

5

- The government's tax increase is not popular _____ voters.
- Mina's mother has worked for the regional bank _____ 2009.

① between – from ② between – since
③ among – from ④ among – since
⑤ among – for

[6-7] 다음 빈칸에 들어갈 말이 나머지 넷과 다른 것을 고르시오.

6

① The crowd celebrated the first day of the new year _____ midnight.
② You have to be _____ home today because of the yellow dust.
③ He always walks his dog _____ the evening.
④ The coach was surprised _____ his team's enthusiasm and desire to win.
⑤ Jane and I meet _____ the bus stop every day.

7

① This monument was built _____ the 19th century.
② The board members decided to close the factory _____ Berlin.
③ The song is internationally popular even though it is sung _____ Korean.
④ Scientists have not yet discovered any signs of intelligent life _____ the universe.
⑤ Neil Armstrong was the first person to walk _____ the Moon.

[8-9] 다음 문장에서 어법상 <u>틀린</u> 부분을 찾아 쓰고 바르게 고쳐 쓰시오.

8

Some trees are dormant during winter and aren't active again by spring.   *dormant: 휴면기의

_____ → _____

9

You can contact us in phone. <학평 응용>

_____ → _____

[10-11] 우리말과 같도록 괄호 안의 말을 알맞게 배열하시오.

10

그녀는 부작용 때문에 그 약을 복용하는 것을 멈췄다. (she, the side effects, taking, of, stopped, because, the medication)

= _____
_____.

11

다른 비용을 줄이는 것 대신에, 그 회사는 제품 가격을 올렸다. (of, other expenses, instead, cutting)

= _____, the company raised product prices.

[12-16] 우리말과 같도록 괄호 안의 말을 활용하여 문장을 완성하시오.

12

너는 충분한 수면 없이 너의 시험에 집중할 수 없다. (can't, your exam, focus on, enough sleep)

= _____.

<학평 응용>

13

그의 고군분투에도 불구하고, 그 오래된 트럭은 작동하지 않았다. (the old truck, work, his struggles)

= _____
_____.

14

너를 제외하고 모든 반 친구들이 나의 생일 파티에 왔다. (come, every classmate, my birthday party)

= _____.

15

그 식당 뒤에 대형 쓰레기 수납기가 있다. (be, there, the restaurant, a dumpster)

= _____.

16

그들은 그들의 장거리 자동차 여행 동안 그 나라를 가로질러 운전했다. (their road trip, drive, the country)

= _____.

17 우리말과 같도록 주어진 <조건>에 맞게 문장을 완성하시오.

> 나는 약간의 통증에도 불구하고 정오까지 연습을 끝냈다.

> <조건>
> 1. finish, noon, the practice, some pain을 활용하시오.
> 2. 11단어로 쓰시오.

= _____ .

[18-19] 다음 글을 읽고 주어진 질문에 답하시오.

> Many woodland animals such as bears and raccoons get through the winter months by hibernating. Hibernation is more complicated than just a deep sleep (A) from / because of the changes animals experience when in this state. Most significantly, an animal's heartbeat and breathing rate drop down to well (B) below / above normal. ⓐ 이것은 그들이 생존을 위해 에너지를 아끼도록 한다 (allow, conserve, energy, survival) as they sleep through the winter in places (C) according to / like burrows, caves, and dens.
>
> *hibernate: 동면하다

18 위 글의 밑줄 친 우리말 ⓐ와 같도록 괄호 안의 말을 활용하여 문장을 완성하시오.

= This _____

19 위 글의 (A), (B), (C)의 각 네모 안에서 어법에 맞는 표현으로 가장 적절한 것은?

	(A)	(B)	(C)
①	from	above	according to
②	from	below	like
③	because of	below	like
④	from	above	like
⑤	because of	below	according to

정답 및 해설 p.11

20 (A), (B), (C)의 각 네모 안에서 어법에 맞는 표현으로 가장 적절한 것은?

> On her way home, Shirley noticed a truck parked (A) through / in front of the house across the street. New neighbors! She was dying to meet them. (B) For / During dinner, Shirley's dad said joyfully, "There's one thing that may be interesting to you. The new neighbors have a daughter just your age. Maybe she wants to be your playmate." Shirley nearly dropped her fork on the floor. How many times had she prayed for a friend? Finally, her prayers (C) answered / were answered! <학평 응용>

	(A)	(B)	(C)
①	in front of	For	answered
②	in front of	During	were answered
③	in front of	During	answered
④	through	During	were answered
⑤	through	For	answered

21 다음 글의 밑줄 친 부분 중, 어법상 틀린 것은?

> Sometimes, it is a simpler product that gives a business a ①competitive advantage. ②Until recent days, bicycles had to have many gears to be considered high-end. But fixed-gear bikes with minimal features have become more popular as those who buy ③them are happy to pay more for much less. The overall profitability of these bikes is much higher than that of the more complex ones because they do a single thing really well ④with the cost of added complexity. Companies should carefully consider whether it's worth adding more features to their products ⑤due to the increased cost and the potential for reduced profitability. <학평 응용>
>
> *high-end: 최고급의

CHAPTER 8
부정사

기출로 적중 POINT

1 명사적 용법

2 형용사적 용법

3 부사적 용법

4 to부정사의 의미상 주어

5 to부정사의 시제와 태

6 부정사를 목적격 보어로 쓰는 동사

7 to부정사 구문

8 독립부정사

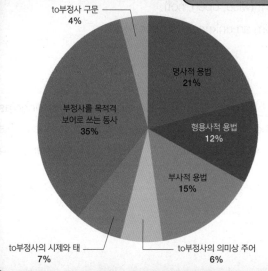

최근 7개년 수능/학평/내신 출제 경향

TOP 1 부정사를 목적격 보어로 쓰는 동사 (35%)
특정 동사에 따라 목적격 보어로 to부정사와 원형부정사 중 어느
것을 쓰는지 묻는 문제가 자주 출제된다.

TOP 2 명사적 용법 (21%)
to부정사의 명사적 용법을 묻는 문제가 자주 출제된다.

TOP 3 부사적 용법 (15%)
to부정사 부사적 용법의 다양한 의미를 묻는 문제가 자주 출제된
다.

명사적 용법

1. to부정사는 「to + 동사원형」의 형태로, 명사처럼 문장 안에서 주어, 목적어, 보어로 쓰인다.

To play the piano well needs much practice. <주어>

The company decided **not[never] to accept** the partner's offer. <목적어>
　　　　　　　　　　↳ to부정사의 부정형: 「not[never] to + 동사원형」

A doctor's main job is **to deliver** the best possible care to patients. <보어>

TIP to부정사(구)가 주어나 5형식 문장의 목적어로 쓰일 때는 주로 해당 자리에 가주어/가목적어 it을 쓰고 to부정사(구)를 뒤로 보낸다.
　　It is rude *to interrupt people when they are speaking*.

2. 「의문사 + to부정사」는 명사처럼 쓰이며, 「의문사 + 주어 + should + 동사원형」으로 바꿔 쓸 수 있다.

She is aware of **how to use** this vacuum cleaner.

→ She is aware of **how she should use** this vacuum cleaner.

[1-4] <보기>의 동사를 한 번씩만 활용하여 문장을 완성하시오.

<보기>	judge	post	create	pay

1 In the past, many artists wanted _____ more realistic paintings.

2 A funeral's purpose is _____ respect to the deceased.

3 It is easy _____ people based on their actions. <학평>

4 The concern of the marketing industry today is where _____ their advertisements. <학평 응용>

[5-7] 우리말과 같도록 괄호 안의 말을 활용하여 문장을 완성하시오.

5 그 연구의 목적은 북극의 야생동물에 대한 정보를 수집하는 것이다. (gather, information)

= The objective of the study is _____ about Arctic wildlife.

6 그 경제학자들은 언제 부동산에 돈을 투자할지 의논했다. (invest, money, when)

= The economists discussed _____ in real estate.

7 잘 모르는 출처로부터의 이메일 첨부파일을 열지 않는 것은 현명하다. (wise, open, not)

= It is _____ e-mail attachments from an unknown source. <학평 응용>

8 다음 글에서 어법상 <u>틀린</u> 부분을 찾아 쓰고 바르게 고쳐 쓰시오.

In 1795, how to prevent food from spoiling was a problem for Napoleon Bonaparte's army. Nicholas Appert eventually invented a method of sterilizing food and keeping it in an airtight container. This technique made it possible supply French troops with adequate food.　　*sterilize: 살균하다

_____ → _____

정답 p.12

POINT 2 형용사적 용법

1. to부정사는 '~할, ~하는'의 의미로 형용사처럼 명사를 수식하며, 이때 명사 뒤에 온다.

He has *homework* **to do** this weekend.
Since we didn't bring anything, our art teacher provided *some tools* **to paint with**.

「to부정사 + 전치사」가 수식하는 명사는 to부정사 뒤에 있는 전치사의 목적어이며, 이때 전치사를 반드시 쓴다.

2. 「be + to부정사」는 예정, 의무, 운명, 의도, 가능을 나타내며 주어를 보충 설명한다.

The passengers **are to board** the ship in 30 minutes. <예정: ~할 예정이다>
Students **are** not **to talk** during the exam. <의무: ~해야 한다>
Unfortunately, they **were** never **to meet** again. <운명: ~할 운명이다>
If you **are to get** good grades, you should review every day. <의도: ~하려고 하다>
Nothing **was to be seen** in the dark forest. <가능: ~할 수 있다>

[1-5] 괄호 안에서 알맞은 것을 고르시오.

1 He always brings a book (read / to read) when he commutes.

2 You are (not access / not to access) confidential documents.

3 I will buy some stamps (to put / to put on) this envelope. <수능 응용>

4 The girl was (become / to become) a renowned dancer one day.

5 Do you have (time to help / to help time) me now?

[6-11] 우리말과 같도록 괄호 안의 말을 활용하여 빈칸에 쓰시오.

6 그 경기들은 세 개의 경기장에서 동시에 시작할 예정이다. (be, the games, start)
= _____ _____ _____ _____ _____ in three stadiums simultaneously.

7 너는 해가 지기 전에 그 목적지에 도착해야 한다. (arrive, be)
= _____ _____ _____ _____ at the destination before the sun sets.

8 아름다운 그림들은 이 미술관에서 찾을 수 있다. (be, beautiful paintings, be found)
= _____ _____ _____ _____ _____ at this art museum.

9 세계화는 우리에게 다른 사회들에 대해 배울 기회를 준다. (a chance, learn)
= Globalization gives us _____ _____ _____ _____ about other societies. <학평>

10 나는 최근에 이 마을로 이사했기 때문에 함께 놀 친구들이 없다. (friends, play with)
= I don't have _____ _____ _____ _____ because I recently moved to this town.

11 만약 네가 실수하는 것을 피하려고 한다면 세심한 주의를 하는 것이 필요하다. (avoid, be, pay, be, necessary)
= _____ _____ _____ _____ _____ close attention if _____ _____
_____ _____ making mistakes.

부사적 용법

to부정사는 부사처럼 동사, 형용사, 부사, 문장 전체를 수식하며, 다양한 의미를 나타낸다.

He exercised hard **to keep** in good shape. <목적: ~하기 위해>
↳ 목적의 의미를 강조하기 위해 to 대신 in order to나 so as to를 쓸 수 있다.

Rebecca was nervous **to meet** her favorite writer. <감정의 원인: ~해서, ~하니>
The reporter was rude **to ask** such personal questions. <판단의 근거: ~하다니>
He woke up **to find** himself in the hospital. <결과: (…해서 결국) ~하다>
To see their appearance, you would not think they were siblings. <조건: ~한다면>
Those flowers are dangerous **to touch** because they have thorns. <형용사 수식: ~하기에>

TIP 부정적인 내용의 결과를 나타낼 때 to부정사 앞에 only나 never를 쓰기도 한다.
He hurried to the station, **only** *to miss* the train.

[1-4] 주어진 문장을 우리말로 해석하시오.

1 We are delighted to invite you to our annual event. <학평 응용>
= _____.

2 To hear her speech, you would be persuaded by her.
= _____.

3 That old building looks unstable to live in.
= _____.

4 Some animals developed useful weapons to protect themselves. <학평 응용>
= _____.

[5-10] 우리말과 같도록 괄호 안의 말을 활용하여 문장을 완성하시오.

5 감정을 상하게 하는 말을 하다니 Nancy는 화가 난 것이 틀림없다. (say, hurtful things)
= Nancy must have been angry _____.

6 나는 과학 박람회에서 일등을 해서 놀랐다. (be surprised, win)
= I _____ first place at the science fair.

7 사업에서의 성공은 짧은 시간 내에 성취하기에 어렵다. (achieve, be, difficult)
= Success in business _____ in a short time.

8 고난을 극복하면서, 나의 삼촌은 자라서 유명한 음악가가 되었다. (become, a famous musician)
= Overcoming hardships, my uncle grew up _____.

9 너는 너의 생각들을 표현하기 위해 복잡한 문장들이 필요하지 않다. (your ideas, express)
= You don't need complex sentences _____. <학평>

10 그 해변에서 일출을 본다면, 너는 평화롭게 느낄 것이다. (the sunrise, watch)
= _____ at the beach, you would feel peaceful.

POINT 4 to부정사의 의미상 주어

정답 p.12

1. to부정사가 나타내는 행위의 주체가 문장의 주어나 목적어와 다를 때, 의미상 주어 「for + 목적격」을 to부정사 앞에 쓴다. 단, 의미상 주어가 사람의 성격이나 성질을 나타내는 형용사 뒤에 쓰일 때는 「of + 목적격」의 형태로 쓴다.

   This recipe is quite easy **for me** *to follow*. <학평 응용>
   It was *careless* **of you** *to spill* coffee. <학평>

2. to부정사의 의미상 주어가 문장의 주어 또는 목적어와 같거나 people, we, they처럼 불특정한 일반인인 경우에는 따로 나타내지 않는다.

   I reminded **my grandmother** *to take* her medication.
   It is scary *to walk* along an empty street at night.

[1-5] 괄호 안에서 알맞은 것을 고르시오.

1 Today's lesson is difficult (me / for me) to follow.

2 It was generous (for him / of him) to forgive their misbehavior.

3 The counselor advised (us / for us) to resolve the problem by communication.

4 It is selfish (her / of her) to leave all of the unpleasant work to me.

5 The program will be a great opportunity (for them / of them) to experience something new. <수능 응용>

[6-13] 우리말과 같도록 괄호 안의 말을 활용하여 문장을 완성하시오.

6 이 지역의 토양은 식물들이 자라기에 열악하다. (plants, grow)

   = The soil in this region is inferior _____.

7 앞에 있는 차에 너무 가까이 운전하는 것은 위험하다. (drive)

   = It is dangerous _____ too close to the car in front.

8 그들은 그 운동선수가 세계 기록을 깨기를 기대하지 않았다. (break, the athlete)

   = They didn't expect _____ the world record.

9 그 도둑이 그의 죄를 고백하다니 정직했다. (the thief, confess)

   = It was honest _____ his guilt.

10 그 판사는 Williams씨가 즉시 벌금을 내라고 명령했다. (pay, Mr. Williams)

   = The judge ordered _____ _____ the fine immediately.

11 Katherine은 그녀의 방을 효율적으로 사용하기를 원했다. (use)

   = Katherine wanted _____ her room efficiently.

12 몇몇 학생들은 사적인 공간들을 제외한 어느 곳에서도 공부하는 것이 불편하다. (some students, study)

   = It is uncomfortable _____ anywhere except in private spaces. <학평 응용>

13 그 사업가가 미래 세대를 위해 친환경적인 제품들을 출시하다니 사려 깊다. (launch, the entrepreneur)

   = It is considerate _____ eco-friendly products for the future generation.

1. to부정사의 시제: 주절의 시제와 같거나 그 이후일 때는 「to + 동사원형」을 쓰고, 주절의 시제보다 앞설 때는 완료형 「to have + p.p.」를 쓴다.

The used vehicle *seems* **to be** in good condition.
(→ It *seems* that the used vehicle *is* in good condition.)

The used vehicle *seems* **to have been** in good condition.
(→ It *seems* that the used vehicle *was* in good condition.)

2. to부정사의 수동태: 주절의 시제와 같거나 그 이후일 때는 「to be + p.p.」를 쓰고, 주절의 시제보다 앞설 때는 완료형 「to have been + p.p.」를 쓴다.

Our stove will probably need **to be replaced** soon.
This structure appeared **to have been built** over a thousand years ago.

[1-4] 괄호 안에서 알맞은 것을 고르시오.

1 I advised Adam not to (discourage / be discouraged) by rejection. <수능 응용>

2 My computer appears to (be infected / have been infected) with a virus last week.

3 The Internet enables people to (find / be found) information on a variety of topics.

4 They seem to (encounter / have encountered) a hurricane when they were in the Pacific.

[5-11] 우리말과 같도록 괄호 안의 말을 활용하여 문장을 완성하시오.

5 그 왕은 그의 후손들에 의해 기억되기를 바란다. (remember)
= The king hopes _____ by his descendants.

6 그 회사는 불법적으로 사용자들의 개인 정보를 이용했다고 말해진다. (exploit)
= The company is said _____ the users' personal information illegally.

7 저 늑대들은 인간에 의해 길들여졌던 것 같다. (domesticate)
= Those wolves seem _____ by humans. <학평 응용>

8 그는 수리되어야 하는 모든 자전거들을 꺼냈다. (repair)
= He took out all the bicycles _____. <학평 응용>

9 몇몇 고래들은 휘파람을 사용해서 의사소통하는 것 같다. (communicate)
= Some whales seem _____ using a whistle.

10 나는 누군가에 의해 방해받기를 원하지 않기 때문에 보통 혼자 공부한다. (disturb)
= I usually study alone because I don't want _____ by anyone.

11 어제 진행된 그 협상들은 결의안 없이 끝났던 것 같다. (end)
= The negotiations held yesterday appear _____ without a resolution.

부정사를 목적격 보어로 쓰는 동사

1. 다음 동사는 to부정사를 목적격 보어로 쓴다.

want	ask	tell	cause	order	persuade
allow	force	advise	encourage	expect	enable

Brian's accountant *advised* him **to save** more money for retirement.

2. 사역동사와 지각동사는 원형부정사를 목적격 보어로 쓴다.

The video recording *made* the woman **admit** that she had lied.
They *felt* the ground **vibrate[vibrating]** suddenly.
　　　　　　　　　↳ 지각동사는 V-ing형을 목적격 보어로 써서 동작이 진행 중임을 강조할 수 있다.

TIP 준사역동사 help는 목적격 보어로 to부정사와 원형부정사를 모두 쓸 수 있고, get은 to부정사만 쓴다.
　　 The classes *helped* him (**to**) **improve** his cooking skills.
　　 My mom *got* me **to adopt** a regular lifestyle.

[1-5] 괄호 안에서 알맞은 것을 고르시오.

1 The teacher didn't allow us (touch / to touch) anything at the museum.

2 The bank's new mobile app helps customers (pay / paid) their bills online.

3 I will let my dogs (play / to play) at the dog park. <수능 응용>

4 Challenging problems force us (to come / coming) up with creative answers. <학평 응용>

5 The visitors watched the presenter (to demonstrate / demonstrating) how to operate the device.

[6-8] 우리말과 같도록 괄호 안의 말을 활용하여 문장을 완성하시오.

6 나는 신호등이 바뀐 것을 알아차렸다. (notice, change, the traffic light)
= I _____.

7 그 새로운 교수법은 학생들이 그들의 사전 지식을 활성화하는 것을 돕는다. (help, students, activate)
= The new teaching method _____ their prior knowledge. <학평 응용>

8 그 남자는 참가자들에게 그들 자신을 작은 집단들로 나눌 것을 요청했다. (divide, ask, the participants)
= The man _____ themselves into small groups. <학평 응용>

9 다음 글에서 어법상 틀린 부분을 찾아 쓰고 바르게 고쳐 쓰시오.

> We want our friends and family members to value us all the time. However, we sometimes take them for granted. Spending time away from those who are close to us often makes us to realize how important they really are.
>
> *value: 소중하게 생각하다

_____ → _____

to부정사 구문

1. 「too + 형용사/부사 + to부정사」: ~하기에 너무 …한/하게

→ 「so + 형용사/부사 + that + 주어 + can't + 동사원형」

I was **too** busy **to help** you with your science project. <학평 응용>

→ I was **so** busy **that** I **couldn't help** you with your science project.

2. 「형용사/부사 + enough + to부정사」: ~할 만큼 충분히 …한/하게

→ 「so + 형용사/부사 + that + 주어 + can + 동사원형」

This knife is sharp **enough to cut** through thick cardboard.

→ This knife is **so** sharp **that** it **can cut** through thick cardboard.

3. 「It takes + 목적어 + 시간 + to부정사」: …가 ~하는 데 (시간)이 걸리다

→ 「It takes + 시간 + for + 목적격 + to부정사」

It takes us an hour **to get** back home. <수능>

→ **It takes** an hour **for us to get** back home.

[1-4] 다음 두 문장의 의미가 같도록 문장을 완성하시오.

1 Jason is so strong that he can carry all those heavy things.

→ Jason _____ all those heavy things.

2 It took several weeks for the man to recover from his injuries.

→ It _____ from his injuries.

3 The wedding hall is too small to accommodate many attendants.

→ The wedding hall _____ many attendants.

4 The food at the buffet was various enough to satisfy everyone's taste.

→ The food at the buffet _____ everyone's taste.

[5-7] 우리말과 같도록 괄호 안의 말을 알맞게 배열하시오.

5 소방관들이 그 숲의 불을 진화하는 데 이틀이 걸렸다. (two days, took, to, firefighters, extinguish)

= It _____ the fire in the forest.

6 Jonathan은 결승에 진출할 만큼 충분히 잘 공연했다. (enough, well, move, performed, to)

= Jonathan _____ on to the final round. <학평 응용>

7 나는 장거리 버스의 표를 사기에 너무 가난했다. (poor, buy, was, to, too)

= I _____ a ticket for a long-distance bus. <학평 응용>

독립부정사

정답 p.13

독립부정사는 독립적인 의미를 갖는 to부정사 표현으로, 문장 전체를 수식한다.

to begin[start] with 우선, 먼저	so to speak 말하자면
to be sure 확실히	strange to say 이상한 얘기지만
to be frank (with you) 솔직히 말하면	to make matters worse 설상가상으로
to tell (you) the truth 사실대로 말하면	to make a long story short 간단히 말하면
needless to say 말할 필요도 없이	to say nothing of ~은 말할 것도 없이

To begin[start] with, I will explain the goal of the research.
To be frank (with you), there is little chance of passing this test.

[1-10] 우리말과 같도록 문장을 완성하시오.

1 사실대로 말하면, 나는 어제 너에게 완전히 솔직하지 않았다.

= _____, I wasn't completely honest with you yesterday.

2 간단히 말하면, 우리는 그 기차를 놓쳐서 또 다른 기차를 탔다.

= _____, we missed the train and took another train.

3 말하자면, 우리는 그 없이 그 경기를 이기지 못했을 수도 있었다.

= We couldn't have won the game without him, _____.

4 이상한 얘기지만, 나는 우주 공간에 외계인들이 존재한다고 생각한다.

= _____, I think that aliens exist in outer space.

5 말할 필요도 없이, 그 영화는 시작부터 끝까지 끔찍했다.

= _____, the movie was terrible from start to finish.

6 재정상의 부담은 말할 것도 없이, 나의 직원들을 해고하는 것은 매우 어려웠다.

= It was very difficult to fire my employees, _____ the financial burdens.

7 솔직히 말하면, 우리는 그 일을 끝낼 더 많은 시간이 필요하다.

= _____, we need more time to finish the task.

8 우선, 나는 나의 실험실의 장비들과 규칙들을 소개할 것이다.

= _____, I will introduce the devices and rules of my laboratory.

9 설상가상으로, 그녀는 그녀의 무례한 태도에 대해 사과하는 것을 거부했다.

= _____, she refused to apologize for her rude attitude.

10 확실히, 너는 다른 가게에서도 비슷한 제품을 살 수 있다.

= _____, you can also buy a similar product at other stores.

Review Test

[1-2] 다음 빈칸에 들어갈 알맞은 것을 고르시오.

1

> The principal wants you _____ her in the office tomorrow.

① meet ② met ③ to meet
④ meeting ⑤ to be met

2

> You should pass the audition so as _____ as a band member.

① accept ② accepted ③ to accept
④ to accepting ⑤ to be accepted

3 다음 문장의 빈칸에 들어갈 말이 순서대로 짝지어진 것은?

> It is mature _____ you _____ acknowledge your flaws and weaknesses.

① to – to ② of – to ③ for – to
④ of – for ⑤ for – for

[4-5] 다음 중 밑줄 친 to부정사의 용법이 나머지 넷과 다른 것을 고르시오.

4

① You are very open-minded to listen to an argument you disagree with.
② She missed the opportunity to work abroad.
③ Charlie was upset to recognize the field trip had been canceled.
④ The government increased its spending to stimulate the economy.
⑤ To hear him read the script, you would know he is a voice actor.

5

① A good performer desires to understand the meaning of music. <학평 응용>
② I found it hard to breathe in higher places.
③ It is customary to call the first name here.
④ Does this camera have the capacity to take high-definition photos?
⑤ The main purpose of our foundation is to fight for equality.

[6-7] 다음 중 밑줄 친 부분이 어법상 틀린 것을 고르시오.

6

① The woman had the store clerk to wrap her purchase carefully.
② Some people are too arrogant to listen to others.
③ He seems to have been popular when he was young.
④ The decision to reduce wages brought complaints from the laborers.
⑤ The witness saw the suspect running down the street.

7

① To be frank, the lecture is a little long and a bit confusing.
② The driver maintained a constant speed to save fuel.
③ Since I was sick, my mom made me stay home.
④ The salesperson persuaded the couple to buy the home appliances.
⑤ The station employee told us when leave for the platform.

[8-9] 다음 문장에서 어법상 틀린 부분을 찾아 쓰고 바르게 고쳐 쓰시오.

8

My father generally just agrees with my mother in order avoid an argument. <학평 응용>

_____ → _____

9

Ms. Anderson got her children help her clean the front porch.

_____ → _____

10 다음 글에서 어법상 틀린 부분을 찾아 쓰고 바르게 고쳐 쓰시오.

The band released a new song, but the lyrics were negative and unattractive. Needless saying, it didn't seem to fulfill anyone's expectations.

_____ → _____

[11-13] 다음 두 문장의 의미가 같도록 문장을 완성하시오.

11

He was so shy that he couldn't ask the celebrity for her autograph.

→ He _____ the celebrity for her autograph.

12

It seems that the jury was persuaded by the lawyer.

→ The jury _____ by the lawyer.

13

The disease was so infectious that it could spread all over Europe.

→ The disease _____ all over Europe.

[14-15] 우리말과 같도록 괄호 안의 말을 알맞게 배열하시오.

14

선원들은 그 상어가 보트로 오는 것을 보고 있었다. (come, the sailors, the shark, to the boat, were watching)

= _____.

15

그가 무엇을 먹을지 결정하는 데 적어도 한 시간이 걸릴 것이다. (to, what, to, at least an hour, him, decide, will take, it, eat)

= _____.

[16-17] 우리말과 같도록 괄호 안의 말을 활용하여 문장을 완성하시오.

16

말하자면, 인플레이션은 생활비가 증가하게 했다. (speak, inflation, living expenses, make, increase)

= _____, _____.

17

어른들이 그들의 아이들의 의견을 무시하는 것은 바람직하지 않다. (ignore, be, adults, desirable)

= It _____ their children's opinions.

18 우리말과 같도록 주어진 <조건>에 맞게 문장을 완성하시오.

> 뉴스 보도에 따르면, 주가의 하락은 정부의 규제에 의해 야기됐던 것 같다.

> <조건>
> 1. the decline in stock price, cause, seem을 활용하시오.
> 2. 10단어로 쓰시오.

= According to the news report, _____
_____ by the
government's regulation.

[19-20] 다음 글을 읽고 주어진 질문에 답하시오.

> The last time I watched a film in a theater, I suddenly heard my phone ⓐ rang. (A) 그러나, 나의 가방 안에 있는 휴대폰을 찾기에 너무 어두웠다. (find, be, dark, the cell phone, too, it) I thought it rude ⓑ to disrupt the film for everyone else, so I exited the theater. It is unusual ⓒ me to forget to turn off the phone, so I was embarrassed ⓓ to make such a mistake. ⓔ To prevent this from happening again, I will double-check my phone beforehand.

19 위 글의 밑줄 친 우리말 (A)와 같도록 괄호 안의 말을 활용하여 문장을 완성하시오.

= However, _____
in my bag.

20 위 글의 밑줄 친 ⓐ~ⓔ 중 어법상 틀린 것의 기호를 쓰고 바르게 고쳐 쓰시오.

(1) _____ → _____

(2) _____ → _____

수능형

21 (A), (B), (C)의 각 네모 안에서 어법에 맞는 표현으로 가장 적절한 것은?

> Some years ago, a psychologist named Richard Lippa called a group of introverts to his lab and asked them (A) act / to act like extroverts while pretending to teach a math class. He measured how extroverted they appeared based on their speech and body language. He found that some of the introverts did a surprisingly convincing job of acting like extroverts. Thus, this experiment shows that most of us seem to (B) know / be known how to fake it to some extent. Whether or not we're aware that the way we act marks us as introverts or extroverts, we know it (C) unconscious / unconsciously . <학평 응용>
>
> *introvert: 내성적인 사람

	(A)	(B)	(C)
①	act	know	unconscious
②	act	be known	unconsciously
③	to act	know	unconscious
④	to act	know	unconsciously
⑤	to act	be known	unconscious

수능형

22 다음 글의 밑줄 친 부분 중, 어법상 틀린 것은?

> The belief that animals aren't moral beings is such a longstanding assumption that it is hard ① for some to break. A lot of people have this assumption because ② it is easier to deny animals have morality than to accept it. This tendency is strong enough to make people ③ to cling to the status quo. The denial of who animals are conveniently allows us ④ to maintain stereotypes about their capacities. Clearly, a major paradigm shift ⑤ is needed for people's opinions to change. <학평 응용> *status quo: 현재 상태

CHAPTER 9
동명사

기출로 적중 POINT

최근 7개년 수능/학평/내신 출제 경향

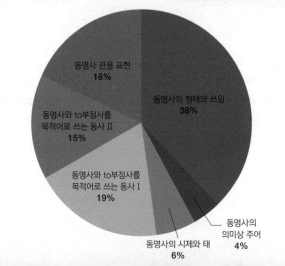

동명사 관용 표현
18%

동명사와 to부정사를
목적어로 쓰는 동사 II
15%

동명사와 to부정사를
목적어로 쓰는 동사 I
19%

동명사의 형태와 쓰임
38%

동명사의 시제와 태
6%

동명사의
의미상 주어
4%

TOP 1 동명사의 형태와 쓰임 (38%)
동명사의 형태와 쓰임을 묻는 문제가 자주 출제된다.

TOP 2 동명사와 to부정사를 목적어로 쓰는 동사 I (19%)
특정 동사에 따라 목적어로 동명사와 to부정사 중 어느 것을 쓰는
지 묻는 문제가 자주 출제된다.

TOP 3 동명사 관용 표현 (18%)
동명사 관용 표현의 의미와 형태를 묻는 문제가 자주 출제된다.

동명사의 형태와 쓰임

정답 p.14

동명사는 V-ing의 형태로, 명사처럼 문장 안에서 주어, 목적어, 보어로 쓰인다.

Starting a new business *requires* a lot of effort and dedication. <주어>
↳ 주어로 쓰인 동명사(구)는 항상 단수 취급한다.

Have you ever *considered* **entering** a law school? <동사의 목적어>

I apologized *for* **not[never] returning** the bike. <전치사의 목적어>
↳ 동명사의 부정형: 「not[never] + V-ing」

Her mistake was **sending** the letter to a different address. <보어>

[1-5] 밑줄 친 동명사의 쓰임을 <보기>에서 골라 그 기호를 쓰시오.

<보기>	ⓐ 주어	ⓑ 동사의 목적어	ⓒ 전치사의 목적어	ⓓ 보어

1 An effective way to make friends is <u>joining</u> a local sports club.　　[　　]

2 The problem with <u>staying</u> up late is that you feel tired the next day.　　[　　]

3 The Sun will keep <u>shining</u> for billions of years.　　[　　]

4 <u>Arranging</u> the shelf took much longer than Lisa anticipated.　　[　　]

5 That restaurant is known for <u>serving</u> authentic Mexican food.　　[　　]

[6-9] 우리말과 같도록 동명사와 괄호 안의 말을 활용하여 문장을 완성하시오.

6 그 정부의 목표는 실업률을 줄이는 것이다. (reduce, the unemployment rate)

= The government's aim is _____.

7 그 회의에 제시간에 도착하지 못한 것은 나의 잘못이었다. (be, at the meeting on time, arrive, not)

= _____ my fault.

8 그녀는 책을 읽는 것을 좋아하기 때문에 항상 도서관에 간다. (books, read)

= She always goes to the library because she loves _____.

9 실패의 위험은 우리가 더 큰 보상을 성취하기 위해 지불해야 하는 대가이다. (achieve, greater rewards)

= A risk of failure is the price we must pay for _____. <학평 응용>

10 다음 글에서 어법상 틀린 부분을 찾아 쓰고 바르게 고쳐 쓰시오.

> Jackson Pollack tried to express his unconscious ideas by pouring paint directly onto a canvas. However, determining which works he created himself are now difficult because of his unusual painting method. As a result, collectors sometimes unintentionally purchase fakes.
>
> *unconscious: 무의식적인

_____ → _____

POINT 2 동명사의 의미상 주어

정답 p.14

1. 동명사가 나타내는 행위의 주체가 문장의 주어나 목적어와 다를 때, 소유격이나 목적격 형태의 의미상 주어를 동명사 앞에 쓴다.

We were surprised at **his[him]** *appearing* in the movie.
I really hated **Rachel('s)** *gossiping* at the party last night.

2. 동명사의 의미상 주어가 문장의 주어 또는 목적어와 같거나 people, we, they처럼 불특정한 일반인인 경우에는 따로 나타내지 않는다.

He finished *building* a model airplane with his son.
Having too much food late at night causes many diseases.

[1-5] <보기>와 같이 두 문장의 의미가 같도록 동명사를 이용하여 문장을 완성하시오.

> **<보기>** They are aware that Karen has a secret.
> → They are aware of _Karen('s) having a secret_ .

1 I really appreciated that you invited us to Korea.
   → I really appreciated _____ . <학평>

2 We were all satisfied that Luke planned for the group project.
   → We were all satisfied with _____ .

3 Surprisingly, my parents didn't mind that I came home late.
   → Surprisingly, my parents didn't mind _____ .

4 The professor insists that we sit at the same desk each class.
   → The professor insists on _____ .

5 He respects that firefighters sacrifice themselves to rescue people.
   → He respects _____ .

[6-9] 우리말과 같도록 동명사와 괄호 안의 말을 활용하여 문장을 완성하시오.

6 나는 그녀가 바쁜 척하는 것을 좋아하지 않는다. (pretend, like)
   = I _____ that she is busy.

7 Terrence씨는 어젯밤에 늑대가 울부짖는 것에 깜짝 놀랐다. (be startled at, a wolf, howl)
   = Mr. Terrence _____ last night.

8 그 광대를 보고 있는 아이들은 그가 저글링하는 것에 감명을 받았다. (juggle, be impressed by)
   = The children watching the clown _____ .

9 Alena는 그녀의 남편이 불필요한 물건에 돈을 쓰는 것에 넌더리 난다. (be tired of, spend, her husband)
   = Alena _____ money on unnecessary stuff.

1. **동명사의 시제:** 주절의 시제와 같거나 그 이후일 때는 V-ing를 쓰고, 주절의 시제보다 앞설 때는 완료형 「having + p.p.」를 쓴다.

   He always explains the advantages of **getting** regular exercise.
   The author was famous for **having written** several best-selling novels.

2. **동명사의 수동태:** 주절의 시제와 같거나 그 이후일 때는 「being + p.p.」를 쓰고, 주절의 시제보다 앞설 때는 완료형 「having been + p.p.」를 쓴다.

   She is annoyed at **being stuck** in traffic now.
   The man denied **having been involved** in the crime.

[1-4] 다음 두 문장의 의미가 같도록 동명사를 이용하여 문장을 완성하시오.

1 I appreciated that I was promoted to the supervisor position.

   → I appreciated _____ to the supervisor position.

2 Dennis was embarrassed that he fell on the street.

   → Dennis was embarrassed about _____ on the street.

3 Michael is upset that he lost his wallet at the bus terminal yesterday.

   → Michael is upset about _____ his wallet at the bus terminal yesterday.

4 The soccer player remembered that he had been awarded a trophy.

   → The soccer player remembered _____ a trophy.

[5-10] 우리말과 같도록 동명사와 괄호 안의 말을 활용하여 빈칸에 쓰시오.

5 많은 어린 아이들은 무엇을 해야 하는지 말해지는 것을 싫어한다. (tell)

   = Many young children dislike _____ _____ what to do.

6 그의 불충분한 수면은 질병이 생기는 것의 가능성을 증가시켰다. (develop)

   = His insufficient sleep increased the possibility of _____ diseases. <학평 응용>

7 그녀는 운전면허 시험에 떨어졌던 것에 좌절한 것 같다. (fail)

   = She seems frustrated at _____ _____ the driver's license test.

8 오늘날의 환경 문제를 만들었던 것에 대해 기술을 비판하는 것은 일반적이다. (create)

   = It is common to criticize technology for _____ _____ today's environmental issues. <수능 응용>

9 Edward는 마침내 그의 아들이 결백하다고 밝혀진 것으로부터 안도감을 느꼈다. (determine)

   = Edward finally felt relief from his son's _____ _____ innocent.

10 그 고객은 그가 예상했던 것보다 더 많이 청구받았던 것에 대해 항의했다. (charge)

   = The client complained about _____ _____ _____ more than he had expected.

기출로작중 POINT 4 동명사와 to부정사를 목적어로 쓰는 동사 I

정답 p.14

1. 다음 동사는 동명사를 목적어로 쓴다.

enjoy	avoid	mind	finish	keep	deny	stop
quit	admit	delay	postpone	consider	give up	put off

Many desert animals *avoid* **moving** around in the daytime.
When will you *finish* **preparing** for the exam? <학평 응용>

2. 다음 동사는 to부정사를 목적어로 쓴다.

want	hope	expect	decide	plan	choose	promise
agree	pretend	desire	wish	prepare	refuse	need

The artist *expects* **to display** several paintings in the gallery.
He is *planning* **to plant** flowers in the backyard.

[1-5] 괄호 안에서 알맞은 것을 고르시오.

1 Sally pretended (to understand / understanding) what the teacher was saying.

2 Loyal employees do not mind (to put / putting) in much more effort. <학평 응용>

3 They agreed (to make / making) huge changes to the contract.

4 You'd better not postpone (to visit / visiting) the dentist if you have serious pain.

5 I am grateful for your job offer and am strongly considering (to accept / accepting) it. <학평 응용>

[6-9] 우리말과 같도록 괄호 안의 말을 활용하여 문장을 완성하시오.

6 그 후보자는 대중에게 그의 재산을 밝히는 것을 거절했다. (reveal, refuse)
   = The candidate _____ his asset to the public.

7 나는 이번 달 말까지 그 아파트에서 이사를 나가는 것을 미뤘다. (delay, move)
   = I _____ out of the apartment until the end of this month. <학평 응용>

8 Brenner씨는 내년 여름에 2주 동안 유럽을 여행하기를 원한다. (travel, hope)
   = Ms. Brenner _____ in Europe for two weeks next summer.

9 그 도둑은 귀중품들을 모으는 것을 포기하고 빠르게 그 가게를 떠났다. (give up, collect)
   = The thief _____ valuables and left the store quickly. <학평 응용>

10 다음 글에서 어법상 <u>틀린</u> 부분을 찾아 쓰고 바르게 고쳐 쓰시오.

> Wanda has always enjoyed making food for her family members. So, she decided taking cooking classes at the local community college. This month, she will be learning how to cook Asian dishes.

_____ → _____

동명사와 to부정사를 목적어로 쓰는 동사 II

정답 p.14

1. 다음 동사는 목적어로 동명사를 쓸 때와 to부정사를 쓸 때의 의미가 같다.

begin	start	like	love	hate	prefer	continue

It *started* **raining[to rain]** right when we arrived at the beach.

2. 다음 동사는 목적어로 동명사를 쓸 때와 to부정사를 쓸 때의 의미가 다르다.

forget + 동명사 (과거에) ~한 것을 잊다 **forget + to부정사** (미래에) ~할 것을 잊다	**regret + 동명사** ~한 것을 후회하다 **regret + to부정사** ~하게 되어 유감이다
remember + 동명사 (과거에) ~한 것을 기억하다 **remember + to부정사** (미래에) ~할 것을 기억하다	**try + 동명사** (시험 삼아) ~해보다 **try + to부정사** ~하려고 노력하다

I'll never *forget* **attending** my favorite singer's concert.
He *forgot* **to bring** his wallet today, so I bought him lunch.

TIP 「stop + 동명사」(~하는 것을 멈추다)에서의 동명사는 stop의 목적어이며, 「stop + to부정사」(~하기 위해 멈추다)에서의 to부정사는 부사적 용법으로 쓰여 목적을 나타낸다.
The museum *stopped* **selling** discounted passes to students.
The tourists *stopped* **to watch** a street performer.

[1-3] 괄호 안에서 알맞은 것을 고르시오.

1 Mr. Nolan hates (talk / talking) about his private life.

2 He regretted (to fix / fixing) up the woman's bike because she left without paying. <학평 응용>

3 A lack of sunlight causes many types of plants to stop (to grow / growing).

[4-6] 우리말과 같도록 괄호 안의 말을 활용하여 문장을 완성하시오.

4 나는 자러 가기 전에 나의 휴대폰 배터리를 충전할 것을 잊었다. (charge, forget)

= I _____ my cell phone battery before I went to bed. <학평 응용>

5 공산품들의 가격은 연료비 때문에 계속 오를 것이다. (continue, rise)

= The price of industrial products _____ because of the gas price.

6 우리는 Dave에 대해 친절하려고 노력했지만, 그는 우리의 노력을 무시했다. (be, try)

= We _____ friendly toward Dave, but he ignored our effort.

7 다음 글에서 어법상 틀린 부분을 찾아 쓰고 바르게 고쳐 쓰시오.

> If something seems impossible, trying to convince yourself otherwise will rather increase your anxiety. Therefore, sometimes the best way to accomplish a difficult objective is to stop to think that it is possible and just take things one step at a time. <학평 응용>   *convince: 납득시키다

_____ → _____

기출로작중 POINT 6 동명사 관용 표현

정답 p.14

다음은 동명사를 쓰는 관용 표현이다.

feel like + V-ing ~하고 싶다	**be worth + V-ing** ~할 가치가 있다
on[upon] + V-ing ~하자마자	**be busy + V-ing** ~하느라 바쁘다
by + V-ing ~함으로써, ~해서	**cannot help V-ing** ~하지 않을 수 없다
look forward to + V-ing ~하는 것을 기대하다	**spend + 시간/돈 + V-ing** ~하는 데 시간/돈을 쓰다
when it comes to + V-ing ~하는 것에 관한 한	**have difficulty[trouble] + V-ing** ~하는 데 어려움이 있다
be used to + V-ing ~하는 데 익숙하다	**keep[prevent] … from + V-ing** …가 ~하지 못하게 하다
make a point of + V-ing ~하기로 정하다	**It is no use + V-ing** ~해도 소용없다
dream of + V-ing ~하는 것을 꿈꾸다	**There is no + V-ing** ~할 수 없다

I **feel like jogging** in the park because the weather is nice today.
She **cannot help getting** angry about her cousin's rude behavior.

[1-10] 우리말과 같도록 괄호 안의 말을 활용하여 문장을 완성하시오.

1 Jonas는 그의 첫 번째 현장 학습에 가는 것을 기대하고 있었다. (go)

= Jonas _____ on his first field trip. <수능 응용>

2 그 배우들은 그들의 곧 있을 공연을 위해 리허설하느라 바쁘다. (rehearse)

= The actors _____ for their upcoming performance.

3 네가 바꿀 수 없는 것에 대해 불평해도 소용없다. (complain)

= _____ about things you cannot change.

4 Alice는 매일 건강에 좋은 음식을 먹기로 정했다. (eat)

= Alice _____ a healthy diet every day.

5 바깥의 소음은 어젯밤에 내가 잘 자지 못하게 했다. (sleep)

= The sound outside _____ well last night.

6 만약 네가 모험 이야기에 흥미가 있다면 이 책은 읽을 가치가 있다. (read)

= This book _____ if you are interested in adventure stories.

7 나의 교수님은 연구 논문을 쓰는 데 그의 시간의 대부분을 쓴다. (most of his time, write)

= My professor _____ a research paper.

8 그 쓰러진 코끼리는 그것의 무게 때문에 호흡하는 데 어려움이 있을 것 같다. (breathe)

= The fallen elephant is likely to _____ because of its weight. <학평 응용>

9 재활용을 늘림으로써, 우리는 종이에 사용되는 나무의 양을 줄일 수 있다. (increase)

= _____ recycling, we can reduce the amount of wood used for paper. <학평 응용>

10 그녀의 항공편이 취소되었다는 것을 알게 되자마자, Anna는 또 다른 것을 예약하기 위해 서둘렀다. (learn)

= _____ her flight was canceled, Anna hurried to book another.

Review Test

[1-3] 다음 빈칸에 들어갈 알맞은 것을 고르시오.

1

> Ms. Brown regrets _____ at her neighbor about the conflicts yesterday.

① yell   ② yelled   ③ to yell
④ yelling   ⑤ to be yelled

2

> The mayor desires _____ a new expressway.

① build   ② to build   ③ building
④ to be built   ⑤ being built

3

> We are only capable of _____ meaningful relationships with a maximum of about 150 people. <학평 응용>

① form   ② forming
③ to be formed   ④ being formed
⑤ having been formed

[4-6] 다음 중 어법상 **틀린** 것을 고르시오.

4

① Donating to children makes me happy. <수능 응용>
② Keep following this path, and you will reach the lake.
③ When did you begin to work at your company?
④ Megan once dreamed of becoming a model.
⑤ As the flooding got worse, we needed evacuating our home.

5

① He stopped to ask for directions to the stadium.
② Bruce seems quite sure about the soccer team's winning the match.
③ Do you remember telling me one of your secrets?
④ Wearing seatbelts are mandatory for everyone in the vehicle.
⑤ The politician entered his office without answering any questions from reporters.

6

① Critics could not help focusing on the unbelievable plot of the movie.
② Thomas admitted breaking his sister's new toy.
③ My uncle quit to drink alcohol after he was diagnosed with cancer.
④ We regret to tell you that your application has been rejected.
⑤ The organization's goal is raising money for ecological programs.

7 다음 중 어법상 바른 것끼리 묶인 것은?

> ⓐ Matt appreciated me for helping him.
> ⓑ They love to go to the beach in the evening to watch the sun set.
> ⓒ She went back to the office because she forgot bringing an important document.
> ⓓ Jenny is the most talented person I know when it comes to bake.
> ⓔ Neal was sad about having been refused to ride the roller coaster.

① ⓐ, ⓑ, ⓒ   ② ⓐ, ⓑ, ⓔ   ③ ⓐ, ⓒ, ⓓ
④ ⓑ, ⓓ, ⓔ   ⑤ ⓒ, ⓓ, ⓔ

[8-10] 다음 문장에서 어법상 틀린 부분을 찾아 쓰고 바르게 고쳐 쓰시오.

8

It is no use persuade him because he hates listening to others.

_____ → _____

9

Laura didn't feel like going outside on the rainy day, so she chose staying home.

_____ → _____

10

Since my parents had heard about my skipping classes, I was afraid of punishing.

_____ → _____

[11-12] 다음 두 문장의 의미가 같도록 동명사를 이용하여 문장을 완성하시오.

11

The ruling party is confident that Mr. Brown will win the election.
→ The ruling party is confident of _____ _____ the election.

12

The security guard denied that he had noticed the alarm at midnight.
→ The security guard denied _____ the alarm at midnight.

[13-14] 우리말과 같도록 괄호 안의 말을 알맞게 배열하시오.

13

이 붐비는 도시에서는 교통 문제를 해결할 수 없다. (the traffic problems, is, solving, no, there)

= _____ in this crowded city.

14

나는 네가 여기에 너의 차를 주차하는 것을 신경 쓰지 않는다. (you, mind, not, parking, I, your car, do)

= _____ here.

[15-17] 우리말과 같도록 괄호 안의 말을 활용하여 문장을 완성하시오.

15

그 교수는 그의 조수에게 계속 전화했지만, 그녀는 전화를 받지 않았다. (call, keep, his assistant)

= The professor _____, but she didn't answer the phone.

16

만약 우리가 자연 서식지를 계속 파괴한다면, 야생동물들은 더 이상 이 지역에서 살 수 없을 것이다. (continue, natural habitats, destroy)

= If we _____, the wildlife can no longer live in these areas. <학평 응용>

17

그 학생은 공정하게 대우받지 못하는 것에 대해 걱정했다. (treat, be worried about, not)

= The student _____ fairly.

18 우리말과 같도록 주어진 <조건>에 맞게 문장을 완성하시오.

> 아이들의 행동을 통제하는 것은 경험이 풍부한 선생님에게도 어렵다.

> <조건>
> 1. difficult, children's behaviors, control, be를 활용하시오.
> 2. 5단어로 쓰시오.

= _____ even for the experienced teacher.

[19-20] 다음 글을 읽고 주어진 질문에 답하시오.

> To slow the rate of global warming, people must take immediate action (A) reduce / to reduce the amount of energy they use. Considering the severity of the problem, being reluctant to make personal sacrifices (B) is / are not an option. One method to limit energy use is to avoid (C) wasting / to waste hot water. Another important consideration is that much electricity is used for lighting. ⓐ그것들이 불필요할 때 조명들을 끄지 않음으로써, (turn off, lights, not) you are directly contributing to global warming.
>
> *severity: 심각성 **reluctant: 꺼리는

19 위 글의 밑줄 친 우리말 ⓐ와 같도록 괄호 안의 말을 활용하여 문장을 완성하시오.

= _____ when they are unnecessary

20 위 글의 (A), (B), (C)의 각 네모 안에서 어법에 맞는 표현으로 가장 적절한 것은?

	(A)	(B)	(C)
①	reduce	is	wasting
②	reduce	are	to waste
③	to reduce	is	wasting
④	to reduce	is	to waste
⑤	to reduce	are	wasting

21 (A), (B), (C)의 각 네모 안에서 어법에 맞는 표현으로 가장 적절한 것은?

> Some people prefer to stay in their comfort zone. They have difficulty (A) to give / giving a public presentation because it makes them nervous. Others reject a chance (B) to study / studying abroad because they don't consider themselves adventurous. People become trapped by their own conception of their limits, so they become angry at (C) asking / being asked to step beyond them. This attitude toward life, however, is a huge mistake. You should welcome new challenges at every turn. <학평 응용>

	(A)	(B)	(C)
①	to give	to study	asking
②	to give	studying	being asked
③	giving	to study	asking
④	giving	to study	being asked
⑤	giving	studying	asking

22 다음 글의 밑줄 친 부분 중, 어법상 틀린 것은?

> Thank you for agreeing ①to send an engineer to repair the washing machine you supplied. However, I noticed that the product warranty says that although replacement parts are free, you charge for labor. This sounds ②unfair. I believe the machine's failure ③was caused by a manufacturing defect. Initially, it made a lot of noise, and later, it stopped ④to operate entirely. Given this, I hope you will not insist on ⑤my paying for the labor. <수능 응용>

CHAPTER 10
분사

기출로 적중 POINT

최근 7개년 수능/학평/내신 출제 경향

주의해야 할 분사구문
4%

분사의 형태와 쓰임
8%

분사구문의 시제와 태
37%

현재분사와 과거분사
42%

분사구문의 다양한 의미
5%

분사구문 만드는 법 4%

TOP 1 현재분사와 과거분사 (42%)
명사와 분사의 관계에 따른 현재분사와 과거분사의 쓰임을 구별하는 문제가 자주 출제된다.

TOP 2 분사구문의 시제와 태 (37%)
문맥에 따라 능동형 분사구문과 수동형 분사구문을 구별하는 문제가 자주 출제된다.

TOP 3 분사의 형태와 쓰임 (8%)
명사를 수식하는 분사(구)의 형태와 쓰임을 묻는 문제가 자주 출제된다.

분사의 형태와 쓰임

정답 p.15

분사는 V-ing(현재분사)나 p.p.(과거분사)의 형태로, 형용사처럼 명사를 수식하거나 문장 안에서 보어로 쓰인다. 분사가 명사를 수식할 때 단독으로 쓰이면 명사 앞에 오고, 구를 이루어 쓰이면 명사 뒤에 온다.

You should not bother the **sleeping** animals. <명사 수식>
The historical item **discovered** *in the cave* is kept in the museum. <명사 수식>
The man stood **waiting** for the bus. <주격 보어>
I found *the building's construction* **unfinished**. <목적격 보어>

[1-6] 밑줄 친 부분의 쓰임과 같은 것을 <보기>에서 골라 그 기호를 쓰시오.

> **<보기>** ⓐ There were lots of <u>shining</u> stars in the sky.
> ⓑ We had the room <u>cleaned</u> after we used it.

1 The tornado left the region severely <u>damaged</u>.   [   ]

2 Peter sat <u>watching</u> the ducks in the lake.   [   ]

3 We learned about some mushrooms <u>growing</u> on the forest floor.   [   ]

4 The <u>broken</u> copy machine has not been replaced for three months.   [   ]

5 She looked <u>distracted</u> while driving and almost caused an accident.   [   ]

6 Some people waste electricity <u>generated</u> by burning fuels. <학평 응용>   [   ]

[7-13] 우리말과 같도록 괄호 안의 말을 알맞게 배열하시오.

7 직업을 찾는 모든 사람들은 같은 목표를 가지고 있다. (a job, everyone, searching for)
= _____ has the same goal. <학평>

8 나의 부모님은 나의 성적표에 실망한 것 같았다. (my report card, disappointed at, seemed)
= My parents _____.

9 그 고객은 그의 이름이 은행원에 의해 불린 것을 들었다. (a bank teller, called by, heard, his name)
= The client _____.

10 그 맛있는 요리들은 요리사들의 놀라운 재능을 보여줬다. (amazing, of the chefs, talents)
= The delicious dishes demonstrated the _____. <학평 응용>

11 어른들은 소셜 미디어에서 사용되는 언어를 알고 싶어 한다. (language, social media, used in)
= Adults would like to be aware of the _____. <학평 응용>

12 오늘 밤에 비가 많이 올 것이기 때문에, 너는 창문들이 닫혀 있게 해야 한다. (the windows, keep, closed)
= Because it will rain a lot tonight, you must _____.

13 그 쇼핑몰은 크리스마스 선물을 사는 쇼핑객들로 가득 차 있었다. (Christmas gifts, shoppers, buying)
= The mall was full of _____.

POINT 2 현재분사와 과거분사

정답 p.16

1. 현재분사는 능동이나 진행의 의미를 나타내고, 과거분사는 수동이나 완료의 의미를 나타낸다.

It was an **embarrassing** moment.　　　They noticed a stranger **wandering** around.
I bought spices **imported** from India.　　The **rotten** tomato smells awful.

TIP 현재분사는 능동이나 진행의 의미로 명사를 수식하지만, 동명사는 명사의 용도나 목적을 나타낸다.
　　　Look at the **running** boy. <현재분사>　　　I need new **running** shoes. <동명사>

2. 분사가 수식하거나 설명하는 대상이 감정을 일으키는 주체인 경우 현재분사를 쓰고, 감정을 느끼는 대상인 경우 과거분사를 쓴다.

We heard the **surprising** news at the meeting.
We were **surprised** at the news about oil prices.

[1-5] 괄호 안에서 알맞은 것을 고르시오.

1 He remained (involving / involved) in the project until it was finished.

2 My mentor always cheers me with (encouraging / encouraged) words.

3 I was very (exciting / excited) to be able to bring a souvenir for them. <학평 응용>

4 Curiosity makes us view a tough problem as an (interesting / interested) challenge. <학평 응용>

5 Fred saw a spider (crawling / crawled) along the side of his desk.

[6-10] 우리말과 같도록 괄호 안의 말을 활용하여 문장을 완성하시오.

6 그 이야기의 결말은 감동적이어서, 그들은 울었다. (touch, be)
= The ending of the story _____, so they cried.

7 기후 변화는 개인들의 행동의 축적된 결과이다. (accumulate, result)
= Climate change is an _____ of individuals' behaviors. <학평 응용>

8 그 회사는 잠재적인 고객으로부터 만족스러운 응답을 받았다. (response, satisfy)
= The company received a _____ from the potential client.

9 나의 삼촌은 자동차 정비소에서 그의 차가 수리되게 했다. (his car, repair)
= My uncle had _____ at the auto repair shop.

10 네가 무서워할 때, 너의 몸은 아드레날린을 생산한다. (terrify, be)
= When you _____, your body produces adrenalin. <학평 응용>

11 다음 문장에서 어법상 틀린 부분을 찾아 쓰고 바르게 고쳐 쓰시오.

> Mild stimulants commonly finding in beverages can make you more focused. <학평 응용>　　*stimulant: 자극제

_____ → _____

분사구문 만드는 법

분사구문은 분사를 이용하여 「접속사 + 주어 + 동사」 형태의 부사절을 부사구로 바꾼 것이다. 부사절과 주절의 주어가 같을 때 부사절의 접속사와 주어를 생략하고 동사를 V-ing형으로 바꿔서 만든다.

As she realized her mistake, she immediately apologized.

→ **Realizing** her mistake, she immediately apologized.

Since I did not know his address, I couldn't write him a letter.

→ **Not[Never] knowing** his address, I couldn't write him a letter.
  └→ 분사구문의 부정형: 「not[never] + 분사」

After he arrived at the hotel, he went to the reception desk.

→ *After* **arriving** at the hotel, he went to the reception desk.
  └→ 분사구문의 의미를 분명하게 하기 위해 접속사를 생략하지 않기도 한다.

[1-5] 다음 두 문장의 의미가 같도록 분사구문을 완성하시오. (단, 접속사를 생략하시오.)

1 Since I felt pain in my stomach, I took a digestive medicine.

→ _____, I took a digestive medicine.

2 If you try to do too much at once, you might accomplish nothing.

→ _____, you might accomplish nothing.

3 While she cleaned her room, she was talking on the phone.

→ _____, she was talking on the phone.

4 After he retired in 1952, he remained active in teaching and writing.

→ _____, he remained active in teaching and writing. <수능 응용>

5 Because I did not understand the instructions, I asked for clarification.

→ _____, I asked for clarification.

[6-10] 우리말과 같도록 괄호 안의 말을 활용하여 분사구문을 완성하시오.

6 바쁘기 때문에, 그들은 점심시간에도 일해야 한다. (be, since, busy)

= _____, they have to work even at lunchtime.

7 손님들을 맞으면서, 그는 그들에게 어디로 가야 하는지 안내했다. (greet, the guests)

= _____, he guided them where to go.

8 그의 생각을 바꾼 후에, 그는 그 회의에 참석하기로 동의했다. (change, his mind, after)

= _____, he agreed to attend the meeting.

9 안경을 쓰지 않아서, 나는 칠판 위의 작은 글씨들을 읽을 수 없었다. (wear, not, glasses)

= _____, I couldn't read the small letters on the blackboard.

10 편집장으로 일하면서, 그녀는 많은 잘 알려진 작가들을 만났다. (an editor, work as)

= _____, she met many well-known writers. <학평 응용>

POINT 4 분사구문의 다양한 의미

정답 p.16

분사구문은 시간, 이유, 동시동작, 연속동작, 조건, 양보 등의 의미를 나타낸다.

시간	when/after/while/as soon as ~할 때/한 후에/하는 동안/하자마자	**Swimming** in the ocean, he saw a shark. (← *When he swam* in the ocean)
이유	because/since/as ~하기 때문에	**Needing** some sugar, we went to the supermarket. (← *As we needed* some sugar)
동시동작	while/as ~하면서	**Checking** the messages, she drank some coffee. (← *While she checked* the messages)
연속동작	and ~하고 나서	I called the ambulance, **explaining** the situation. (← *and I explained* the situation)
조건	if 만약 ~한다면	**Watching** the film, you will understand why it is popular. (← *If you watch* the film)
양보	although/though 비록 ~이지만	**Admitting** he was right, I could not forgive him. (← *Although I admitted* he was right)

[1-4] 다음 두 문장의 의미가 같도록 괄호 안에서 가장 알맞은 것을 고르시오.

1 Turning left at the corner, you will easily find the destination.
→ (Although / If) you turn left at the corner, you will easily find the destination.

2 Not having enough time, we should move quickly.
→ (As soon as / As) we don't have enough time, we should move quickly.

3 The airplane leaves Incheon at 3:30, landing in Jejudo at 4:30.
→ The airplane leaves Incheon at 3:30, (and / after) it lands in Jejudo at 4:30.

4 Preparing breakfast, I usually listen to the radio.
→ (While / If) I prepare breakfast, I usually listen to the radio.

[5-8] <보기>의 접속사를 한 번씩만 활용하여 다음 밑줄 친 부분을 부사절로 바꿔 쓰시오.

<보기> as soon as   since   if   although

5 Being short, he was pretty good at basketball.
→ _____, he was pretty good at basketball.

6 Arriving at the theater late, we missed the opening credits.
→ _____, we missed the opening credits.

7 Visiting other countries, you will experience and learn new things.
→ _____, you will experience and learn new things.

8 Hearing a familiar voice behind me, I turned around.
→ _____, I turned around.

분사구문의 시제와 태

1. 분사구문의 시제: 주절의 시제와 같을 때는 V-ing를 쓰고, 주절의 시제보다 앞설 때는 완료형 「having + p.p.」를 쓴다.

Listening to music, I am more productive at work.
(← *When I listen* to music, I am more productive at work.)

Having slept for three hours last night, she is very sleepy now.
(← *As she slept* for three hours last night, she is very sleepy now.)

2. 분사구문의 수동태: 주절의 시제와 같을 때는 「being + p.p.」를 쓰고, 주절의 시제보다 앞설 때는 완료형 「having been + p.p.」를 쓴다. 이때 being이나 having been은 생략할 수 있다.

(Being) Offered a job opportunity, she was excited.
(← *When she was offered* a job opportunity, she was excited.)

(Having been) Injured in an accident, he had to walk on crutches.
(← *Because he had been injured* in an accident, he had to walk on crutches.)

[1-7] 다음 두 문장의 의미가 같도록 분사구문을 완성하시오. (단, 접속사를 생략하시오.)

1 As he had witnessed the car crash firsthand, he called the police.
→ _____, he called the police.

2 Since she is known to the public, she doesn't go to crowded places.
→ _____, she doesn't go to crowded places.

3 After they had heard the judge's solution, everybody in the court agreed.
→ _____, everybody in the court agreed. <학평 응용>

4 While she baked a cake, Stella accidentally set off the smoke detector.
→ _____, Stella accidentally set off the smoke detector.

5 As it was hurt by the economic recession, the company planned to dismiss some employees.
→ _____, the company planned to dismiss some employees.

6 Because it had been stored in the refrigerator, the soup needed to be warmed up.
→ _____, the soup needed to be warmed up.

7 When it is used together with a pain reliever, caffeine is effective in treating headaches.
→ _____, caffeine is effective in treating headaches. <학평 응용>

8 다음 글에서 어법상 틀린 부분을 찾아 쓰고 바르게 고쳐 쓰시오. (단, 두 단어로 고쳐 쓰시오.)

> Though knowing for his sculptures and paintings, Michelangelo was also an architect. His most famous contribution to this field was St. Peter's Basilica. Having served as the model for the United States Capitol building, this building gained popularity among many imitators.   *St. Peter's Basilica: 성 베드로 대성전

_____ → _____

POINT 6 주의해야 할 분사구문

정답 p.16

1. 분사구문을 만들 때 부사절과 주절의 주어가 다르면 부사절의 주어를 생략하지 않으며, 이를 독립분사구문이라고 한다.

It being a public holiday, many shops are closed.
(← *As it is* a public holiday, many shops are closed.)

TIP 부사절이 「there + be동사」인 경우, 분사구문에서 being 앞에 there를 쓴다.
There being no evidence, the police released the suspect.
(← *Since there was* no evidence, the police released the suspect.)

2. 분사구문의 주어가 불특정한 일반인인 경우 관용적으로 주어를 생략하며, 이를 비인칭 독립분사구문이라고 한다.

Generally speaking 일반적으로 말하면	Frankly speaking 솔직히 말하면	Strictly speaking 엄밀히 말하면
Speaking of ~에 대해 말하자면	Judging from ~으로 판단하건대	Considering ~을 고려하면

Frankly speaking, I don't like Shannon because she is selfish.

3. 「with + 명사 + 분사」는 '…이 ~한 채로/하면서'라는 의미로, 동시동작을 나타낸다. 이때 명사와 분사의 관계가 능동이면 현재분사를 쓰고, 수동이면 과거분사를 쓴다.

Flowers are starting to bloom **with spring beginning.**
He was sitting **with his legs crossed**.

[1-3] 다음 두 문장의 의미가 같도록 분사구문을 완성하시오. (단, 접속사를 생략하시오.)

1 As the dress fit nicely, I decided to buy it.
→ _____, I decided to buy it.

2 When his business succeeded, he was filled with a sense of accomplishment.
→ _____, he was filled with a sense of accomplishment.

3 Since there was more work to complete, the workers couldn't go home.
→ _____, the workers couldn't go home.

[4-6] 우리말과 같도록 괄호 안의 말을 활용하여 문장을 완성하시오.

4 한 어린 소녀가 눈물이 흐르는 채로 그녀의 부모님을 찾고 있었다. (tears, with, run)
= A young girl was looking for her parents _____ down.

5 그 환자는 머리가 붕대에 감긴 채로 침대 위에 누워 있었다. (his head, bandage, with)
= The patient was lying on the bed _____.

6 일반적으로 말하면, 학생들은 선생님들의 몸짓 언어에 세심한 주의를 기울인다. (speak)
= _____, students pay close attention to teachers' body language. <학평 응용>

Review Test

[1-3] 다음 빈칸에 들어갈 알맞은 것을 고르시오.

1

I got air purifiers _____ in both the living room and my room.

① install   ② installs   ③ to install
④ installed   ⑤ installing

2

Learning a foreign language is _____ for me.

① being interested   ② interested
③ interesting   ④ to interest
⑤ having interested

3

_____ by his best friend, Julian got skeptical about friendships with others.

① Betray   ② Betrays
③ Betraying   ④ Having betrayed
⑤ Having been betrayed

[4-5] 다음 두 문장의 의미가 같도록 빈칸에 들어갈 알맞은 것을 고르시오.

4

While she read the article, she discovered several spelling mistakes.
→ _____ the article, she discovered several spelling mistakes.

① Read   ② Reading   ③ To read
④ Having read   ⑤ Being read

5

Having waited in the lobby for a long time, we became impatient.
→ Since we _____ in the lobby for a long time, we became impatient.

① wait   ② were waiting   ③ will wait
④ have waited   ⑤ had waited

[6-7] 다음 중 어법상 틀린 것을 고르시오.

6

① She was satisfied with the product she ordered online.
② The man wearing a uniform told us to sign in.
③ Some organizations try to save endangering animals around the world.
④ She looked very exhausted, so I made her go to bed. <학평 응용>
⑤ The baby is sleeping with his hands lifted above his head.

7

① Having experienced a few engine problems, the car didn't run smoothly.
② Born in a small town, he knew every villager around.
③ Judging from the color, the bananas will take a few more days to ripen.
④ Giving detailed guidelines, they finished their research without any difficulty.
⑤ There being no ingredients to cook with, I ordered pizza instead.

[8-9] 다음 문장에서 어법상 <u>틀린</u> 부분을 찾아 쓰고 바르게 고쳐 쓰시오.

8

When taking a picture of himself, the tourist noticed his wallet stealing.

_____ → _____

9

The constant barking of the neighbor's dog is incredibly annoyed.

_____ → _____

[10-12] 다음 두 문장의 의미가 같도록 분사구문을 완성하시오. (단, 접속사를 생략하시오.)

10

Since she had been hurt seriously, she spent several days in the hospital.
→ _____, she spent several days in the hospital.

11

As the shuttle bus arrived, he carried his bag and got ready to go.
→ _____, he carried his bag and got ready to go.

12

I opened the box because I thought that Mom had hidden my new phone inside it.
→ I opened the box _____
_____. <학평 응용>

[13-14] 우리말과 같도록 괄호 안의 말을 알맞게 배열하시오.

13

많은 사람들이 그들의 일상 생활에서 원유로 만들어진 플라스틱 제품들을 사용한다. (use, plastic products, crude oil, made from, many people)

= _____
in their daily lives. <학평 응용>

14

그를 속상하게 만들고 싶지 않았기 때문에, 나는 그에게 그의 공연이 환상적이었다고 말했다. (wanting, not, to upset, him)

= _____, I told him that his performance was fantastic.

[15-16] 우리말과 같도록 분사와 괄호 안의 말을 활용하여 문장을 완성하시오.

15

이 섬은 현대 문명으로부터 여전히 고립되어있다. (remain, isolate, this island)

= _____ from modern civilization.

16

그 어머니는 그녀의 아기가 우는 채로 편하게 식사할 수 없었다. (her baby, cry)

= The mother couldn't have a meal comfortably
_____.

17 우리말과 같도록 주어진 <조건>에 맞게 분사구문을 완성하시오.

방사능에 노출되었기 때문에, 저 야채들은 폐기되어야 한다.

<조건>

1. the radiation, expose to를 활용하시오.
2. 6단어로 쓰시오.

= _____, those vegetables have to be discarded.

[18-19] 다음 글을 읽고 주어진 질문에 답하시오.

(A) 탄광에서 사용된 중력 철도에 의해 영감을 받아, (inspire, use in, by the gravity railroads, coal mines) Thompson designed America's first roller coaster at Coney Island in 1884. It was nothing like the exciting rides ⓐ enjoying today. Modern thrill-seekers might look forward to ⓑ riding a fast roller coaster. They will cheerfully scream during their ride with the wind ⓒ blowing through their hair. However, ⓓ being slow at only six miles per hour, the roller coaster at Coney Island hardly sounded enjoyable. Yet it was a great success, ⓔ generated hundreds of dollars each day.

*gravity railroad: 중력 철도

18 위 글의 밑줄 친 우리말 (A)와 같도록 괄호 안의 말을 활용하여 빈칸에 쓰시오.

= _____ _____ _____ _____

_____ _____ _____ _____

19 위 글의 밑줄 친 ⓐ~ⓔ 중 어법상 틀린 것의 기호를 쓰고 바르게 고쳐 쓰시오. (단, 한 단어로 고쳐 쓰시오.)

(1) _____ → _____
(2) _____ → _____

수능형
20 (A), (B), (C)의 각 네모 안에서 어법에 맞는 표현으로 가장 적절한 것은?

Nonverbal communication is not a substitute for verbal communication. Rather, it should function as a supplement, (A) serving / served to enhance the richness of the content of the message. Imagine you are in an uncomfortable position while talking to someone. Nonverbal communication will help you (B) get / getting the message across to him or her and give you some time to get comfortable before continuing a conversation. Nonverbal communication also offers you the opportunity to express emotions and attitudes properly. For example, responding to news with your eyebrows (C) raising / raised shows that you are surprised at what you have heard. <학평 응용> *substitute: 대신하는 것

(A)	(B)	(C)
① serving	get	raising
② serving	get	raised
③ serving	getting	raising
④ served	get	raising
⑤ served	getting	raised

수능형
21 다음 글의 밑줄 친 부분 중, 어법상 틀린 것은?

Charlie knew something was wrong. The lake was ① gone. He paused and scanned the field, but he could not see ② anything familiar. Suddenly, several dogs barked behind him. The ③ unexpected sound startled him, so he began to run away. He was terribly ④ frightening and ran with increasing awkwardness, tearing at the weeds with his hands so that everything about him seemed to be moving except his slow feet. With his movements ⑤ slowed, he soon heard the dogs getting closer and closer. <학평 응용>

CHAPTER 11
관계사

기출로 적중 POINT

최근 7개년 수능/학평/내신 출제 경향

복합관계사 4%
관계사의 계속적 용법 16%
관계부사 17%
전치사 + 관계대명사 12%
관계대명사 what 17%
관계대명사 that 4%
소유격 관계대명사 2%
목적격 관계대명사 8%
주격 관계대명사 20%

TOP 1 **주격 관계대명사 (20%)**
주격 관계대명사의 역할과 쓰임을 묻는 문제가 자주 출제된다.

TOP 2 **관계대명사 what (17%)**
관계대명사 what과 that의 쓰임을 구분하는 문제가 자주 출제된다.

TOP 3 **관계부사 (17%)**
관계부사와 관계대명사의 쓰임을 구분하는 문제가 자주 출제된다.

1. 관계대명사는 관계대명사절을 이끄는 접속사와 대명사 역할을 하며, 관계대명사절은 선행사를 수식한다.

Rachel is a *singer*. **She** is very popular.
→ Rachel is *a singer* **who** is very popular.

2. 선행사의 종류와 관계대명사절에서의 선행사의 역할에 따라 어느 관계대명사를 쓸지 결정된다.

선행사 ＼ 관계대명사의 격	주격	목적격	소유격
사람	who	who(m)	whose
사물, 동물	which	which	whose
사람, 사물, 동물	that	that	-

I know *a carpenter* **who** has devoted himself to his work for years. <주격> <학평>
Mark displays *every trophy* **that** he won at the tournament. <목적격>
The firefighter helped *the girl* **whose** cat was stuck in a tree. <소유격>

[1-6] 밑줄 친 관계대명사의 쓰임을 <보기>에서 골라 그 기호를 쓰시오.

<보기> ⓐ 주격   ⓑ 목적격   ⓒ 소유격

1 The pizza <u>which</u> I ate last night was delicious.   [   ]

2 This is Alexis, the student <u>whom</u> I told you about.   [   ]

3 He was a powerful Babylonian king <u>whose</u> name was Hammurabi.   [   ]

4 Insects <u>that</u> bite can be repelled with an effective bug spray.   [   ]

5 We visited an old castle <u>whose</u> walls were at least 30 feet high.   [   ]

6 They were impressed by the fireworks <u>which</u> lit up the night sky.   [   ]

[7-12] 다음 빈칸에 알맞은 말을 <보기>에서 골라 쓰시오.

<보기> who   whom   which   whose

7 The class _____ I took last semester is no longer being offered.

8 I met the architect _____ designed this café three years ago.

9 I got a chance to talk to the man _____ presentation was really interesting.

10 The hairdresser _____ I see regularly is unavailable for appointments this week.

11 My mother buys eggs from a local farmer _____ chickens eat only organic grains.

12 Cleaning the house is the household chore _____ I dislike the most.

1. 주격 관계대명사는 관계대명사절에서 주어 역할을 하며, 선행사의 종류에 따라 who, which, that을 쓴다.

I have *a dog*. **It** has beautiful eyes.
→ I have *a dog* **which[that]** has beautiful eyes.
↳ 주격 관계대명사절의 동사는 선행사에 수일치시킨다.

2. 「주격 관계대명사 + be동사」 뒤에 형용사나 분사가 올 때는 「주격 관계대명사 + be동사」를 생략할 수 있다.

Tom ate everything (**that was**) *placed* in front of him.

[1-6] 관계대명사를 이용하여 다음 두 문장을 한 문장으로 연결하시오. (단, that은 쓰지 마시오.)

1   Cindy is the one. She came up with the idea.
    → Cindy is _____.

2   We learned about the astronauts. They walked on the moon.
    → We learned about _____.

3   He bought a nice house. It overlooked the whole city.
    → He bought _____.

4   The doctor found a treatment. It was effective for the patient.
    → The doctor found _____.

5   They arrested the thief. He stole some jewelry.
    → They arrested _____.

6   It was the film. It was praised by both critics and audiences.
    → It was _____.

[7-10] 밑줄 친 부분이 어법상 맞으면 O를 쓰고, 틀리면 바르게 고쳐 쓰시오. (단, that으로 고쳐 쓰지 마시오.)

7   There are several lakes in this region <u>who</u> contain a variety of fish.   → _____

8   The company created new commercials which <u>advertises</u> healthy cat food.   → _____

9   Amy met a beautiful woman <u>who</u> wore a dress as white as snow. <학평>   → _____

10 Make sure you don't hand in an assignment that <u>is</u> full of errors.   → _____

11 다음 글에서 어법상 <u>틀린</u> 부분을 찾아 쓰고 바르게 고쳐 쓰시오.

> Completed in 1965, the Gateway Arch in St. Louis, Missouri, is a 193-meter tourist attraction which is visited by an estimated 2.5 million people a year. To get to the top, visitors can take a special elevator that run up both legs of the arch every 10 minutes.

_____ → _____

목적격 관계대명사

1. 목적격 관계대명사는 관계대명사절에서 목적어 역할을 하며, 선행사의 종류에 따라 who(m), which, that을 쓴다.

The baseball team has *a coach*. The players respect **him**.
→ The baseball team has *a coach* **who(m)[that]** the players respect.

2. 목적격 관계대명사는 생략할 수 있다.

The bush (**that**) I planted is finally starting to grow flowers.

[1-7] 관계대명사를 이용하여 다음 두 문장을 한 문장으로 연결하시오. (단, that은 쓰지 마시오.)

1 The software is a bit difficult to use. I installed it yesterday.
→ The software _____ is a bit difficult to use.

2 The story has many adventurous characters. Anna likes them.
→ The story has many adventurous characters _____.

3 I picked up the pencil. I dropped it on the floor.
→ I picked up the pencil _____.

4 The television show is about to enter its third season. I watched it every Friday night.
→ The television show _____ is about to enter its third season.

5 I ran into a woman. I met her at a conference many years ago.
→ I ran into a woman _____.

6 Old ideas are replaced with new information. Scientists sometimes can't explain it.
→ Old ideas are replaced with new information _____. <학평 응용>

7 The photographer was very talented. We hired him for the event.
→ The photographer _____ was very talented.

[8-13] 밑줄 친 부분을 생략할 수 있으면 O를 쓰고, 생략할 수 없으면 X를 쓰시오.

8 Several people <u>whom</u> I wasn't expecting showed up at the party.   → _____

9 I reported the crime to a police officer <u>who</u> was nearby.   → _____

10 Tara called the lawyer <u>who was</u> handling her case to provide an update. → _____

11 I understand the excitement <u>which</u> you felt when you traveled abroad. → _____

12 Our body produces some hormones <u>that make</u> us calm.   → _____

13 I was not familiar with the car <u>which was</u> coming up the driveway.   → _____

POINT 4 소유격 관계대명사

정답 p.17

소유격 관계대명사는 관계대명사절에서 소유격 역할을 하며, 선행사와 상관없이 whose를 쓴다.

Carl has *a sister*. **Her** *goal* is to become a scientist.

→ Carl has *a sister* **whose** *goal* is to become a scientist.

TIP 선행사가 사물인 경우 「whose + 명사」를 「명사 + of which」나 「of which + 명사」로 바꿔 쓸 수 있다.

I visited *the Eiffel Tower* **whose height** is 324 meters.
→ I visited *the Eiffel Tower* **the height of which** is 324 meters.
→ I visited *the Eiffel Tower* **of which the height** is 324 meters.

[1-4] 소유격 관계대명사를 이용하여 다음 두 문장을 한 문장으로 연결하시오.

1 The child won a prize. His drawing was the best.

→ The child _____ won a prize.

2 The national park employs rangers. Their jobs include protecting the animals.

→ The national park employs rangers _____.

3 The students had to take a makeup test. Their grades were low.

→ The students _____ had to take a makeup test.

4 There are some techniques to revive patients. Their hearts have stopped beating.

→ There are some techniques to revive patients _____. <학평 응용>

[5-11] 우리말과 같도록 괄호 안의 말을 알맞게 배열하시오.

5 정부는 집이 허리케인으로 파괴된 사람들을 도왔다. (were destroyed, people, houses, whose)

= The government helped _____ in the hurricane.

6 그 사서는 표지가 파란색인 책을 내밀었다. (of which, blue, the cover, was, a book)

= The librarian held out _____.

7 벤자민 프랭클린은 얼굴이 미국 100달러 지폐에 있는 사람이다. (face, the person, whose, is)

= Benjamin Franklin is _____ on the American $100 bill.

8 그는 초능력이 순간이동인 슈퍼히어로이다. (is, whose, teleportation, a superhero, superpower)

= He is _____.

9 우리는 나뭇가지가 눈으로 덮여 있는 나무들 근처에서 사진을 찍었다. (of which, trees, were covered, branches)

= We took a photo near _____ with snow.

10 휴가 동안, 그들은 내부가 궁전같이 보이는 호텔에 머물렀다. (the interior, looked, of which, a hotel)

= During vacation, they stayed at _____ like a palace.

11 그는 연구가 경영학에 초점을 맞춘 경제학자였다. (whose, an economist, focused, study)

= He was _____ on business administration. <학평 응용>

기출로픽중 POINT 5 관계대명사 that

정답 p.17

1. 관계대명사 that은 선행사와 상관없이 주격이나 목적격 관계대명사로 쓸 수 있다.

They made *important discoveries* **that** led to the invention of the automobile. <학평 응용>

TIP that은 지시대명사, 지시형용사, 명사절 접속사로도 쓰인다.

That is my house over there on the corner. <지시대명사>
I've been on **that** big cruise before. <지시형용사>
Charlie realized **that** his parents had already arrived home. <명사절 접속사>

2. 선행사에 다음이 포함될 때는 주로 관계대명사 that을 쓴다.

최상급, 서수	Durian is *the smelliest fruit* **that** I have tried.
the same/only/very	Of all the rules, this is *the only one* **that** I disagree with.
-thing/-body로 끝나는 대명사	Walking is *something* **that** most people do every day. <학평 응용>
all, no, little, much 등	She gave him *all the money* **that** she had.

[1-6] 밑줄 친 that과 바꿔 쓸 수 있는 관계대명사를 <u>모두</u> 쓰시오.

1 Most residents think that he was the mayor <u>that</u> the city needed. → _____

2 The plane tickets <u>that</u> I purchased are non-refundable. → _____

3 When you're upset, talk to a friend <u>that</u> listens to you. → _____

4 The street <u>that</u> George usually takes is closed for construction. → _____

5 Daniel wrote an essay <u>that</u> described his last winter. → _____

6 The company announced a list of employees <u>that</u> it promoted this year. → _____

[7-12] 밑줄 친 that의 쓰임과 같은 것을 <보기>에서 골라 그 기호를 쓰시오.

<보기> ⓐ The woman <u>that</u> moved in next door seems nice.
　　　　ⓑ Did you already finish the food <u>that</u> I gave you?
　　　　ⓒ I hope <u>that</u> I see you again soon.

7 The apartment <u>that</u> I rented was beautifully decorated. [　　　]

8 The painting <u>that</u> hangs in my kitchen was a gift from my grandfather. [　　　]

9 My teacher informed us <u>that</u> the school would have a fire drill today. [　　　]

10 Members <u>that</u> forget to pay their fees will receive a reminder letter. [　　　]

11 The scuba diving instructor said <u>that</u> I would be safe underwater. [　　　]

12 The chair <u>that</u> the clerk showed me was too small. [　　　]

POINT 6 관계대명사 what

정답 p.18

관계대명사 what은 선행사를 포함하고 있으며, 문장 안에서 주어, 목적어, 보어로 쓰이는 명사절을 이끈다. '~한 것'이라는 의미이며, the thing(s) which[that]으로 바꿔 쓸 수 있다.

Curiosity is a way of adding value to **what** you see. <학평>
→ Curiosity is a way of adding value to **the thing which[that]** you see.

TIP 관계대명사 what은 선행사를 포함하고 있지만 관계대명사 that은 선행사를 포함하고 있지 않은 것에 주의한다.
Alex imagined (~~that~~, **what**) the world would be like in 100 years.

[1-5] 우리말과 같도록 관계대명사 what과 괄호 안의 말을 활용하여 문장을 완성하시오.

1 그들이 상자 안에서 발견한 것은 그들을 놀라게 했다. (find, in the box)
= _____ surprised them.

2 현실적인 목표를 세우는 것은 네가 먼저 고려해야 하는 것이다. (consider first, have to)
= Setting a realistic goal is _____.

3 너는 너의 의사가 어제 너에게 말했던 것을 기억하니? (tell, yesterday, your doctor)
= Do you remember _____?

4 만화책을 읽는 것은 그녀가 그녀의 여가 시간에 하는 것이다. (in her free time, do)
= Reading comic books is _____.

5 내가 Frank에 대해 감탄하는 것은 그의 멋진 유머 감각이다. (admire about)
= _____ is his wonderful sense of humor.

[6-11] 괄호 안에서 알맞은 것을 고르시오.

6 (What / That) is important is how you feel about yourself.

7 I saved the money (what / that) I earned from my part-time job.

8 Species (what / that) evolved on the Galapagos Islands are unlike animals anywhere else.

9 You are free to choose (what / that) you want to make of your life. <학평>

10 Being there for you is (what / that) good buddies do to show their support.

11 Health concerns are not the only reason (what / that) young adults change their diets. <학평 응용>

12 다음 글의 밑줄 친 ⓐ~ⓒ 중 어법상 틀린 것의 기호를 쓰고 바르게 고쳐 쓰시오.

In ancient Roman times, gladiators fought in large arenas ⓐ<u>which</u> spectators eagerly visited. Today, many people believe ⓑ<u>which</u> they see in movies and think that a "thumbs up" gesture from the crowd meant saving the gladiator's life. However, some historians argue that ⓒ<u>what</u> determined a gladiator's fate was in fact a turned thumb.

*gladiator: (고대 로마의) 검투사

_____ → _____

전치사 + 관계대명사

관계대명사가 전치사의 목적어인 경우, 그 전치사는 관계대명사절 맨 뒤나 관계대명사 바로 앞에 온다.

This is the notebook (**which**[**that**]) Eric writes all of his schedules **in**.

→ This is the notebook **in which** Eric writes all of his schedules.

TIP   전치사가 관계대명사 바로 앞에 올 때는 관계대명사 who와 that을 쓸 수 없고, 목적격 관계대명사를 생략할 수 없다.
Judy sent a text message to the friend **with** (~~who~~, **whom**) she was going to play.
I think this is a job **for** (~~that~~, **which**) I am perfectly suited.

[1-3] <보기>와 같이 관계대명사를 이용하여 다음 두 문장을 한 문장으로 연결하시오.

> <보기>   Saint Basil's Cathedral is a landmark. Moscow is famous for it.
> → Saint Basil's Cathedral is a landmark *which[that] Moscow is famous for* .
> → Saint Basil's Cathedral is a landmark *for which Moscow is famous* .

1   The teacher will resign. I took yoga classes with her.

→ The teacher _____ will resign.

→ The teacher _____ will resign.

2   The staff toured the new office building. They would soon work in it.

→ The staff toured the new office building _____.

→ The staff toured the new office building _____.

3   I'm planning to have dinner with the man. I spoke about him before.

→ I'm planning to have dinner with the man _____ before.

→ I'm planning to have dinner with the man _____ before.

[4-8] 밑줄 친 부분이 어법상 맞으면 O를 쓰고, 틀리면 바르게 고쳐 쓰시오.

4   One writer <u>in whom</u> I have an interest is Edgar Allen Poe.   → _____

5   The man <u>from who</u> I purchased my bicycle let me test it out first.   → _____

6   Some nutrition that plants get comes from the soil <u>that</u> they grow in.   → _____

7   You should check the sources <u>from that</u> you get your information.   → _____

8   The mechanic <u>to whom</u> I brought my car to found the problem.   → _____

9   우리말과 같도록 괄호 안의 말을 알맞게 배열하시오.

> 과거에, 텔레비전 기자들이 기사를 제출하는 한 중심적인 장소가 있었다.
> (submitted, one central place, to, television reporters, which)

= In the past, there was _____ stories. <학평 응용>

관계부사 when(시간), where(장소), why(이유), how(방법)는 관계부사절을 이끄는 접속사와 부사 역할을 하며, 「전치사 + 관계대명사」로 바꿔 쓸 수 있다.

I shopped a lot in *December*. Many stores were having sales **during that month**.

→ I shopped a lot in *December* **when**(= **during which**) many stores were having sales.

TIP   관계부사의 선행사가 the time, the place, the reason처럼 시간, 장소, 이유를 나타내는 일반적인 명사인 경우, 선행사나 관계부사 중 하나를 생략할 수 있다. 단, 선행사 the way와 관계부사 how는 둘 중 하나만 쓸 수 있다.

Can you tell me (*the reason*) **why** you were late?
= Can you tell me *the reason* (**why**) you were late?

Sarah showed me **how** she did the magic trick.
= Sarah showed me *the way* she did the magic trick.

[1-4] 관계부사를 이용하여 다음 두 문장을 한 문장으로 연결하시오.

1   Do you remember the day? We got lost while hiking on that day.

→ Do you remember the day _____?

2   That's the reason. Steve and Charlie are no longer teammates for that reason.

→ That's the reason _____.

3   I know a website. You can learn foreign languages there.

→ I know a website _____. <학평>

4   I can teach you the way. The artist drew such detailed pictures in that way.

→ I can teach you _____.

[5-9] 괄호 안에서 알맞은 것을 모두 고르시오.

5   I look forward to the day (when / on which / where) I graduate from university.

6   Carol visited an island (which / at which / where) is full of her childhood memories.

7   The weather can affect (the way how / the way / how) you feel when you exercise.

8   They ran to (the place / where / the place where) the treasures were buried.

9   A home is a safe zone (which / at which / where) we can express our feelings. <학평 응용>

10   (A), (B)의 각 네모 안에서 어법에 맞는 표현으로 가장 적절한 것을 고르시오.

> The remains of the *Titanic* were discovered in 1985. The ship's location was unknown partially because the area of the ocean (A) which / where the surviving passengers had escaped from was too deep to search. With the development of online navigation services, it is now possible to see the exact spot (B) which / where the tragedy occurred.

관계사의 계속적 용법은 관계사가 선행사에 부가적인 설명을 덧붙일 때 사용하며, 이때 관계사 앞에 콤마(,)를 쓴다.

❶ 관계대명사는 계속적 용법에서 「접속사 + 대명사」의 의미이다. 관계대명사 that과 what은 계속적 용법으로 쓸 수 없다.

This is *my father*, **who**(= **and he**) is a doctor.

The robbery barely opened *the vault*, **which**(= **but it**) was empty.

My best friend is moving away, **which**(= **and it**) upsets me greatly.
↳ 관계대명사 which는 계속적 용법으로 쓸 때 구나 절을 선행사로 쓸 수 있다.

TIP 콤마 뒤에 「부정대명사(all, most, some, both, one 등) + of + whom[which]」를 써서 선행사의 전체나 일부를 나타낼 수 있다.
The couple has *three children*, **one of whom** plays the piano very well.

❷ 관계부사는 계속적 용법에서 「접속사 + 부사」의 의미이다. 관계부사 why와 how는 계속적 용법으로 쓸 수 없다.

The plant normally grows in *the shade*, **where**(= **and there**) the sunlight doesn't reach. <학평 응용>

[1-4] 우리말과 같도록 관계사와 괄호 안의 말을 활용하여 문장을 완성하시오.

1 Alex는 소파 위에서 자고 있었는데, 그 큰 소리에 짜증이 났다. (was sleeping)

= Alex, _____ on the couch, was annoyed at the loud noise.

2 그 나무 위의 집은 내가 지었는데, 폭풍우 동안 손상되었다. (built)

= The tree house, _____, was damaged during the storm.

3 그 직원들은 금요일을 좋아하는데, 그때 직장에 티셔츠와 청바지를 입고 갈 수 있다. (can wear)

= The employees love Fridays, _____ T-shirts and jeans to work.

4 많은 투자자들이 그 지역을 방문했는데, 그곳에 새로운 공항이 건설될 것이다. (will be constructed, a new airport)

= Many investors visited the region, _____.

[5-10] 밑줄 친 부분이 어법상 맞으면 O를 쓰고, 틀리면 바르게 고쳐 쓰시오.

5 Our math teacher, <u>that</u> I admire, will retire next year. → _____

6 The woman owns several restaurants, all of <u>them</u> have good reputations. → _____

7 Vincent went to the pool with his son, <u>what</u> enjoys swimming. → _____

8 I learned how to fish in Alaska, <u>where</u> I spent summers as a child. → _____

9 Galileo made spyglasses, <u>which</u> were later named telescopes. <학평 응용> → _____

10 The boy gave the dog a snack, <u>that</u> made it happy. → _____

---

11 다음 글에서 어법상 틀린 부분을 찾아 쓰고 바르게 고쳐 쓰시오.

> An idiom is an expression that does not have a literal meaning. There are many idioms in English like "Every cloud has a silver lining," that means that there is always something to be hopeful about, even in bad situations.
>
> *literal: 문자 그대로의

_____ → _____

POINT 10 복합관계사

1. 복합관계대명사는 「관계대명사 + -ever」의 형태로 명사절이나 부사절을 이끈다.

복합관계대명사	명사절	부사절
who(m)ever	anyone who(m) ~하는 누구든지	no matter who(m) 누가/누구를 ~하더라도
whichever	anything that ~하는 어느 것이든지	no matter which 어느 것이/것을 ~하더라도
whatever	anything that ~하는 무엇이든지	no matter what 무엇이/무엇을 ~하더라도

Since it's your birthday party, you can invite **who(m)ever** you like.

2. 복합관계부사는 「관계부사 + -ever」의 형태로 시간·장소·방법이나 양보 부사절을 이끈다.

복합관계부사	시간·장소·방법의 부사절	양보 부사절
whenever	at any time when ~할 때는 언제나	no matter when 언제 ~하더라도
wherever	at any place where ~하는 곳은 어디든지	no matter where 어디서 ~하더라도
however	in whatever way that ~하는 어떤 방법으로든지	no matter how 아무리 ~하더라도

However *painful the truth is*, don't be afraid to be honest with yourself. <학평 응용>
↳ 복합관계부사 however가 양보 부사절을 이끌 때는 「however + 형용사/부사 + 주어 + 동사」의 형태로 쓴다.

[1-5] 다음 두 문장의 의미가 같도록 복합관계사를 이용하여 문장을 완성하시오.

1 The man didn't open the door, no matter who visited his house.

→ The man didn't open the door, _____.

2 No matter how hard she tried, Monica could not remember his name.

→ _____, Monica could not remember his name.

3 You can get tomatoes from my garden at any time when you want.

→ You can get tomatoes from my garden _____. <수능 응용>

4 I'm sure the games will be fun, no matter which you choose to play.

→ I'm sure the games will be fun, _____.

5 The actors continued their performance, no matter what was happening backstage.

→ The actors continued their performance, _____.

[6-9] 괄호 안에서 알맞은 것을 모두 고르시오.

6 You can pick (whomever / anyone whom) you would like to be on your team.

7 I'll answer the phone immediately, no matter (when / whenever) you call me.

8 He planted trees (wherever / at any place where) people needed them.

9 Focus entirely on (whatever / whenever) you're doing at the moment. <학평 응용>

Review Test

[1-2] 다음 빈칸에 들어갈 알맞은 것을 고르시오.

1

> Sherry is a nurse _____ responsibilities include helping patients in urgent situations.

① whom   ② that   ③ whose
④ who   ⑤ which

2

> Wild animals need space _____ they can avoid human activity. <학평 응용>

① which   ② what   ③ why
④ how   ⑤ where

[3-4] 다음 빈칸에 공통으로 들어갈 알맞은 것을 고르시오.

3

> · Copenhagen is the safest city _____ I can think of.
> · Jane believes _____ her vegetarian diet is the reason for her good health.

① whom   ② which   ③ where
④ that   ⑤ what

4

> · The suspect _____ the witness identified is being questioned by the police.
> · The movie star, _____ everyone had hoped to see, quickly walked into the building.

① whose   ② whom   ③ that
④ which   ⑤ what

[5-6] 다음 중 어법상 **틀린** 것을 고르시오.

5

① Martin decided to stand up to the bullies who teased him.
② I always drink a cup of black tea on the day when there's a full moon. <학평 응용>
③ A delicious selection of food is that you expect when you go to a buffet restaurant.
④ The speech contest, which lasted all afternoon, ended with an awards ceremony.
⑤ Whoever made the shelf must be a good carpenter.

6

① I think that you shouldn't be angry with me.
② The customer whom I helped returned a shirt.
③ The field on which the football team practices needs to be carefully maintained.
④ Keep whatever you consider valuable in a safe.
⑤ The apartment is shared by two men, both of them work as computer programmers.

7 다음 중 어법상 **틀린** 것끼리 묶인 것은?

> ⓐ She glanced at the old man whom face looked familiar.
> ⓑ I like the way how Simon speaks.
> ⓒ This is the art exhibition which drew a great deal of public interest recently.
> ⓓ Do you know the reason February is the shortest month of the year?
> ⓔ Through the Internet, we can contact people instantly, no matter wherever they are. <학평 응용>

① ⓐ, ⓑ, ⓒ   ② ⓐ, ⓑ, ⓔ   ③ ⓐ, ⓒ, ⓔ
④ ⓑ, ⓓ, ⓔ   ⑤ ⓒ, ⓓ, ⓔ

[8-11] 다음 문장에서 어법상 틀린 부분을 찾아 쓰고 바르게 고쳐 쓰시오. (단, 한 단어로 고쳐 쓰시오.)

8

> Some people think that cows which eats grass instead of other crops produce better milk.

_____ → _____

9

> The 1970s was a time which disco music was very popular in the United States.

_____ → _____

10

> To learn languages, an infant must make sense of the context in that languages occur. <학평 응용>

_____ → _____

11

> His mother found that he bought for her under the bed.

_____ → _____

[12-14] 우리말과 같도록 괄호 안의 말을 활용하여 문장을 완성하시오.

12

> 윌리엄 셰익스피어는 많은 새로운 단어들과 표현들을 만들어낸 극작가였다. (invent, a playwright, many new words and expressions)

= William Shakespeare was _____
_____.

13

> 아무리 바쁘더라도, 나는 그 콘서트에 갈 것이다. (busy, be)

= _____, I will go to the concert.

14

> 노벨상은 연구나 활동이 인류를 이롭게 한 사람들에게 주어진다. (research or actions, benefit, people)

= Nobel Prizes are given to _____
_____ humanity.

[15-17] 다음 두 문장의 의미가 같도록 관계사를 이용하여 문장을 완성하시오.

15

> That was the year in which the construction of the Statue of Liberty was completed.
> → That was the year _____
> _____ was completed.

16

> Astronomers are not sure of the reason for which the universe is expanding so quickly.
> → Astronomers are not sure of the reason ____
> _____ so quickly.

17

> Carbon dioxide gas is released into the air, and it contributes to global warming.
> → Carbon dioxide gas is released into the air,
> _____. <학평 응용>

18 우리말과 같도록 주어진 <조건>에 맞게 문장을 완성하시오.

> 그 직원들이 원한 것은 좋은 근무 환경과 적정한 임금이었다.

> <조건>
> 1. want, the employees를 활용하시오.
> 2. 4단어로 쓰시오.

= _____ was a good work environment and fair wages.

[19-20] 다음 글을 읽고 주어진 질문에 답하시오.

> (A) 새끼를 가진 암컷 바다거북들은 알을 낳기 위해 그들이 태어났던 장소로 돌아온다. (the place, be) Sea turtles ⓐ whose nesting ground is in Florida arrive at beaches in the state from March to October. After emerging from the water, they search for a spot ⓑ where is above the high water mark. Then, they dig a large hole ⓒ in which they can make a nest. After she lays eggs, the mother turtle returns to the ocean. The eggs, ⓓ which incubate in the warm sand for about 60 days, hatch in unison. ⓔ That determines their survival is whether they can avoid predators and other dangers long enough to make it to the water.
>
> *incubate: 성장하다

19 위 글의 밑줄 친 우리말 (A)와 같도록 관계사와 괄호 안의 말을 활용하여 문장을 완성하시오.

= Pregnant female sea turtles return to _____ _____ born to lay eggs.

20 위 글의 밑줄 친 ⓐ~ⓔ 중 어법상 틀린 것의 기호를 쓰고 바르게 고쳐 쓰시오.

(1) _____ → _____

(2) _____ → _____

수능형
21 (A), (B), (C)의 각 네모 안에서 어법에 맞는 표현으로 가장 적절한 것은?

> We have an idea of (A) that / what is possible and impossible. These ideas make up the box we live in, which limits our possibilities. We generally don't go outside the box (B) which / where society creates for us. Instead, we follow the patterns we've learned from our friends, family, and culture. But sometimes, trying a new pattern might open up a new possibility for you. For example, the next time (C) which / when it rains, go for a walk without an umbrella. Even this small adventure can help you break out of your box. <학평 응용>

	(A)	(B)	(C)
①	that	where	which
②	that	where	when
③	what	where	when
④	what	which	when
⑤	what	which	which

수능형
22 다음 글의 밑줄 친 부분 중, 어법상 틀린 것은?

> Emotions are quite situational. Something in the here and now makes you mad. The emotion itself is tied to the situation ① from which it originates. As long as you remain in that emotional situation, you're likely to stay ② angry. If you leave the situation, the emotion begins to disappear. Moving away from the situation prevents it from ③ taking hold of you. Counselors often advise clients to get some distance from ④ that is bothering them. To take the first step to do so, try separating ⑤ yourself from the source of your anger. <학평 응용>

CHAPTER 12
접속사

기출로 적중 POINT

최근 7개년 수능/학평/내신 출제 경향

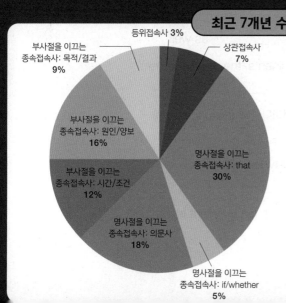

부사절을 이끄는 종속접속사: 목적/결과 9%

등위접속사 3%

상관접속사 7%

부사절을 이끄는 종속접속사: 원인/양보 16%

부사절을 이끄는 종속접속사: 시간/조건 12%

명사절을 이끄는 종속접속사: 의문사 18%

명사절을 이끄는 종속접속사: if/whether 5%

명사절을 이끄는 종속접속사: that 30%

TOP 1 명사절을 이끄는 종속접속사: that (30%)
명사절 접속사 that의 역할과 쓰임을 묻는 문제가 자주 출제된다.

TOP 2 명사절을 이끄는 종속접속사: 의문사 (18%)
의문사가 이끄는 명사절의 역할과 형태를 묻는 문제가 자주 출제된다.

TOP 3 부사절을 이끄는 종속접속사: 원인/양보 (16%)
원인이나 양보를 나타내는 부사절 접속사의 의미와 쓰임을 묻는 문제가 자주 출제된다.

등위접속사 and, but, or, so는 문법적으로 대등한 단어와 단어, 구와 구, 절과 절을 연결하며, 이때 so는 절과 절만 연결한다.

There are *restaurants* **and** *a supermarket* close to my apartment building.
He felt *tired* **but** *happy* after finishing his essay.
  ↳ 분사는 형용사 역할을 하므로, 접속사로 형용사와 분사를 연결할 수 있다.

Application forms must be submitted *in person* **or** *by e-mail*. <학평 응용>
I forgot my bank account password, **so** *I contacted the bank*.

TIP 「명령문 + and ~」는 '…해라, 그러면 ~'이라는 의미이고, 「명령문 + or ~」는 '…해라, 그렇지 않으면 ~'이라는 의미이다.
  Water this plant every day, **and** it will grow quickly.

[1-9] 괄호 안에서 가장 알맞은 것을 고르시오.

1 The hotel room we booked was clean (but / so) a little small.

2 My father (but / or) my mother will give me a ride to school.

3 Dr. Meyers told the patient to stay home (and / so) get plenty of rest.

4 I woke up late this morning, (or / so) I missed the bus.

5 Take the broken fan to the service center, (and / but) a technician will repair it.

6 A panda bear looks incredibly cute, (but / so) it is actually very dangerous.

7 Drive carefully when it's snowing, (and / or) you might cause an accident.

8 Redwood trees have highly durable bark, (or / so) it is rarely harmed by forest fires.

9 Lisa bought her brother a shirt, (and / or) he was pleased with the gift.

[10-15] 우리말과 같도록 등위접속사와 괄호 안의 말을 활용하여 문장을 완성하시오.

10 Nate는 점심에 산책을 하고 싶었지만, 너무 바빴다. (too busy, be)
= Nate wanted to take a walk at lunch, _____.

11 Anne은 첼로를 연주할 수 있고, 피아노 치는 것도 배우고 있다. (the piano, learn, to play)
= Anne is able to play the cello, _____ as well.

12 로비가 페인트칠 되고 있어서, 주민들은 옆문을 이용했다. (the residents, the side door, use)
= The lobby was being painted, _____.

13 그 뜨거운 냄비를 만지지 마라, 그렇지 않으면 너는 손가락을 델 것이다. (your fingers, burn)
= Do not touch the hot pot, _____.

14 Beth는 하루 종일 일한 후에 지쳐서, 일찍 파티를 떠났다. (the party, leave)
= Beth was exhausted after working all day, _____ early.

15 시험을 위해 열심히 공부해라, 그러면 너는 우수한 점수를 받을 것이다. (an excellent score, get)
= Study hard for the test, _____.

상관접속사는 두 개 이상의 단어가 짝을 이뤄 문법적으로 대등한 단어와 단어, 구와 구, 절과 절을 연결한다.

both A and B A와 B 둘 다	**Both** *Poland* **and** *Bulgaria* are located in Eastern Europe.
not only A but (also) B = B as well as A A뿐만 아니라 B도	**Not only / but** **(also)** *my sister* plays soccer every weekend. = *My sister* **as well as** *I* plays soccer every weekend.
not A but B A가 아니라 B	To get to the train station, turn **not** *left* **but** *right* at the intersection.
either A or B A나 B 둘 중 하나	**Either** *some statues* **or** *a fountain* is going to be placed in front of city hall.
neither A nor B A도 B도 아닌	You should **neither** *eat* **nor** *drink* for 12 hours before the surgery.

TIP 「both A and B」로 연결된 주어 뒤에는 항상 복수동사를 쓰고, 나머지 상관접속사로 연결된 주어 뒤에 오는 동사는 B에 수일치시킨다.

[1-5] 우리말과 같도록 괄호 안의 말을 알맞게 배열하시오.

1 Owen이 아니라 Jason이 우리 반에서 가장 키가 큰 학생이다. (but, Owen, is, Jason, not)

= _____ the tallest student in our class.

2 우리는 식당에서 피자와 감자튀김 둘 다 주문했다. (ordered, French fries, both, and, pizza)

= We _____ at the restaurant.

3 Jensen씨나 나 둘 중 한 명이 지원자들의 면접을 볼 것이다. (I, or, Mr. Jensen, will interview, either)

= _____ the candidates.

4 그 새로운 예술 센터는 현대적일 뿐만 아니라 아름답기도 하다. (also, modern, is, only, not, beautiful, but)

= The new arts center _____.

5 Andrew는 전에 연극을 본 적도 콘서트에 간 적도 없다. (attended, nor, a play, neither, a concert, watched)

= Andrew has _____ before.

[6-10] 밑줄 친 부분이 어법상 맞으면 O를 쓰고, 틀리면 바르게 고쳐 쓰시오.

6 A whale as well as dolphins <u>was</u> seen during the boat trip.　→ _____

7 Either he or you <u>has</u> to clean the kitchen.　→ _____

8 As the store sold <u>either</u> candy nor snacks, I didn't buy anything.　→ _____

9 Not Canada but Russia <u>is</u> the largest country in the world.　→ _____

10 The amusement park can be reached easily both by bus <u>or</u> by subway.　→ _____

1. that이 이끄는 명사절은 문장 안에서 주어, 목적어, 보어로 쓰인다.

That the Great Pyramid was built over 4,000 years ago is impressive. <주어>

→ *It* is impressive **that** the Great Pyramid was built over 4,000 years ago.

⤷ 명사절이 주어로 쓰일 때는 주로 주어 자리에 가주어 it을 쓰고 진주어 명사절을 뒤로 보낸다.

Her rude behavior shows (**that**) she is not a nice person. <목적어>

⤷ that절이 목적어로 쓰일 때는 that을 생략할 수 있다.

The policy is **that** all employees must wear an ID badge. <보어>

TIP 감정을 나타내는 형용사(glad, happy, shocked, pleased 등) 뒤에 오는 that절은 감정의 원인을 나타낸다.
The children were *glad* **that** their mother bought them ice cream.

2. that은 fact, news, idea, opinion, possibility 등의 명사를 부연 설명하는 동격절을 이끌기도 하며, 이때 that은 생략할 수 없다.

The boy learned judo despite *the fact* **that** he had lost his arm. <학평 응용>

[1-6] 밑줄 친 that절의 쓰임을 <보기>에서 골라 그 기호를 쓰시오.

<보기>   ⓐ 주어   ⓑ 목적어   ⓒ 보어   ⓓ 동격

1   The company says that it will open a new branch office next year.   [   ]

2   The customer's complaint was that the food was served cold.   [   ]

3   It is important that we treat others with respect.   [   ]

4   We cheered when we heard the news that the athlete had won a gold medal.   [   ]

5   The security guard told me that parking was not allowed in front of the building.   [   ]

6   That the airline canceled the flight came as a shock to the passengers.   [   ]

[7-9] 밑줄 친 부분이 어법상 맞으면 O를 쓰고, 틀리면 바르게 고쳐 쓰시오.

7   Jill's point is what her friends should have remembered her birthday.   → _____

8   Charles Darwin discovered that species evolve over long periods of time.   → _____

9   I'm worried that I will not be able to attend your dinner party next weekend. → _____

10 (A), (B)의 각 네모 안에서 어법에 맞는 표현으로 가장 적절한 것을 고르시오.

> Scientists have found out (A) what / that a type of bacteria actually consumes plastic. As a result, there is a possibility (B) which / that the large quantities of plastic waste in landfills can be destroyed safely.

명사절을 이끄는 종속접속사: if/whether

정답 p.19

명사절을 이끄는 접속사 if와 whether는 '~인지'라는 의미이다. whether가 이끄는 명사절은 문장 안에서 주어, 목적어, 보어로 쓰이지만, if가 이끄는 명사절은 주로 동사의 목적어로 쓰인다.

Whether the marketing campaign will be accepted (or not) is uncertain. <주어>
→ *It* is uncertain **whether** the marketing campaign will be accepted (or not).

I can't choose **if**[**whether**] we should go out for dinner (or not). <동사의 목적어>
Donators are interested in **whether** the charity is really helping others (or not). <전치사의 목적어> <수능 응용>
The question is **whether** the development of AI will benefit humanity or hurt it. <보어>

TIP or not은 whether 바로 뒤에 쓸 수 있지만, if 바로 뒤에는 쓸 수 없다.
People used to bite gold coins to see (if, **whether**) *or not* they were real.

[1-5] 괄호 안에서 알맞은 것을 <u>모두</u> 고르시오.

1   (If / Whether) the judge provided a fair ruling is still being debated.

2   It is hard to predict (if / whether) or not the economy will improve.

3   I forgot (if / whether) I turned the light off before leaving this morning.

4   I don't know (if / whether) Gary was in class today or not.

5   Do not worry about (if / whether) you are musically talented or not. <학평 응용>

[6-10] 우리말과 같도록 괄호 안의 말을 알맞게 배열하시오.

6   알려지지 않은 것은 그 화재가 우연히 시작됐는지이다. (the fire, whether, started)
    = What is unknown is _____ accidentally.

7   그 행사가 야외에서 개최되는지 아닌지는 날씨에 의존한다. (the event, or not, whether, takes place)
    = _____ outside relies on the weather.

8   Cassie는 정장을 입을지 입지 않을지 결정하는 데 어려움을 겪고 있다. (will wear, or not, she, a suit, if)
    = Cassie is having trouble deciding _____.

9   그들은 방을 예약해야 하는지에 대한 문제를 논의했다. (they, a room, whether, should book)
    = They discussed the matter of _____.

10   공항으로 떠나기 전에 우리의 비행기 시간이 바뀌었는지 확인하자. (has changed, if, our flight time)
    = Let's check _____ before leaving for the airport.

11   다음 글에서 어법상 <u>틀린</u> 부분을 찾아 쓰고 바르게 고쳐 쓰시오.

Some people wonder what they should go to a bank to request a housing loan or not. This is because they are not always sure that they will be qualified to receive one. Whether a person qualifies for a mortgage is usually related to one's credit score.   *mortgage: 담보 대출

_____ → _____

명사절을 이끄는 종속접속사: 의문사

의문사가 이끄는 명사절은 「의문사 + 주어 + 동사」의 형태로 문장 안에서 주어, 목적어, 보어로 쓰이며, 이를 간접의문문 이라고 하기도 한다. 단, 의문사가 명사절(간접의문문)의 주어인 경우 「의문사 + 동사」의 형태로 쓴다.

Why *the concert was canceled* is not announced yet. <학평 응용>
→ *It* is not announced yet **why** *the concert was canceled*.

The students were talking about **how** difficult *the math test had been*.
She is trying to figure out **who** *gave* her the letter.

TIP 주절이 do you think[believe, guess, suppose 등]의 형태인 의문문에서는 의문사를 문장 맨 앞에 쓴다.
When *do you think* the children will wake up?

[1-8] 우리말과 같도록 괄호 안의 말을 알맞게 배열하시오.

1 그들은 그가 왜 늦게 도착했는지 알지 못한다. (he, why, arrived)
= They don't know _____ late.

2 나는 이 약이 얼마나 효과적인지 확실하지 않다. (how, is, this medicine, effective)
= I am not sure _____.

3 누가 우리의 조장이 되어야 하는지는 매우 분명하다. (be, should, our group leader, who)
= _____ is very clear.

4 최근에, 연구원들은 웃음이 우리의 몸에 어떻게 영향을 주는지 입증했다. (our bodies, how, affects, laughing)
= Recently, researchers have demonstrated _____. <수능>

5 TV의 가격은 네가 그것을 어디에서 사는지에 따라 달라질 것이다. (buy, you, where, it)
= The price of the TV will vary depending on _____.

6 너는 우리가 우주를 언제 여행할 수 있을 것이라고 생각하니? (think, will, you, when, be, we, do)
= _____ able to travel space?

7 내가 오늘 배운 것은 겨울 동안 날씨가 어떻게 더 추워지는지이다. (colder, gets, how, the weather)
= What I learned today is _____ during winter.

8 너는 탁자 위의 꽃병을 누가 깨뜨렸다고 추측하니? (do, broke, who, guess, you)
= _____ the vase on the table?

[9-13] 밑줄 친 부분이 어법상 맞으면 O를 쓰고, 틀리면 바르게 고쳐 쓰시오.

9 Writing gives you time to think about <u>what do you want</u> to say. <수능> → _____

10 My teacher asked me <u>why did I fail</u> to turn in my assignment. → _____

11 I couldn't help but notice <u>how clean the city was</u> when I visited. → _____

12 <u>What do you suppose</u> Kevin has in his mind? → _____

13 <u>Do you believe why</u> she felt more energetic this morning? → _____

부사절을 이끄는 종속접속사: 시간/조건

1. 시간: when(~할 때), before(~하기 전에), after(~한 후에), as(~하면서, ~하고 있을 때), while(~하는 동안), until[till](~할 때까지), since(~한 이후로), as soon as(~하자마자), once(~할 때)

My headache disappeared **after** I took a nap.

He dropped his wallet **while** he was getting out of the taxi.

TIP 접속사 while 뒤에는 절이 오고, 전치사 during(~ 동안) 뒤에는 명사(구)가 온다.

2. 조건: if(만약 ~한다면), unless(= if ~ not)(만약 ~하지 않는다면), once(일단 ~하면), in case(~할 경우에 대비해서), as[so] long as(~하는 한)

You will get cold **if** you don't put(= **unless** you put) on your jacket.

The rich merchant was always prepared **in case** thieves came to his house. <학평 응용>

TIP 시간이나 조건을 나타내는 부사절에서는 미래의 일을 나타낼 때 미래시제가 아닌 현재시제를 쓴다.
I will arrive on time **unless** there (~~will be~~, **is**) a lot of traffic.

[1-6] 우리말과 같도록 <보기>의 접속사와 괄호 안의 말을 한 번씩만 활용하여 문장을 완성하시오.

| <보기> | while | in case | until | when | as long as | unless |

1 Sarah는 어렸을 때 발레리나가 되고 싶었다. (young, be)

= Sarah wanted to be a ballerina _____.

2 만약 네가 서두르지 않는다면, 버스를 놓칠 것이다. (hurry up)

= _____, you will miss the bus.

3 사고가 일어날 경우에 대비해서 우리는 집에 구급상자를 가지고 있다. (happen, an accident)

= We have a first aid kit at home _____.

4 그녀는 1906년에 죽을 때까지 그녀의 믿음을 위해 계속 싸웠다. (die, in 1906)

= She kept fighting for her belief _____. <학평>

5 어린이들은 어른에 의해 동행되는 한 환영된다. (an adult, be accompanied by)

= Children are welcome _____. <학평 응용>

6 Tony는 그 편지를 읽고 있는 동안 걱정스러워 보였다. (the letter, be reading)

= Tony looked worried _____.

[7-10] 밑줄 친 부분이 어법상 맞으면 O를 쓰고, 틀리면 바르게 고쳐 쓰시오.

7 Please check your phone often in case I <u>will call</u> you. → _____

8 The settlers began building a colony <u>after</u> they arrived in Virginia. → _____

9 It is rude to talk loudly <u>during</u> you are watching a movie in a theater. → _____

10 We will arrange a delivery time as soon as the product <u>will be</u> ready. <학평 응용> → _____

1. 원인: because/since/as/now that(~하기 때문에)

The company postponed the presentation **because** the key speaker was ill.

Now that I'm an adult, I can finally register to vote.

> TIP ① 접속사 because 뒤에는 절이 오고, 전치사 because of(~ 때문에) 뒤에는 명사(구)가 온다.
>
> ② 접속사 as는 '~처럼, ~하듯이'의 의미를 나타낼 수도 있다.
>   **As** you know, carrots are good for your eyes.

2. 양보: although/though/even though(비록 ~이지만), even if(비록 ~일지라도), while/whereas(~인 반면에)

Even though my grandfather is 80 years old, he jogs every day.

Some babies might be calmed by noise, **whereas** others favor quiet. <학평 응용>

> TIP '~에도 불구하고'라는 의미의 전치사 despite와 in spite of 뒤에는 명사(구)가 온다.

[1-4] 괄호 안에서 가장 알맞은 것을 고르시오.

1 Tim gave his mother some flowers (since / whereas) it was her birthday.

2 (Though / Despite) Sam and Elliot are identical twins, they have very different personalities.

3 (Now that / While) crime has dropped nationwide, citizens still report feeling unsafe.

4 I was late for work (because / because of) the traffic congestion in the city center.

[5-10] 우리말과 같도록 <보기>와 괄호 안의 말을 한 번씩만 활용하여 문장을 완성하시오.

<보기> even if	since	despite	while	although	because of

5 비록 나는 어젯밤에 충분한 잠을 잤지만 오늘 매우 피곤하게 느낀다. (enough sleep, get)

= _____ last night, I feel very tired today.

6 그 용감한 군인은 그의 많은 부상에도 불구하고 계속 싸웠다. (his many injuries)

= The brave soldier continued to fight _____.

7 나는 그 지역에 익숙하지 않았기 때문에 내비게이션 어플리케이션을 사용했다. (familiar, not, be)

= I used a navigation application _____ with the area.

8 비록 네가 그 두 액체를 함께 섞을지라도 기름과 물은 합쳐질 수 없다. (the two liquids, stir)

= Oil and water cannot be combined _____ together.

9 몇몇 사람들은 그들의 종교 때문에 고기를 먹지 않는다. (their religion)

= Some people don't eat meat _____.

10 나의 언니는 휴가 때 관광을 가는 것을 좋아하는 반면에, 나는 쉬는 것을 선호한다. (my sister, to go, like)

= _____ sightseeing on vacation, I prefer to relax.

1. **목적:** 「so that ~」(~하기 위해, ~할 수 있도록)

   We should give him a microphone **so that** everyone can hear him.

2. **결과:** 「so + 형용사/부사 + that ~」 「such + (a/an) + (형용사) + 명사 + that ~」(너무 …해서/이어서 ~한)

   The film was **so** *funny* **that** the entire audience laughed throughout it.

   You are **such** *a talented writer* **that** you'll become famous soon.

[1-4] 우리말과 같도록 괄호 안의 말을 활용하여 문장을 완성하시오.

1 그 방은 너무 지저분해서 우리는 전문 청소부를 고용했다. (messy, the room, be)

= _____ we hired a professional cleaning crew.

2 너는 사람들이 공부할 수 있도록 도서관에서 조용히 해야 한다. (study, people, can)

= You must be silent in the library _____.

3 그는 너무 좋은 선생님이어서 나는 그의 다른 수업들을 들을 것이다. (a good teacher, be)

= _____ I will take his other classes.

4 과학자들은 더 정확하게 날씨를 예측할 수 있도록 정보를 모은다. (can, the weather, predict)

= Scientists collect information _____ more accurately. <학평 응용>

[5-7] 다음 두 문장의 의미가 같도록 빈칸에 알맞은 말을 쓰시오.

5 It was such an old book that I was worried it would fall apart.

→ The book was _____ _____ _____ I was worried it would fall apart.

6 The journey was so long that I slept as soon as I got home.

→ It was _____ _____ _____ _____ _____ I slept as soon as I got home.

7 Cyclists should wear bright clothing at night. They need to be more visible to drivers.

→ Cyclists should wear bright clothing at night _____ _____ they are more visible to drivers.

8 다음 글의 밑줄 친 ⓐ~ⓒ 중 어법상 틀린 것의 기호를 쓰고 바르게 고쳐 쓰시오.

NASA is advancing its technology ⓐ so that it can send astronauts to Mars by the 2030s. The idea of a manned mission to Mars is ⓑ such exciting that most Americans support this goal. This is significant as it will come at such a high cost ⓒ which NASA's budget may need to be increased.

(1) _____ → _____

(2) _____ → _____

Review Test

[1-2] 다음 빈칸에 들어갈 알맞은 것을 고르시오.

1

> When faced with danger, our physical reaction prepares us _____ to fight the danger or to escape it. <학평 응용>

① both   ② not only   ③ as well as
④ either   ⑤ neither

2

> Kyle shared his opinion _____ video games are more entertaining than movies.

① which   ② what   ③ that
④ despite   ⑤ if

[3-4] 다음 빈칸에 공통으로 들어갈 가장 알맞은 것을 고르시오.

3

> · She showed the guard her ID _____ she entered the laboratory.
> · _____ the cost of living in cities has gotten expensive, people are moving to towns.

① unless   ② as   ③ even if
④ so that   ⑤ although

4

> · I can't remember _____ I selected the correct answer.
> · The popularity of a new word determines _____ or not it makes it into the dictionary.

① that   ② what   ③ how
④ if   ⑤ whether

[5-6] 다음 중 어법상 틀린 것을 고르시오.

5

① Set your alarm clock, or you will oversleep.
② Many people argue that the government should enhance the subway system.
③ Dan asked me what did Carol cook for dinner.
④ They wonder if Tina is married or not.
⑤ The song was such a success that it was played on radio stations for several months.

6

① George purchased not one but two jackets.
② How do you think my new haircut is?
③ The students practice playing their musical instruments every day so that they improve.
④ They will go on a hike as soon as the sun will come up.
⑤ Sarah was sad that her favorite café had closed the business.

7 다음 중 어법상 틀린 것끼리 묶인 것은?

> ⓐ Neither my brother nor my sister want to go to the park now.
> ⓑ The magician described how he performed the magic trick.
> ⓒ Brian walked into the room such quietly that I was startled.
> ⓓ Ms. Parker's suggestion is that the project deadline should be extended.
> ⓔ I turned on the light because of it had gotten dark outside.

① ⓐ, ⓑ, ⓓ   ② ⓐ, ⓒ, ⓔ   ③ ⓑ, ⓒ, ⓓ
④ ⓑ, ⓒ, ⓔ   ⑤ ⓒ, ⓓ, ⓔ

[8-10] 다음 문장에서 어법상 <u>틀린</u> 부분을 찾아 쓰고 바르게 고쳐 쓰시오.

8

> Despite the war ended, people are still suffering from the aftereffects of the war.

_____ → _____

9

> The book looks into the idea which modern life is too stressful.

_____ → _____

10

> I'm aware of where does she work because I sometimes give her a ride.

_____ → _____

[11-13] 접속사를 이용하여 다음 두 문장을 한 문장으로 연결하시오.

11

> · It is commonly believed.
> · History always glorifies the winners.

→ It is commonly believed _____

_____ .

12

> · I don't know.
> · Why did Sam quit playing football?

→ I don't know _____ .

13

> · Do you suppose?
> · When will the economy recover?

→ _____ ?

[14-16] 우리말과 같도록 괄호 안의 말을 활용하여 문장을 완성하시오.

14

> Sean뿐만 아니라 Paul도 그 테니스 토너먼트에 출전할 것이다. (compete, Paul, but, Sean)

= _____ in the tennis tournament.

15

> 창문을 닫아 두어라, 그렇지 않으면 방이 너무 추워질 것이다. (become, the room, too cold)

= Keep the windows closed, _____

_____ .

16

> 비록 인간은 몇 세기 동안 커피를 마셔왔지만, 커피가 어디에서 유래했는지는 확실하지 않다. (drink, humans, coffee, where, originate)

= _____ coffee for centuries, it is not clear _____ . <학평 응용>

17 우리말과 같도록 주어진 <조건>에 맞게 문장을 완성하시오.

> 수소는 폭발성이기 때문에 산소에 노출되자마자 불이 붙는다.

> <조건>
> 1. expose to, oxygen을 활용하시오.
> 2. 수동태를 활용하시오.
> 3. 8단어로 쓰시오.

= As hydrogen is explosive, it catches on fire _____
_____ .

[18-19] 다음 글을 읽고 주어진 질문에 답하시오.

> Northern Americans will harvest sap from trees and turn it into maple syrup when the weather ⓐ will begin to warm up. There are various types of maple trees, but the sugar maple is the most popular for this purpose. This is since sap from this type of tree has the highest sugar content, ⓑ as its name suggests. First, a hole which is ⓒ such small that it doesn't cause any damage is drilled into the tree. Then, a tap ⓓ and a container to catch the sap are attached. After the sap has been collected, it is filtered ⓔ so that any debris is removed. (A) 마지막으로, 수액은 시럽이 될 때까지 끓여진다. (syrup, become)
>
> *sap: 수액 **debris: 이물질, 파편

18 위 글의 밑줄 친 우리말 (A)와 같도록 괄호 안의 말을 활용하여 문장을 완성하시오.

= Finally, the sap is boiled _____ .

19 위 글의 밑줄 친 ⓐ~ⓔ 중 어법상 틀린 것의 기호를 쓰고 바르게 고쳐 쓰시오.

(1) _____ → _____
(2) _____ → _____

20 (A), (B), (C)의 각 네모 안에서 어법에 맞는 표현으로 가장 적절한 것은?

> Touring caravans are mobile homes which are connected to the back of your car (A) so that / now that you can enjoy traveling from place to place. Many families can go anywhere they want (B) if / although there is a camp site or caravan park. Touring caravan parks have basic services such as shower blocks, toilet blocks, and a small shop. It is up to the family to make sure they have food, water, electricity, gas, and whatever else is needed (C) during / while they are staying. <학평 응용>

	(A)	(B)	(C)
①	now that	although	while
②	now that	if	while
③	so that	if	while
④	so that	if	during
⑤	so that	although	during

21 다음 글의 밑줄 친 부분 중, 어법상 틀린 것은?

> People are cautioned not to look at the sun at the time of a solar eclipse ① because the brightness and the ultraviolet light of direct sunlight are damaging to the eyes. This advice is often misunderstood by those who think ② what sunlight is more damaging at this time. Staring at the sun when it is high in the sky is harmful ③ even if an eclipse is not occurring. In fact, staring at the sun directly is much more ④ harmful than looking at it when the moon is blocking part of it. The reason people are told to take special precautions is simply that more people are interested in ⑤ looking at the sun during this time. <학평 응용>   *solar eclipse: 일식

CHAPTER 13
비교구문

기출로 적중 POINT

최근 7개년 수능/학평/내신 출제 경향

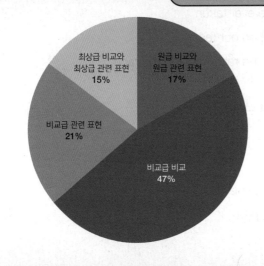

TOP 1 비교급 비교 (47%)

비교급 비교와 비교급 강조 표현의 형태 및 쓰임을 묻는 문제가 자주 출제된다.

TOP 2 비교급 관련 표현 (21%)

비교급 관련 표현의 형태와 쓰임을 묻는 문제가 자주 출제된다.

TOP 3 원급 비교와 원급 관련 표현 (17%)

원급 비교와 원급 관련 표현의 형태 및 쓰임을 묻는 문제가 자주 출제된다.

비교급과 최상급 만드는 법

형용사나 부사를 그대로 사용하거나 형태를 바꿔 원급, 비교급, 최상급 비교를 표현할 수 있다.

❶ 규칙 변화

비교급과 최상급 만드는 법		원급 – 비교급 – 최상급
대부분의 형용사/부사	+ -er/-est	smart – smart**er** – smart**est**
-e로 끝나는 형용사/부사	+ -r/-st	wide – wide**r** – wide**st**
「자음 + y」로 끝나는 형용사/부사	y를 i로 바꾸고 + -er/-est	scary – scar**ier** – scar**iest**
「단모음 + 단자음」으로 끝나는 형용사/부사	마지막 자음을 한 번 더 쓰고 + -er/-est	thin – thin**ner** – thin**nest**
대부분의 2음절 이상인 형용사/부사 (-y로 끝나는 형용사 제외)	more/most + 원급	helpful – **more** helpful – **most** helpful
분사 형태의 형용사		tired – **more** tired – **most** tired
「형용사 + ly」 형태의 부사		quietly – **more** quietly – **most** quietly

Drinking tea is **healthier** than drinking coffee. <학평>

❷ 불규칙 변화

good/well – **better** – **best**	late(시간이 늦은) – **later** – **latest**
bad/badly/ill – **worse** – **worst**	late(순서가 늦은) – **latter** – **last**
many/much – **more** – **most**	far(거리가 먼) – **farther** – **farthest**
little – **less** – **least**	far(정도가 더욱) – **further** – **furthest**
old(나이 든, 오래된) – **older** – **oldest**	
old(연상의) – **elder** – **eldest**	

China has **more** people than Russia. It has the **most** people in the world.

[1-5] 괄호 안에서 알맞은 것을 고르시오.

1 The Mariana Trench is the (most deep / deepest) part of the Pacific Ocean.

2 A photograph can depict nature (gooder / better) than a painting. <수능 응용>

3 The history test was the (easiest / easyest) exam I have ever taken.

4 Wanda's score in the game was the (most bad / worst) on our team.

5 Although the turtle moved more (slowly / slowlier) than the rabbit, it won the race.

[6-9] 밑줄 친 부분이 어법상 맞으면 O를 쓰고, 틀리면 바르게 고쳐 쓰시오.

6 The woman is the <u>eldest</u> of three daughters. <학평 응용>   → _____

7 James sang the <u>loudliest</u> of all the choir members.   → _____

8 An elephant is <u>biger</u> than all the other land animals on the planet.   → _____

9 My new apartment is <u>closer</u> than my old one to Central Park.   → _____

POINT 2 원급 비교와 원급 관련 표현

정답 p.21

1. 「as + 원급 + as」는 '…만큼 ~한/하게'라는 의미로, 비교하는 두 대상의 정도가 비슷하거나 같음을 나타낸다.

The recent earthquake was **as disastrous as** the previous one.

The curry I made was <u>**not as[so] spicy as**</u> I expected.
　　　　　　　　↳ 「not + as[so] + 원급 + as」: …만큼 ~하지 않은/않게

I went to bed **as early as** my little sister *did*(= *went* to bed) yesterday.
　　　　　　　　　　　　　　↳ do/does/did는 대동사로서 동사(구)의 반복을 피할 때 쓴다.

2. 원급 관련 표현

❶ 「as + 원급 + as + possible」: 가능한 한 ~한/하게 (= 「as + 원급 + as + 주어 + can」)

Please drive us to the airport **as quickly as possible**.

(= Please drive us to the airport **as quickly as you can**.)

❷ 「배수사 + as + 원급 + as」: …보다 ─배 더 ~한/하게

In 2014, computer usage was **three times as high as** e-reader usage. <학평 응용>

❸ 「not so much A as B」: A라기보다는 B인 (= B rather than A)

Losing my favorite earrings was **not so much sad as irritating**.

(= Losing my favorite earrings was **irritating rather than sad**.)

[1-6] 우리말과 같도록 괄호 안의 말을 활용하여 문장을 완성하시오. (단, 원급을 사용하시오.)

1 우리는 우리가 대해지기를 원하는 만큼 다른 사람들을 잘 대해야 한다. (well)

= We should treat others ＿＿＿＿＿＿＿＿＿＿＿＿＿＿＿＿＿＿ we want to be treated. <학평 응용>

2 고릴라는 보통의 인간보다 약 아홉 배 더 힘이 세다. (strong, nine times)

= A gorilla is about ＿＿＿＿＿＿＿＿＿＿＿＿＿＿＿＿ a typical human.

3 Kim씨는 다른 구직자만큼 긴장하지 않았다. (nervous)

= Ms. Kim was ＿＿＿＿＿＿＿＿＿＿＿＿＿＿＿＿ the other job applicant.

4 Dillon에게, 만화책을 모으는 것은 취미라기보다는 집착이었다. (a hobby, an obsession)

= For Dillon, collecting comics was ＿＿＿＿＿＿＿＿＿＿＿＿＿＿＿＿.

5 물리적인 서점은 가상의 것만큼 많은 책들을 가지고 있을 수 없다. (many books)

= Physical bookstores can't stock ＿＿＿＿＿＿＿＿＿＿＿＿＿＿＿＿ virtual ones. <학평 응용>

6 가능한 한 조심스럽게 바닥에서 깨진 유리를 집어라. (carefully, possible)

= Pick up the broken glass from the floor ＿＿＿＿＿＿＿＿＿＿＿＿＿＿＿＿.

7 다음 글의 밑줄 친 ⓐ~ⓒ 중 어법상 틀린 것의 기호를 쓰고 바르게 고쳐 쓰시오.

> Few species were ⓐ<u>as endangered as</u> the Amur leopard. People used to kill these animals ⓑ<u>as often</u>
> <u>as possible</u> for their beautiful fur. Fortunately, there are now about 110 Amur leopards in the wild, which
> is ⓒ<u>twice as more as</u> there were ten years ago. 　　　　*Amur leopard: 아무르표범

＿＿＿＿ → ＿＿＿＿＿＿＿

1. 「비교급 + than」은 '…보다 더 ~한/하게'라는 의미로, 비교하는 두 대상 간 정도의 차이를 나타낸다.

When it comes to health, some foods are **better than** others. <학평 응용>

My English teacher is **less strict than** my science teacher.

↳ 「less + 원급 + than」은 '…보다 덜 ~한/하게'라는 의미로, 「not + as[so] + 원급 + as」로 바꿔 쓸 수 있다.

TIP than 대신 to를 쓰는 비교급: superior(우수한), inferior(열등한), prior(이전의), senior(상위의, 연장자의), junior(하위의, 손아래의) 등
The man is five years **senior to** his business partner.

2. 비교급 앞에 much, even, still, far, a lot을 써서 '훨씬'이라는 의미로 비교급을 강조할 수 있다.

The horror movie was **much[even/still/far/a lot]** *more terrifying than* it is advertised.

[1-5] 우리말과 같도록 괄호 안의 말을 활용하여 문장을 완성하시오. (단, 비교급을 사용하시오.)

1 그 작가의 첫 번째 책은 그의 두 번째 것보다 더 재미있었다. (interesting)

= The author's first book was ＿＿＿＿＿＿＿＿＿＿ his second one.

2 이 스마트폰 모델은 나의 것보다 더 우수하다. (superior)

= This smartphone model is ＿＿＿＿＿＿＿＿＿＿ mine.

3 너의 목표를 네가 가능하다고 생각하는 것보다 훨씬 더 높게 설정해라. (much, high)

= Set your goals ＿＿＿＿＿＿＿＿＿＿ you consider possible. <학평 응용>

4 지하철은 어제 아침에 평소보다 덜 붐볐다. (crowded)

= The subway was ＿＿＿＿＿＿＿＿＿＿ usual yesterday morning.

5 캘리포니아에 있는 그 브리슬콘 소나무는 다른 모든 나무들보다 더 오래됐다. (old)

= The bristlecone pine in California is ＿＿＿＿＿＿＿＿＿＿ all the other trees.

[6-9] 밑줄 친 부분이 어법상 맞으면 O를 쓰고, 틀리면 바르게 고쳐 쓰시오.

6 Some weaknesses make a laptop inferior <u>than</u> a desktop computer. <학평 응용>   → ＿＿＿＿＿＿

7 The renovation work was <u>far</u> more extensive than originally planned.   → ＿＿＿＿＿＿

8 Mammals tend to be less colorful <u>as</u> reptiles. <학평 응용>   → ＿＿＿＿＿＿

9 My high school uniform is a lot <u>fancy</u> than my middle school one. <학평 응용>   → ＿＿＿＿＿＿

---

10 다음 글에서 어법상 틀린 부분을 찾아 쓰고 바르게 고쳐 쓰시오.

> A Norse explorer traveled to North America prior to the voyage of Christopher Columbus. His followers established a settlement in modern-day Canada very earlier than other Europeans. Experts believe that this Norse village was built more than 1,000 years ago.   *Norse: 고대 스칸디나비아의

＿＿＿＿＿＿ → ＿＿＿＿＿＿

POINT 4 비교급 관련 표현

정답 p.21

1. 「the + 비교급, the + 비교급」: ···하면 할수록 더 ~하다

The more people you know, **the brighter** your life becomes. <학평 응용>

2. 「비교급 + and + 비교급」: 점점 더 ~한/하게

Tigers are getting **rarer and rarer** as their habitats are destroyed.

The actor became **more and more famous** over her long career.

↳ 비교급이 「more + 원급」의 형태인 경우 「more and more + 원급」으로 쓴다.

3. 「배수사 + 비교급 + than」: ···보다 -배 더 ~한/하게 (= 「배수사 + as + 원급 + as」)

The Golden Gate Bridge is **three times longer than** the Brooklyn Bridge.

(= The Golden Gate Bridge is **three times as long as** the Brooklyn Bridge.)

4. 「the + 비교급 + of the two」: 둘 중 더 ~한/하게

There are two hotels in the town. The hotel near the beach is **the newer of the two.**

5. 「no more than」: 겨우 ~밖에, 「no less than」: ~만큼이나

The library allows us to check out **no more than** four books at once.

I visited **no less than** 15 museums during my trip to Paris.

[1-5] 우리말과 같도록 괄호 안의 말을 활용하여 문장을 완성하시오. (단, 비교급을 사용하시오.)

1 태양의 중심은 화산의 용암보다 약 12,000배 더 뜨겁다. (hot, 12,000 times)

= The center of the Sun is about _____ the lava of a volcano. <학평 응용>

2 나는 스페인어를 오래 공부하면 할수록 더 유창해졌다. (long, fluent)

= _____ I studied Spanish, _____ I became.

3 나의 할아버지는 그의 은퇴 후에 점점 더 우울해지셨다. (depressed)

= My grandfather got _____ after his retirement. <학평 응용>

4 David은 그의 엄마를 위한 선물에 500달러만큼이나 썼다. (500 dollars)

= David spent _____ on a present for his mom.

5 우리는 이번 주에 퀴즈 두 개를 봤다. 오늘의 퀴즈는 둘 중 더 어려웠다. (difficult)

= We took two quizzes this week. Today's quiz was _____.

6 우리말과 같도록 괄호 안의 말을 알맞게 배열하시오.

> 날씨가 추워지면 질수록 나는 밖에 나가는 것을 더 주저한다.
> (I, becomes, reluctant, the, more, the weather, colder, the, am)

= _____, _____ to go outside.

최상급 비교와 최상급 관련 표현

정답 p.21

1. 「the + 최상급」은 '가장 ~한/하게'라는 의미로 셋 이상의 비교 대상 중 하나의 정도가 가장 높음을 나타내며, 보통 in이나 of를 사용하여 비교 범위를 나타낸다.

She is **the most talented** musician *in the band*. ‹in + 장소/집단›
My father wakes up **(the) earliest** *of my family members*. ‹of + 시간/비교 대상›
     ↳ 부사의 최상급 앞에는 the를 생략하기도 한다.

TIP 최상급 앞에 much, by far, quite을 써서 '단연코'라는 의미로 최상급을 강조할 수 있다.
  I am **much[by far/quite]** *the most skilled* chef in the restaurant.

2. **최상급 관련 표현**

❶ 「one of the + 최상급 + 복수명사」: 가장 ~한 것들 중 하나
 The elevator is **one of the greatest advances** in building technology. ‹학평 응용›

❷ 「the + 최상급 + 명사 + (that) + 주어 + have + (ever) + p.p.」: …해본 것 중에서 가장 ~한
 The Taj Mahal was **the most amazing structure (that) I had (ever) visited**.

❸ 「the + 서수 + 최상급 + 명사」: …번째로 가장 ~한
 He is considered to be **the second best player** on the hockey team.

[1-6] 우리말과 같도록 괄호 안의 말을 활용하여 문장을 완성하시오.

1 흑사병은 중세의 가장 치명적인 전염병이었다. (deadly, epidemic)
 = The Black Plague was _____ of the middle ages.

2 비둘기는 도시에서 발견되는 가장 흔한 새들 중 하나이다. (bird, common)
 = The pigeon is _____ found in cities.

3 늦게 도착한 사람들은 무대로부터 가장 멀리 앉았다. (far)
 = People who arrived late sat _____ from the stage.

4 번지 점프하는 것은 내가 시도해본 것 중에서 가장 신나는 활동이다. (exciting, try, activity)
 = Bungee jumping is _____.

5 내가 먹어본 단연코 최고의 빵은 저 빵집에서 만들어졌다. (good, quite, bread)
 = _____ I have eaten was made at that bakery.

6 티타늄은 지구의 지각에서 아홉 번째로 가장 풍부한 금속이다. (ninth, metal, abundant)
 = Titanium is _____ in the earth's crust.

7 우리말과 같도록 괄호 안의 말을 알맞게 배열하시오.

> Frank Knight은 20세기의 가장 영향력 있는 경제학자들 중 한 명이었다.
> (economists, one, most, Frank Knight, of, was, the, influential)

 = _____ of the 20th century. ‹수능 응용›

원급과 비교급을 이용한 최상급 비교 표현

원급이나 비교급을 이용하여 최상급 비교의 의미를 나타낼 수 있다.

> **the + 최상급** 가장 ~한/하게
> = **No (other) + 단수명사 ~ as[so] + 원급 + as** (다른) 어떤 –도 …만큼 ~하지 않은
> = **No (other) + 단수명사 ~ 비교급 + than** (다른) 어떤 –도 …보다 더 ~하지 않은
> = **비교급 + than any other + 단수명사** 다른 어떤 …보다 더 ~한
> = **비교급 + than all the other + 복수명사** 다른 모든 …보다 더 ~한

India exported **the most rice** in 2012.
= **No (other) country** exported **as[so] much rice as** India in 2012.
= **No (other) country** exported **more rice than** India in 2012. <학평>
= India exported **more rice than any other country** in 2012.
= India exported **more rice than all the other countries** in 2012.

[1-4] 다음 문장들의 의미가 같도록 문장을 완성하시오.

1 The inland taipan is the most venomous snake.

→ _____ the inland taipan.

→ _____ the inland taipan.

→ The inland taipan is _____.

→ The inland taipan is _____.

2 The Westwood Grill is the busiest restaurant in San Francisco.

→ _____ The Westwood Grill in San Francisco.

→ _____ The Westwood Grill in San Francisco.

→ The Westwood Grill is _____ in San Francisco.

→ The Westwood Grill is _____ in San Francisco.

3 Kara was the most diligent member on the marketing team.

→ _____ Kara on the marketing team.

→ _____ Kara on the marketing team.

→ Kara was _____ on the marketing team.

→ Kara was _____ on the marketing team.

4 Diamond is the hardest material on our planet.

→ _____ diamond on our planet.

→ _____ diamond on our planet.

→ Diamond is _____ on our planet.

→ Diamond is _____ on our planet.

Review Test

[1-3] 다음 빈칸에 들어갈 말이 순서대로 짝지어진 것을 고르시오.

1

> · The Trans-Siberian railway runs _____ than other railway lines.
> · He is the _____ student in my class.

① far – more ambitious
② far – most ambitious
③ farther – ambitiousest
④ farther – most ambitious
⑤ further – more ambitious

2

> · A grizzly bear can run two times _____ as a person.
> · It took _____ shorter than estimated to complete the art project.

① fast – very   ② faster than – by far
③ as fast – by far   ④ faster than – even
⑤ as fast – even

3

> · Death Valley is hotter than any other _____ in the United States.
> · Watching online lectures is one of the most efficient _____ to learn.

① place – ways   ② place – way
③ places – ways   ④ places – way
⑤ places – a way

[4-5] 다음 중 어법상 <u>틀린</u> 것을 <u>모두</u> 고르시오.

4

① The movers took as more care as possible when unloading the furniture.
② The manual was less detailed than I expected.
③ The older we grow, the wise we turn.
④ Jim's house is eight times more expensive than ours.
⑤ She made the most annoying sound I had ever heard. <학평 응용>

5

① In 2011, he was the tenth most successful entrepreneur in the country.
② Early humans became intelligenter and intelligenter as time passed.
③ Is the new version of the software as effective than the former one?
④ Jane is a far more talented piano player than her friends.
⑤ Staying in New York is one of the best decisions Greg has made.

6 다음 중 어법상 바른 것끼리 묶인 것은?

> ⓐ Chess is less difficult than baduk to learn.
> ⓑ He tried to make as fewer mistakes as he could during the driving test.
> ⓒ Michael cheered loudest for his team.
> ⓓ A baby's brain makes up no less than 65 percent of its body weight. <학평 응용>
> ⓔ Antarctica is the third smaller continent on earth.

① ⓐ, ⓑ   ② ⓐ, ⓔ   ③ ⓑ, ⓒ
④ ⓐ, ⓒ, ⓓ   ⑤ ⓒ, ⓓ, ⓔ

[7-8] 다음 문장에서 어법상 틀린 부분을 찾아 쓰고 바르게 고쳐 쓰시오.

7

No other lake of the North American Great Lakes is as deeper than Lake Superior.

_____ → _____

8

Traffic on Sunday was very heavier than it was on weekday.

_____ → _____

9 우리말과 같도록 괄호 안의 말을 알맞게 배열하시오.

나의 학교에 두 명의 새로운 선생님이 있다. 생물 선생님은 둘 중 더 경험이 있다. (of, two, is, more, the biology teacher, experienced, the, the)

= There are two new teachers at my school. _____
_____.

[10-14] 우리말과 같도록 괄호 안의 말을 활용하여 문장을 완성하시오.

10

대면 상호 작용은 창의적인 생각을 자극하는 가장 좋은 방법들 중 하나이다. (good, way)

= Face-to-face interaction is _____ to stimulate creative thinking. <학평 응용>

11

우리는 성 역할이 과거에 그랬던 것만큼 엄격하지 않은 사회에 산다. (strict)

= We live in a society where gender roles are _____ _____ they were in the past. <학평 응용>

12

Susan의 개는 나의 고양이보다 여섯 배 더 무겁다. (six times, heavy, my cat)

= Susan's dog is _____.
= Susan's dog is _____.

13

우리는 공항에 일찍 도착하면 할수록 탑승구에서 더 오래 기다릴 것이다. (early, long, get, wait)

= _____ to the airport, _____ _____ at the gate.

14

나는 청소하는 데 가능한 한 많은 노력을 들였다. (great effort)

= I put _____ into cleaning.
= I put _____ into cleaning.

15 우리말과 같도록 주어진 <조건>에 맞게 문장을 완성하시오.

> 피카소는 19세기의 다른 모든 화가들보다 더 획기적이었다.

> <조건>
> 1. Picasso, innovative, be, painter를 활용하시오.
> 2. 9단어로 쓰시오.

= _____

of the 19th century.

[16-17] 다음 글을 읽고 주어진 질문에 답하시오.

> Craig was nervous about participating in the Fashion Design Competition. He was worried that his clothes were (A) less / not so stylish as the other contestants'. In fact, he felt that other participants were superior (B) than / to him. However, he did not withdraw because he knew that ⓐ그가 더 많은 경험을 쌓으면 쌓을수록 더 숙련될 것이다. (he, the, would, more, he, experience, skilled, got, the, become, more) Surprisingly, the judges selected Craig's outfit as one of the best (C) entry / entries and awarded him the second-place prize.
>
> *withdraw: 기권하다

16 위 글의 밑줄 친 우리말 ⓐ와 같도록 괄호 안의 말을 알맞게 배열하시오.

= _____

_____

17 (A), (B), (C)의 각 네모 안에서 어법에 맞는 표현으로 가장 적절한 것은?

	(A)	(B)	(C)
①	less	to	entries
②	less	than	entry
③	not so	to	entry
④	not so	than	entry
⑤	not so	to	entries

18 (A), (B), (C)의 각 네모 안에서 어법에 맞는 표현으로 가장 적절한 것은?

> We are more successful when we are positive. For example, doctors put in a positive mood before making a diagnosis show almost three times (A) much / more intelligence and creativity than doctors in a neutral state. Salespeople who are optimistic sell (B) very / a lot more than those who are pessimistic. It turns out (C) what / that our brains are literally programmed to perform at their best not when we feel negative or even neutral, but when we feel positive. <학평 응용>
>
> *diagnosis: 진단

	(A)	(B)	(C)
①	much	very	what
②	more	very	what
③	more	a lot	what
④	more	a lot	that
⑤	much	a lot	that

19 다음 글의 밑줄 친 부분 중, 어법상 틀린 것은?

> Our message to you is brief, but ①important: Your subscription to *Winston Magazine* will end soon and we haven't ②heard from you about renewing it. We're sure you won't want to miss even one upcoming issue. Renew now to make sure that the service will continue. You'll get continued delivery of the excellent stories and news that make *Winston Magazine* the ③faster growing magazine in America. To make it as easy as ④possible for you to act now, we've sent a reply card for you to complete. Simply send back the card today, and you'll continue ⑤to receive your monthly issue of *Winston Magazine*. <학평>

CHAPTER 14

가정법

기출로 적중 POINT

최근 7개년 수능/학평/내신 출제 경향

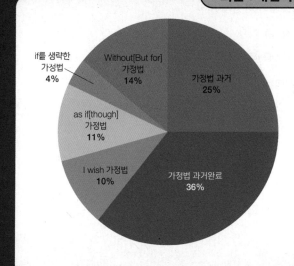

TOP 1 가정법 과거완료 (36%)
가정법 과거완료의 형태를 묻고 가정법 과거완료시제에 맞게 영작하는 문제가 자주 출제된다.

TOP 2 가정법 과거 (25%)
가정법 과거의 형태를 묻는 문제가 자주 출제된다.

TOP 3 Without[But for] 가정법 (14%)
Without[But for] 가정법을 활용하여 영작하는 문제가 자주 출제된다.

가정법 과거: 「If + 주어 + 동사의 과거형 ~, 주어 + 조동사의 과거형 + 동사원형 …」

'만약 ~한다면, …할 텐데'의 의미로, 현재의 사실과 반대되거나 실현 가능성이 거의 없는 일을 가정할 때 쓴다.

If I **had** a million dollars, I **could buy** a bigger house.

(← As I *don't have* a million dollars, I *can't buy* a bigger house.)

If I **were** younger, I **would move** abroad for work.
↳ if절의 be동사는 주어에 상관없이 were를 쓰는 것이 원칙이다.

(← As I'*m not* younger, I *won't move* abroad for work.)

TIP 실현 가능성이 매우 낮은 현재나 미래의 일을 가정할 때는 if절에 were to나 should를 쓸 수도 있다.

If the sun **were to** rise in the west, I would forgive him.

If it **should** snow tomorrow, we could go to a ski resort.

[1-6] 괄호 안에서 알맞은 것을 고르시오.

1 If he arrived at the shop early, he (can buy / could buy) the new sneakers.

2 If the politician (run / ran) for president, he would have a lot of support.

3 It (will be / would be) foolish of you to buy a cow if you lived in an apartment. <학평 응용>

4 If I (am to / were to) find the answer, I would share it with you.

5 I wouldn't make a change in the speech script if I (am / were) you. <수능 응용>

6 If she (should meet / meets) her favorite actor, she would be very pleased.

[7-12] 우리말과 같도록 괄호 안의 말을 활용하여 문장을 완성하시오.

7 만약 내가 그 주제에 대해 충분히 안다면, 의견을 제안할 텐데. (offer, know)

= If I _____ enough about the topic, I _____ an opinion.

8 만약 David이 너무 수줍어하지 않는다면 대중 앞에서 공연할 텐데. (be, perform)

= David _____ in public if he _____ so shy.

9 만약 그가 더 열심히 공부한다면, 더 좋은 점수를 받을 수 있을 텐데. (get, study)

= If he _____ harder, he _____ better grades.

10 만약 내가 너라면, 파티에 늦은 것에 대해 사과할 텐데. (be, apologize)

= If I _____ you, I _____ for being late to the party.

11 만약 Jane이 아무 숙제도 없다면, 우리와 함께 영화를 볼 텐데. (have, watch)

= If Jane _____ any homework, she _____ the movie with us.

12 만약 Richard가 자동차를 소유하고 있다면 그의 조부모님을 볼 수 있을 텐데. (own, see)

= Richard _____ his grandparents if he _____ a car.

가정법 과거완료: 「If + 주어 + had + p.p. ~, 주어 + 조동사의 과거형 + have + p.p. …」

'만약 ~했더라면, …했을 텐데'의 의미로, 과거의 사실과 반대되는 일을 가정할 때 쓴다.

If she **had applied**, she **could have gotten** the scholarship.
(← As she *didn't apply*, she *couldn't get* the scholarship.)

If I **hadn't rescued** the dog, it **would have died** of starvation. <수능 응용>
(← As I *rescued* the dog, it *didn't die* of starvation.)

[1-4] 우리말과 같도록 괄호 안의 말을 활용하여 문장을 완성하시오.

1 만약 그 요리사가 알맞은 재료들을 준비했더라면, 그 요리를 만들 수 있었을 텐데. (make, prepare)

= If the chef _____ the right ingredients, he _____ the dish.

2 만약 그 코트가 덜 비싸다면, 나는 그것을 살 텐데. (buy, be)

= If the coat _____ less expensive, I _____ it.

3 만약 그녀가 승무원이 되었더라면 세계를 여행할 수 있었을 텐데. (travel, become)

= She _____ the world if she _____ a flight attendant.

4 만약 그 남자가 너무 빠르게 운전하지 않았더라면, 사고를 일으키지 않았을 텐데. (cause, drive)

= If the man _____ so fast, he _____ an accident.

[5-8] 다음 문장을 가정법 문장으로 바꿔 쓰시오.

5 As the witness came forward, the criminal couldn't avoid jail.

→ If _____.

6 As the boss acted rudely, the employee quit the job.

→ If _____.

7 As the wait wasn't less than an hour, we didn't stand in line.

→ If _____.

8 As the tourist doesn't speak the local language, she can't ask for directions.

→ If _____.

9 다음 글의 밑줄 친 @~ⓒ 중 어법상 틀린 것의 기호를 쓰고 바르게 고쳐 쓰시오.

> If the couple had had enough money, they @ would have taken the train to Paris from London. But if they ⓑ didn't stay more in London, they wouldn't have enjoyed the city as much. They went to incredible restaurants and museums. If they ⓒ had more time, they would stay there longer.

_____ → _____

혼합 가정법

정답 p.23

혼합 가정법: 「If + 주어 + had + p.p. ~, 주어 + 조동사의 과거형 + 동사원형 …」

'만약 ~했더라면, …할 텐데'의 의미로, 과거의 사실과 반대되는 일이 현재까지 영향을 미치는 상황을 가정할 때 쓴다.

If I **had finished** my essay yesterday, I **could play** video games today.

(← As I *didn't finish* my essay yesterday, I *can't play* video games today.)

If they **hadn't watched** the horror movie, they **wouldn't be** scared now.

(← As they *watched* the horror movie, they *are* scared now.)

[1-5] 우리말과 같도록 괄호 안의 말을 활용하여 문장을 완성하시오.

1 만약 내가 지시를 따랐더라면, 지금 너의 도움이 필요하지 않을 텐데. (follow, need)

= If I _____ instructions, I _____ your assistance now.

2 만약 그녀가 그 책을 읽었더라면, 그 등장인물을 좋아할 텐데. (love, read)

= If she _____ the book, she _____ the character.

3 만약 Tom이 헬멧을 쓰지 않았더라면, 심하게 다쳤을 텐데. (wear, injure)

= If Tom _____ a helmet, he _____ himself badly.

4 만약 그가 난방기를 켰더라면, 이렇게 춥지 않을 텐데. (turn, be)

= If he _____ the heater on, it _____ so cold.

5 만약 우리가 더 일찍 표를 예매했더라면, 그 축제를 방문할 수 있을 텐데. (visit, reserve)

= If we _____ tickets earlier, we _____ the festival.

[6-11] 다음 문장을 가정법 문장으로 바꿔 쓰시오.

6 As the bank isn't open today, I don't have cash now.

→ If _____.

7 As the hikers didn't pack snacks, they are hungry.

→ If _____.

8 As you didn't take the medicine, you don't feel better now.

→ If _____.

9 As we fought yesterday, my friend doesn't talk to me.

→ If _____.

10 As I didn't save your cell phone number, I couldn't send you a message.

→ If _____.

11 As people didn't watch the news, they don't know about the crisis.

→ If _____.

POINT 4 ｜ I wish 가정법

정답 p.23

1. 「I wish + 가정법 과거」는 '~한다면 좋을 텐데'라는 의미로, 현재 이룰 수 없거나 실현 가능성이 거의 없는 일을 소망할 때 쓴다.

   I wish I **spoke** Italian more fluently.
   (← I'm sorry that I *don't speak* Italian more fluently.)

2. 「I wish + 가정법 과거완료」는 '~했더라면 좋을 텐데'라는 의미로, 과거에 이루지 못한 일에 대한 아쉬움을 나타낼 때 쓴다.

   I wish the guests **had arrived** for the event on time.
   (← I'm sorry that the guests *didn't arrive* for the event on time.)

   TIP ｜ 「It's (about) time + 주어 + 동사의 과거형」은 '~해야 할 때이다'라는 의미로, 했어야 하는 일을 하지 않은 것에 대한 유감을 나타낼 때 쓴다.
   It's (about) time we **bought** a new table for the living room.

[1-5] 우리말과 같도록 괄호 안의 말을 활용하여 문장을 완성하시오.

1 나의 가족이 나에게 더 가까이 산다면 좋을 텐데. (live)
   = I wish my family _____ closer to me.

2 내가 그녀가 견과류에 알레르기가 있다는 것을 알았더라면 좋을 텐데. (know)
   = I wish I _____ that she was allergic to nuts.

3 Mike가 스스로 그의 침실을 청소한다면 좋을 텐데. (clean)
   = I wish Mike _____ his bedroom for himself.

4 그 바리스타가 오늘 아침 나의 커피에 우유를 추가하지 않았더라면 좋을 텐데. (add)
   = I wish the barista _____ milk to my coffee this morning.

5 정부가 전국의 대중교통을 개선해야 할 때이다. (improve)
   = It's time the government _____ public transportation around the country.

[6-9] 다음 두 문장의 의미가 같도록 문장을 완성하시오.

6 I'm sorry that she doesn't keep quiet during class.
   → I wish _____ during class.

7 I'm sorry that I didn't see the eclipse of the moon with my own eyes.
   → I wish _____ with my own eyes. <학평 응용>

8 I wish I hadn't wasted all my allowance on those jeans.
   → I'm sorry that _____ on those jeans.

9 I wish he cooked pasta for us more often.
   → I'm sorry that _____ for us more often.

1. 「as if[though] + 가정법 과거」는 '마치 ~인 것처럼'이라는 의미로, 주절의 시제와 같은 시점의 사실과 반대되는 일을 가정할 때 쓴다.

   He *speaks* **as if**[**though**] he **were** an expert on the subject.
   (← In fact, he *isn't* an expert on the subject.)

   The student *looked* **as if**[**though**] she **had** a question.
   (← In fact, the student *didn't have* a question.)

2. 「as if[though] + 가정법 과거완료」는 '마치 ~이었던 것처럼'이라는 의미로, 주절의 시제보다 앞선 시점의 사실과 반대되는 일을 가정할 때 쓴다.

   I *feel* **as if**[**though**] he **had ignored** me yesterday.
   (← In fact, he *didn't ignore* me yesterday.)

   The security guard *treated* us **as if**[**though**] we **had broken** a rule.
   (← In fact, we *hadn't broken* a rule.)

[1-4] 우리말과 같도록 괄호 안의 말을 활용하여 문장을 완성하시오.

1 그녀는 마치 내가 일부러 그녀를 밀었던 것처럼 나에게 소리 질렀다. (push)

= She yelled at me as though I _____ her on purpose.

2 나의 친구는 마치 속도 제한이 없는 것처럼 그의 차를 운전한다. (be)

= My friend drives his car as if there _____ no speed limit.

3 그는 스키 타는 것을 배웠을 때, 마치 처음부터 다시 걷는 것을 배우는 것처럼 느꼈다. (learn)

= When he learned skiing, he felt as though he _____ to walk all over again. <학평 응용>

4 그 컴퓨터는 마치 아무도 전에 그것을 사용하지 않았던 것처럼 작동한다. (use)

= The computer works as if no one _____ it before.

[5-8] 다음 두 문장을 한 문장으로 연결하시오.

5 The plant looks like it is close to dying. In fact, it is not close to dying.

→ The plant _____ as though it _____ close to dying.

6 We ate the meal like we hadn't had food in weeks. In fact, we had had food in weeks.

→ We _____ the meal as if we _____ food in weeks.

7 She didn't see a ghost. She screamed like she saw a ghost.

→ She _____ as if she _____ a ghost.

8 They were not good friends for ages. They talk like they were good friends for ages.

→ They _____ as though they _____ good friends for ages.

POINT 6 if를 생략한 가정법

정답 p.23

가정법에서 if절의 동사가 were나 「had + p.p.」인 경우 if를 생략할 수 있으며, 이때 주어와 were/had의 위치가 바뀐다.

Were he taller, he could reach the book on that shelf easily.
(← If he *were* taller, he could reach the book on that shelf easily.)

Had I *practiced* harder, I would have won the match.
(← If I *had practiced* harder, I would have won the match.)

[1-6] 다음 문장을 if를 생략한 가정법 문장으로 바꿔 쓰시오.

1 If I were stronger, I could carry this couch up the stairs.

→ _____, I could carry this couch up the stairs.

2 If I had known the date, I would have put it in my calendar.

→ _____, I would have put it in my calendar.

3 If she were honest, she would tell her friend the truth.

→ _____, she would tell her friend the truth.

4 If I were free for the night, I would meet him at the restaurant.

→ _____, I would meet him at the restaurant.

5 If you had called this morning, you could have made an appointment.

→ _____, you could have made an appointment.

6 If the firefighters had been able to arrive on time, the fire wouldn't have spread so far.

→ _____, the fire wouldn't have spread so far. <수능 응용>

[7-12] 우리말과 같도록 괄호 안의 말을 알맞게 배열하시오.

7 만약 그가 더 협조적이라면, 빨리 풀려날 텐데. (he, were, more cooperative)

= _____, he would be released quickly.

8 만약 Roy가 설거지를 했더라면, 그의 엄마는 기뻤을 텐데. (Roy, the dishes, had, washed)

= _____, his mom would have been happy.

9 만약 이 좌석이 편안하다면, 나는 독서하는 동안 잠이 들 텐데. (this seat, comfortable, were)

= _____, I would fall asleep while reading.

10 만약 그녀가 충분한 물을 마셨더라면, 체육관에서 기절하지 않았을 텐데. (drunk, she, enough water, had)

= _____, she wouldn't have passed out at the gym.

11 만약 나의 생일이라면, 우리는 초콜릿 케이크를 먹을 텐데. (it, were, my birthday)

= _____, we would eat chocolate cake.

12 만약 네가 너의 문제에 대해 나에게 말했더라면, 나는 너를 이해했을 텐데. (about your problem, had, me, you, told)

= _____, I would have understood you.

「Without[But for] + 명사(구)」는 '~이 없다면/없었더라면'이라는 의미로, 가정법의 if절을 대신할 수 있다. 가정법 과거에 쓰일 때는 Without[But for]를 If it were not for로 바꿔 쓸 수 있고, 가정법 과거완료에 쓰일 때는 If it had not been for로 바꿔 쓸 수 있다.

Without[But for] friends, the world **would be** a lonely place. <학평>
→ *If it were not for* friends, the world *would be* a lonely place.
→ *Were it not for* friends, the world *would be* a lonely place.

Without[But for] your help, I **couldn't have submitted** the report in time.
→ *If it had not been for* your help, I *couldn't have submitted* the report in time.
→ *Had it not been for* your help, I *couldn't have submitted* the report in time.

[1-4] 우리말과 같도록 괄호 안의 말을 활용하여 문장을 완성하시오.

1 전화기가 없다면, 우리는 편지를 통해 연락할 텐데. (communicate)

= Without phones, we _____ through letters.

2 너의 추천이 없었더라면, 나는 어디로 가야 할지 몰랐을 텐데. (know)

= Without your recommendation, I _____ where to go.

3 창의력이 없다면, 사람들은 이야기, 예술, 그리고 음악을 창작할 수 없을 텐데. (create)

= Without creativity, people _____ stories, art, and music.

4 비가 없었더라면, 작물들은 수확기 전에 죽었을 텐데. (die)

= Without rain, the crops _____ before harvest time.

[5-8] 다음 두 문장의 의미가 같도록 if를 이용하여 문장을 완성하시오. (단, 혼합 가정법을 쓰지 마시오.)

5 Without a recycling program, we would have a lot more trash.

→ _____, we would have a lot more trash.

6 Without such passion, they would have achieved nothing. <학평>

→ _____, they would have achieved nothing.

7 But for the explanation, the question would seem too difficult.

→ _____, the question would seem too difficult.

8 But for the tornado warning, people couldn't have evacuated in advance.

→ _____, people couldn't have evacuated in advance.

9 without을 활용하여 다음 문장을 가정법 문장으로 바꿔 쓰시오.

> Thanks to the influence of minorities, we have innovation and social change.

→ _____, _____ innovation and social change. <수능 응용>

if절 대용어구

정답 p.23

to부정사구, 분사구문, 부사구, 주어로 쓰인 명사구를 가정법의 if절 대신 쓸 수 있다.

To see the art piece, you would think a professional painted it.
(← *If you saw the art piece*, you would think a professional painted it.)

Treated the right way, the children could grow up to be good people.
(← *If they were treated the right way*, the children could grow up to be good people.)

We could have achieved the goal **with additional time**. <학평 응용>
(← We could have achieved the goal *if we had had additional time*.)

A skilled photographer would know how to use lighting effectively.
(← *If he or she were a skilled photographer*, he or she would know how to use lighting effectively.)

[1-4] 우리말과 같도록 괄호 안의 말을 알맞게 배열하시오.

1 유명한 감독에 의해 만들어졌더라면, 그 영화는 많은 돈을 벌었을 텐데. (made, a famous director, by)

= _____, the movie could have made a lot of money.

2 강 유람선 여행을 경험한다면, 너는 그것이 왜 인기 있는지 알 텐데. (to, the river cruise, experience)

= _____, you would see why it is popular.

3 나의 헤드폰이 있었더라면 나는 통근을 즐길 수 있었을 텐데. (my headphones, with)

= I would have been able to enjoy the commute _____.

4 강력한 지도자라면 좋은 대의명분을 위해 쉽게 지지를 모을 수 있을 텐데. (could, a strong leader, gather)

= _____ support easily for a good cause.

[5-8] 다음 두 문장의 의미가 같도록 문장을 완성하시오. (단, 혼합 가정법을 쓰지 마시오.)

5 To visit her home, you would want to redecorate your house.

→ If you _____, you would want to redecorate your house.

6 Using the correct tools, she could fix the chair herself.

→ If she _____, she could fix the chair herself.

7 To work with him, you would have found tasks more enjoyable.

→ If you _____, you would have found tasks more enjoyable.

8 A good instructor would have taught you how to swim in a month.

→ If he or she _____, he or she would have taught you how to swim in a month.

Review Test

[1-2] 다음 빈칸에 들어갈 알맞은 것을 고르시오.

1

> If I _____ a CEO, I would encourage a positive work culture.

① be   ② am   ③ were
④ being   ⑤ have been

2

> _____ the storm not hit the island, the airline wouldn't have delayed our flights.

① Did   ② Is   ③ Were
④ Have   ⑤ Had

[3-4] 다음 두 문장의 의미가 같도록 빈칸에 들어갈 알맞은 것을 고르시오.

3

> I'm sorry that the city didn't stop the old statue from being destroyed.
> → I wish the city _____ the old statue from being destroyed.

① would stop   ② stopped   ③ has stopped
④ had stopped   ⑤ should stop

4

> As the lifeguard saved the child, she is alive.
> → The child _____ alive if the lifeguard hadn't saved her.

① isn't   ② wasn't   ③ wouldn't be
④ hadn't been   ⑤ wouldn't have been

[5-6] 다음 중 어법상 틀린 것을 고르시오.

5

① If we had time, we would have a cup of coffee.
② He ran in the race as if his life depended on it.
③ If he trained his dog, it wouldn't have bitten me yesterday.
④ I wish I were better at public speaking.
⑤ Without the strawberries, the cake would have tasted awful.

6

① Alice speaks as though she had made the song.
② We had brought coins, we could have played darts.
③ If the air pollution were to get much worse, the government would consider new policies.
④ I could own a business now if I had followed my dream.
⑤ Supposing I visited Seoul, I would stay in the luxury hotel.

7 다음 중 어법상 틀린 것끼리 묶인 것은?

> ⓐ Were I ill, I would rest at home all day.
> ⓑ If it didn't rain, we will have a picnic by the river.
> ⓒ I cheered for my team as if the game hadn't already finished.
> ⓓ I wish the holiday were on a Monday instead of a Wednesday.
> ⓔ She would have cleaned the house last night if she were aware of the dinner party.

① ⓐ, ⓑ   ② ⓑ, ⓒ   ③ ⓑ, ⓔ
④ ⓒ, ⓔ   ⑤ ⓓ, ⓔ

[8-11] 다음 문장에서 어법상 틀린 부분을 찾아 쓰고 바르게 고쳐 쓰시오.

8

If we lived in a world where nothing ever changed, there will be no reason for science. <학평 응용>

_____ → _____

9

If you asked for advice two days ago, I would have told you to buy another car.

_____ → _____

10

I wish we are at the warm beach instead of the office now.

_____ → _____

11

Had the baseball game been on last weekend, my family would attend it.

_____ → _____

[12-14] 우리말과 같도록 괄호 안의 말을 알맞게 배열하시오.

12

대중교통이 없다면, 그 도시는 더 많은 교통 혼잡을 겪을 텐데. (experience, the city, more traffic congestion, would)

= Without public transportation, _____
_____.

13

나의 남동생이 바퀴 두 개가 달린 자전거를 어떻게 타는지 배워야 할 때이다. (it's, how to ride, my little brother, time, learned)

= _____ a bike with two wheels.

14

만약 그녀가 매일 그것에게 물을 주었더라면 그 식물은 죽지 않았을 텐데. (it, if, had, every day, she, watered)

= The plant wouldn't have died _____
_____.

[15-17] 다음 두 문장의 의미가 같도록 문장을 완성하시오.

15

Without sunscreen, we would have suffered from sunburns.
→ If _____, we would have suffered from sunburns.

16

I'm sorry that I didn't watch the movie before you told me the ending.
→ I wish _____ before you told me the ending.

17

If he had received a better grade, his parents would have bought him a new phone.
→ Had _____, his parents would have bought him a new phone.

18 우리말과 같도록 주어진 <조건>에 맞게 문장을 완성하시오.

> 그의 계획표가 없었더라면, 그는 그날의 그의 일정을 잊어버렸을 텐데.

> <조건>
> 1. without, his schedule, forget, his planner를 활용하시오.
> 2. 9단어로 쓰시오.

= _____, _____ for the day.

[19-20] 다음 글을 읽고 주어진 질문에 답하시오.

> We (A) won't / wouldn't have soccer without England. However, variations of the game existed. For example, ⓐ만약 네가 서기 600년쯤에 일본을 방문했더라면, 케마리라고 불리는 비슷한 게임을 봤을 것이다. (visit, see) Or, if you (B) traveled / had traveled to China during the Han Dynasty, you could have watched a Cuju match, the earliest version of soccer. Throughout history, people have enjoyed this sport in one form of another. (C) The English had / Had the English not created soccer, a comparable sport would have probably become popular.

19 위 글의 밑줄 친 우리말 ⓐ와 같도록 괄호 안의 말을 활용하여 문장을 완성하시오.

= if _____ Japan around 600 A.D., _____ a similar game called Kemari

20 위 글의 (A), (B), (C)의 각 네모 안에서 어법에 맞는 표현으로 가장 적절한 것은?

	(A)	(B)	(C)
①	won't	traveled	The English had
②	won't	had traveled	Had the English
③	wouldn't	had traveled	The English had
④	wouldn't	had traveled	Had the English
⑤	wouldn't	traveled	The English had

수능형
21 (A), (B), (C)의 각 네모 안에서 어법에 맞는 표현으로 가장 적절한 것은?

> Years ago, I met a boy who told me (A) that / what his best friend was an elderly man on his street. This type of friendship is a gift not valued by many young people. But if I were young again, I (B) will / would value this type of relationship. I wish I (C) received / had received wise advice from those with much life experience before. We desperately need elders in our lives. Without them, we might make much more mistakes and disregard the past. <학평 응용>

	(A)	(B)	(C)
①	that	will	received
②	that	would	had received
③	that	would	received
④	what	would	had received
⑤	what	will	received

수능형
22 다음 글의 밑줄 친 부분 중, 어법상 틀린 것은?

> When you're eager to get your slice of the pie, why would you give a hand to other people ① so that they can get their piece? If Ernest Hamwi had taken that attitude when he was selling zalabia, a thin Persian waffle, he ② might have ended his days as a street vendor. Hamwi noticed that a nearby ice-cream vendor ran out of bowls to serve to his customers. Most people would have sniffed, 'Not my problem.' They could attract more customers if another business ③ were in trouble. Instead, Hamwi rolled up a waffle and put a scoop of ice cream on top, ④ creating one of the world's first ice-cream cones. So, if he ⑤ didn't help his neighbor, he wouldn't have made a fortune in the end. <학평 응용>
>
> *vendor: 상인 **sniff: 콧방귀를 끼며 말하다

CHAPTER 15
일치와 화법

기출로 적중 POINT

최근 7개년 수능/학평/내신 출제 경향

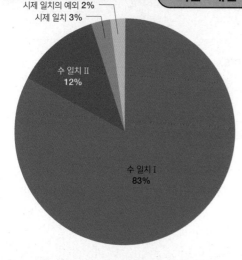

시제 일치의 예외 2%
시제 일치 3%
수 일치 II 12%
수 일치 I 83%

TOP 1 수 일치 I (83%)
주어가 길 때 동사와의 수 일치를 묻는 문제가 자주 출제된다.

TOP 2 수 일치 II (12%)
주어가 부분이나 수량 표현을 포함할 때 동사와의 수 일치를 묻는 문제가 자주 출제된다.

TOP 3 시제 일치 (3%)
주절이 과거시제인 경우 종속절의 시제 일치를 묻는 문제가 자주 출제된다.

1. **주어가 다음과 같은 경우 항상 단수동사를 쓴다.**

each/every가 포함된 주어	*Each student* **has** to give a brief presentation.
-thing, -body, -one	*Something* **is** making a weird noise in the garage.
학과명, 국가명, 질병명	*Mathematics* **is** my favorite subject.
시간, 거리, 무게, 금액 등의 단위	*20 minutes* **was** wasted looking for my train ticket.

TIP 「the + 형용사」는 '~한 사람들'이라는 의미로, 복수명사처럼 쓰여 복수 취급한다.
  The poor **need** to be provided with assistance from the government.

2. **주어가 동명사구나 명사절인 경우 항상 단수동사를 쓴다.**

Chatting with my best friends **is** calming and relaxing. <학평 응용>

3. **주어가 전치사구, to부정사구, 분사구, 관계절 등의 수식을 받을 때는 수식 받는 주어에 동사를 수일치시킨다.**

The notebooks on the counter **have** to be taken back to Marie.
The wind blowing through the trees **moves** the fallen leaves.

[1-5] 괄호 안에서 알맞은 것을 고르시오.

1 Anyone (is / are) allowed to sign up for the online classes.

2 Learning to play a musical instrument (takes / take) a few months.

3 The young often (finds / find) it hard to decide what to do for their future.

4 Where the stadium will be built (was / were) announced this morning.

5 The songs that the Beatles created (remains / remain) popular today.

[6-10] 밑줄 친 부분이 어법상 맞으면 O를 쓰고, 틀리면 바르게 고쳐 쓰시오.

6 The United States <u>is</u> composed of 50 states. → _____

7 Five kilograms <u>are</u> the weight of the package I sent to you. → _____

8 Every planet in our solar system <u>orbits</u> around the Sun. → _____

9 The actors of this movie <u>performs</u> several dangerous stunts. → _____

10 My plan to visit some tourist attractions <u>were</u> canceled because of rain. → _____

11 다음 글의 밑줄 친 ⓐ~ⓒ 중 어법상 틀린 것의 기호를 쓰고 바르게 고쳐 쓰시오.

> Everybody ⓐ <u>requires</u> vitamin C on a regular basis to keep healthy. Eating fresh fruits and vegetables ⓑ <u>is</u> the best way to get sufficient vitamin C. People who do not consume enough of this nutrient ⓒ <u>develops</u> a serious disease known as scurvy.
>
> *scurvy: 괴혈병

_____ → _____

POINT 2 수 일치 II

1. 「부분/수량 표현 + of + 명사」 형태의 주어는 각 표현에 따라 단수동사나 복수동사를 쓴다.

항상 단수동사를 쓰는 표현	one of	much of	the number of	the amount of	
항상 복수동사를 쓰는 표현	many of	a number of			
of 뒤 명사에 동사를 수일치시키는 표현	all of most of	half of majority of	some/any of a lot[lots] of	the rest of plenty of	퍼센트/분수 + of

One of the problems **is** the rising cost of products.
A number of the islands in the Pacific **were** formed by volcanoes.
The majority of animals raised as food **live** in agricultural facilities. <학평 응용>

2. 「both A and B」 형태의 주어는 항상 복수동사를 쓰고, 「not only A but (also) B(= B as well as A)」, 「not A but B」, 「either A or B」, 「neither A nor B」 형태의 주어는 B에 동사를 수일치시킨다.

Not only I but (also) my sister **wants** to join the school band.

[1-6] 괄호 안에서 알맞은 것을 고르시오.

1 Many of the snakes in Brazil (is / are) highly poisonous.

2 Both Sam and William (was / were) helping us empty the shelves.

3 Most of the soccer team members (prefers / prefer) to practice on Saturday mornings.

4 Some of the residents (drives / drive) an hour to shop in larger stores. <학평 응용>

5 A lot of money (was / were) spent on renovating the old palace.

6 Not chocolate but vanilla (is / are) my favorite ice cream flavor.

[7-11] 괄호 안의 동사를 알맞은 형태로 바꿔 빈칸에 쓰시오. (단, 현재시제로 쓰시오.)

7 About 60 percent of the population _____ in urban areas. (live)

8 A number of flaws _____ in the plane engine's design. (exist)

9 Not only strawberries but raspberries _____ in my garden. (grow)

10 The number of car owners _____ expected to decline over the next decade. (be)

11 All of them standing in line _____ waiting for the concert to start. (be)

12 다음 글의 밑줄 친 ⓐ~ⓒ 중 어법상 틀린 것의 기호를 쓰고 바르게 고쳐 쓰시오.

> The amount of air pollution ⓐ is increasing every year. Most of the pollution ⓑ come from factories and other industrial sites. The young, as well as the elderly, ⓒ suffer from many health problems from air pollution, so this issue needs to be addressed soon.

_____ → _____

1. 주절이 현재시제인 경우 종속절에는 의미에 따라 모든 시제를 쓸 수 있다.

I *know* that she **is** a baseball player. <야구 선수인 것을 알고 있다>

I *know* that she **was** a baseball player. <야구 선수였던 것을 알고 있다>

I *know* that she **will be** a baseball player. <야구 선수가 될 것을 알고 있다>

2. 주절이 과거시제인 경우 종속절에는 의미에 따라 과거시제나 과거완료시제를 쓴다.

I *knew* that she **was** a baseball player. <야구 선수인 것을 알고 있었다>

I *knew* that she **had been** a baseball player. <야구 선수였던 것을 알고 있었다>

I *knew* that she **would be** a baseball player. <야구 선수가 될 것을 알고 있었다>

[1-5] 다음 문장의 밑줄 친 부분을 과거시제로 바꿀 때 빈칸에 알맞은 말을 쓰시오.

1 My parents <u>think</u> that I completed my homework.

→ My parents _____ that I _____ _____ my homework.

2 I <u>hope</u> that my flight to Berlin will depart on schedule.

→ I _____ that my flight to Berlin _____ _____ on schedule.

3 The website <u>says</u> that I have to provide my credit card information.

→ The website _____ that I _____ _____ _____ my credit card information.

4 The report <u>suggests</u> that the government failed to reduce poverty.

→ The report _____ that the government _____ _____ to reduce poverty.

5 The book <u>implies</u> that people will live on Mars in the future.

→ The book _____ that people _____ _____ on Mars in the future.

[6-10] 우리말과 같도록 괄호 안의 말을 활용하여 문장을 완성하시오.

6 Norris씨는 그 가게가 파손된 상품들을 파는 것을 불평했다. (complain, sell, the shop)

= Ms. Norris _____ that _____ damaged products.

7 설명서는 그 장비가 정기적으로 청소될 필요가 있다는 것을 설명한다. (need, the equipment, explain)

= The manual _____ that _____ to be cleaned regularly.

8 Eric은 그의 여동생에게 친절할 것을 약속했다. (promise, be)

= Eric _____ that _____ kind to his little sister.

9 나는 그 주민 센터가 무료 주차를 제공했던 것을 기억한다. (the community center, remember, provide)

= I _____ that _____ free parking.

10 그 모험가는 요정들이 그에게 비밀 책을 줬다고 말했다. (say, give, the fairies)

= The explorer _____ that _____ him a secret book. <학평 응용>

시제 일치의 예외

정답 p.25

1. 종속절이 다음과 같은 경우를 나타낼 때는 주절의 시제와 상관없이 항상 현재시제를 쓴다.

현재의 습관이나 반복되는 일	I *heard* that he usually **wears** gloves in winter. She *said* that she **attends** a yoga class on Tuesdays.
일반적·과학적 사실	The expert *explained* that first impressions **matter** a lot. <학평 응용> He *knew* that water **boils** at 100 degrees Celsius.
속담·격언	My grandfather *told* me that all that glitters **is** not gold.

2. 종속절이 역사적 사실을 나타낼 때는 주절의 시제와 상관없이 항상 과거시제를 쓴다.

She *knows* that Vincent Van Gogh **painted** *The Starry Night* in 1889.
They *learned* that Gutenberg **printed** the first book in Europe over 550 years ago.

[1-5] 괄호 안의 동사를 알맞은 형태로 바꿔 빈칸에 쓰시오.

1 I heard that James _____ up at 6 A.M. every day. (wake)

2 She said that the rings of Saturn _____ composed of ice and rock. (be)

3 He knew that Winston Churchill _____ the prime minister of the UK in 1940. (become)

4 My teacher taught us that actions _____ louder than words. (speak)

5 Sam told me that Koreans usually _____ off their shoes before entering their home. (take)

[6-8] 우리말과 같도록 괄호 안의 말을 활용하여 문장을 완성하시오.

6 Brown씨는 인간이 약 10,000년 전에 쌀을 재배하는 것을 시작했다고 말했다. (humans, begin)
= Mr. Brown said that _____ cultivating rice about 10,000 years ago.

7 나의 형은 피는 물보다 더 진하다고 생각했다. (be, blood)
= My brother thought that _____ thicker than water.

8 나는 나일강이 통틀어 10개의 국가를 거쳐 간다는 것을 배웠다. (the Nile River, pass)
= I learned that _____ through 10 countries in total.

[9-12] 밑줄 친 부분이 어법상 맞으면 O를 쓰고, 틀리면 바르게 고쳐 쓰시오.

9 He understood that the Moon <u>travels</u> around Earth once every 27.32 days. → _____

10 My mother always said that every cloud <u>had</u> a silver lining. → _____

11 She explains that both India and Pakistan <u>achieve</u> independence in 1947. → _____

12 I didn't know that the store <u>closes</u> earlier than usual on national holidays. → _____

평서문의 직접 화법 → 간접 화법 전환

Mike said to me, "I want to play this game with you."
→ Mike told me (that) he wanted to play that game with me.
     ⓐ   ⓑ ⓒ   ⓓ   ⓔ   ⓒ

ⓐ 전달동사가 say인 경우 그대로 쓰고, say to인 경우 tell로 바꾼다.

ⓑ 콤마(,)와 큰따옴표(" ")를 없애고 접속사 that으로 두 절을 연결한다. 이때 that은 생략할 수 있다.

ⓒ that절의 인칭대명사를 전달하는 사람의 입장에 맞게 바꾼다.

ⓓ 전달동사가 현재시제인 경우 that절의 시제를 바꾸지 않고, 과거시제인 경우 과거시제나 과거완료시제로 바꾼다.

ⓔ 지시대명사나 부사(구)를 전달하는 사람의 입장에 맞게 바꾼다.

this/these → that/those	~ ago → ~ before	today → that day
here → there	next ~ → the following ~	yesterday → the previous day[the day before]
now → then	last ~ → the previous ~	tomorrow → the next[the following] day

[1-9] 직접 화법은 간접 화법으로, 간접 화법은 직접 화법으로 바꿔 쓰시오.

1 Susan said, "These cookies are quite tasty."

→ Susan _____ that _____.

2 Professor Nelson said to us, "We will review the chapter today."

→ Professor Nelson _____ us that _____.

3 The taxi driver told her that the street had been closed the day before.

→ The taxi driver _____ her, "_____."

4 The man said to them, "I lost my wallet in the park two hours ago."

→ The man _____ them that _____.

5 Steven said that he had seen the woman stealing the car the previous Sunday.

→ Steven _____, "_____."

6 The show host told us that she would introduce her guest then.

→ The show host _____ us, "_____."

7 Mom always says to me, "You need to be humble."

→ Mom always _____ me that _____.

8 Kevin said that his family had lived there ten years before.

→ Kevin _____, "_____."

9 Emily said to me, "I am planning on meeting my friend tomorrow."

→ Emily _____ me that _____.

화법 전환: 의문문/명령문

정답 p.25

1. 의문문의 직접 화법 → 간접 화법 전환

❶ 의문사가 있는 의문문: 「ask (+ 목적어) + 의문사 + 주어 + 동사」

Julie said to me, "What will you do tomorrow?"

→ Julie **asked** me **what I would do** the next[the following] day.

My friend said, "Who made this pasta?"

→ My friend **asked who had made** that pasta.

↳ 의문사가 주어인 경우 「의문사 + 동사」의 형태를 그대로 쓴다.

❷ 의문사가 없는 의문문: 「ask (+ 목적어) + if[whether] + 주어 + 동사」

He said, "Can I get a glass of water?"

→ He **asked if[whether] he could get** a glass of water.

2. 명령문의 직접 화법 → 간접 화법 전환: 「tell[ask, order, advise 등] + 목적어 + to부정사」

The police officer said to me, "Show me your driver's license."

→ The police officer **told** me **to show** him my driver's license.

[1-5] 다음 문장을 간접 화법으로 바꿔 쓰시오.

1 The boy said to the zookeeper, "Are there any lions here?"

→ The boy asked _____.

2 The instructor said to Jenny, "Wear comfortable shoes."

→ The instructor advised _____.

3 My sister said to me, "When are you going to clean up your room?"

→ My sister asked _____.

4 The librarian said to Bill, "Return the books by next Monday."

→ The librarian told _____.

5 My mom said to me, "Who called you last night?"

→ My mom asked _____.

[6-9] 우리말과 같도록 괄호 안의 말을 활용하여 문장을 완성하시오.

6 Henry는 나에게 그가 그 프로그램을 어떻게 설치할 수 있는지 물었다. (install, how, the program)

= Henry asked me _____.

7 법원은 그에게 법을 위반한 것에 대한 벌금을 내라고 명령했다. (a fine, pay)

= The court ordered him _____ for violating the law.

8 Anderson 교수는 나에게 내가 나의 보고서를 왜 제출하지 않았었는지 물었다. (why, my report, turn)

= Professor Anderson asked me _____ in.

9 그 관리자는 노동자들에게 그들의 안전모가 제대로 맞는지 물었다. (their safety helmets, fit)

= The supervisor asked the workers _____ properly. <학평 응용>

Review Test

[1-2] 다음 빈칸에 들어갈 말이 순서대로 짝지어진 것을 고르시오.

1

> · About 165 kilometers _____ the length of the world's longest bridge.
> · The socks lying on the floor _____ to my younger brother.

① is – belongs   ② is – belong
③ is – belonging   ④ are – belongs
⑤ are – belong

2

> · Some of the dishes served in this restaurant _____ for vegetarians.
> · The rich often _____ a higher income tax rate than other people.

① is – pay   ② is – pays   ③ is – paying
④ are – pays   ⑤ are – pay

[3-4] 다음 빈칸에 들어갈 알맞은 것을 고르시오.

3

> I heard that the Lisbon earthquake _____ thousands of deaths in 1755.

① will cause   ② causes   ③ caused
④ has caused   ⑤ causing

4

> I asked him _____ he had told a lie about his job.

① what   ② who   ③ that
④ whether   ⑤ which

[5-6] 다음 중 어법상 <u>틀린</u> 것을 <u>모두</u> 고르시오.

5

① Every patient are required to wear a wristband.
② He worried that the bus had been delayed.
③ Alice asked me who had used her pencil.
④ Ordering some sandwiches were my father's suggestion.
⑤ I know that the dinosaurs died off approximately 65 million years ago.

6

① Something in the fridge is starting to smell bad.
② She asked Tyler who had he met the previous day.
③ My teacher said that breakfast provides essential energy for our body and brain. <학평 응용>
④ Politics is sometimes difficult to understand.
⑤ A number of complaints was about poor customer service.

7 다음 중 어법상 <u>틀린</u> 것끼리 묶인 것은?

> ⓐ A person who wins the lottery is extremely lucky.
> ⓑ He advised me choosing physics as a university major.
> ⓒ The waiter asked the customer if she was ready to order then.
> ⓓ I learned that the Mississippi River flows into the Gulf of Mexico.
> ⓔ Neither Albania nor Serbia are a member of the European Union.

① ⓐ, ⓑ   ② ⓑ, ⓓ   ③ ⓑ, ⓔ
④ ⓐ, ⓒ, ⓓ   ⑤ ⓑ, ⓒ, ⓔ

[8-10] 다음 문장에서 어법상 <u>틀린</u> 부분을 찾아 쓰고 바르게 고쳐 쓰시오.

8

The passengers on the ferry is upset about the crowded conditions.

_____ → _____

9

Chloe asked the store clerk where could she try those pants on.

_____ → _____

10

I heard that killer whales usually lived in groups that have up to 30 members.

_____ → _____

[11-13] 우리말과 같도록 괄호 안의 말을 활용하여 문장을 완성하시오.

11

사과뿐만 아니라 복숭아도 할인 중이다. (not only, peaches, on sale, apples, be)

= _____.

12

나의 코치는 나에게 구르는 돌은 이끼가 끼지 않는다고 자주 말했다. (gather, rolling stones, no moss, tell)

= My coach often _____ me that _____
_____.

13

많은 나의 시간은 미술관들과 다른 문화 시설들을 관람하는 데 쓰였다. (my time, much of, be spent)

= _____ touring galleries and other cultural facilities.

[14-17] 다음 문장을 간접 화법으로 바꿔 쓰시오.

14

The doctor said to me, "I have to run several tests on you today."

→ The doctor _____ me that he _____
_____.

15

The lawyer said to Ms. Miller, "When did you sign this contract?"

→ The lawyer _____ Ms. Miller _____
_____.

16

Nathan said to me, "Can I borrow your textbook tomorrow?"

→ Nathan _____ me _____
_____.

17

The emperor said to his soldiers, "Build a wall."

→ The emperor _____ his soldiers _____
_____. <학평 응용>

18 우리말과 같도록 주어진 <조건>에 맞게 문장을 완성하시오.

> 그 동네에 있는 집들 중 절반은 폭풍에 의해 파손되었다.

> <조건>
> 1. the houses, be damaged, in the neighborhood, half of를 활용하시오.
> 2. 9단어로 쓰시오.

= _____
　　by the storm.

[19-20] 다음 글을 읽고 주어진 질문에 답하시오.

> The bicycle is the perfect transportation for people living in cities. I asked my teacher (A) if / what it had been popular back in the day. However, I was told that urban residents rarely used bicycles to commute prior to the 1990s. A lack of bike lanes, as well as aggressive drivers, (B) was / were the reason. ⓐ다행히도, 새로운 자전거 도로들의 건설에 자금을 조달하는 것은 지금 시 정부에게 우선순위이다. (funding, of new bike lanes, the construction, be) This is because each person who rides a bike to work (C) represents / represent one less car on the road.

19 위 글의 밑줄 친 우리말 ⓐ와 같도록 괄호 안의 말을 알맞게 배열하시오. (단, 필요 시 단어의 형태를 바꾸시오.)

= Fortunately, _____
_____ now a priority for city governments.

20 위 글의 (A), (B), (C)의 각 네모 안에서 어법에 맞는 표현으로 가장 적절한 것은?

	(A)	(B)	(C)
①	if	were	represents
②	if	was	represent
③	if	was	represents
④	what	was	represents
⑤	what	were	represent

수능형
21 (A), (B), (C)의 각 네모 안에서 어법에 맞는 표현으로 가장 적절한 것은?

> When I was a young girl, my room was always a mess. My mother always told me (A) clean / to clean my room, and I resisted her at every opportunity. I was determined to have my room the way I wanted it. Whether I actually liked having a messy room or not (B) was / were another subject altogether. To me, it was more important to get my own way. So, I did not put a lot of thought into the benefits of doing (C) that / what my mother wanted me to do.
> <학평 응용>

	(A)	(B)	(C)
①	clean	were	that
②	clean	was	that
③	to clean	was	that
④	to clean	was	what
⑤	to clean	were	what

수능형
22 다음 글의 밑줄 친 부분 중, 어법상 틀린 것은?

> We usually get along with people who ① are like us. In fact, we seek them out. It's why places like Little Italy, Chinatown, and Koreatown ② exists. But I'm not just talking about race, religion, or skin color. I'm talking about people who share our values and look at the world the same way we do. As the old saying goes, birds of a feather ③ flock together. This is a very common human tendency ④ that is rooted in how our species developed. Similarities make us relate better to other people because we think they'll understand us on a ⑤ deeper level than other people. <학평 응용>

CHAPTER 16
특수구문

기출로 적중 POINT

1 강조
2 부정
3 도치Ⅰ
4 도치Ⅱ
5 병렬
6 동격, 생략

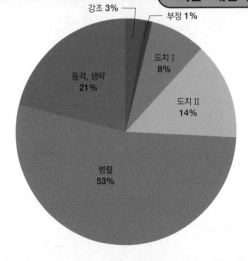

최근 7개년 수능/학평/내신 출제 경향

강조 3%
부정 1%
도치Ⅰ 8%
도치Ⅱ 14%
동격, 생략 21%
병렬 53%

TOP 1 병렬 (53%)
접속사로 문법적인 형태가 같은 것끼리 연결되었는지를 묻는 문제가 자주 출제된다.

TOP 2 동격, 생략 (21%)
명사 뒤에서 동격절을 이끄는 that의 쓰임을 묻는 문제가 자주 출제된다.

TOP 3 도치Ⅱ (14%)
부정의 의미를 가진 말이 도치된 문장의 형태를 묻는 문제가 자주 출제된다.

1. 일반동사를 강조할 때는 「do동사(do/does/did) + 동사원형」의 형태로 쓴다.

   I guess that fashion trends **do repeat**. <학평 응용>
   Janet **did offer** to pay for our meal yesterday evening.

2. it-that 강조 구문은 '…한 것은 바로 ~이다'의 의미로, 동사를 제외한 문장 성분(주어, 목적어, 부사(구/절) 등)을 it과 that 사이에 쓴다.

   Paul bought apples at the market last week.
   → **It** was *Paul* **that[who]** bought apples at the market last week. <주어 강조>
     ↳ 강조하는 대상에 따라 that 대신 who(m), which, where, when을 쓸 수 있다.
   → **It** was *apples* **that[which]** Paul bought at the market last week. <목적어 강조>
   → **It** was *at the market* **that[where]** Paul bought apples last week. <부사구(장소) 강조>
   → **It** was *last week* **that[when]** Paul bought apples at the market. <부사구(시간) 강조>

[1-5] 우리말과 같도록 괄호 안의 말을 알맞게 배열하시오. (단, 필요 시 단어의 형태를 바꾸시오.)

1 그 놀이공원은 아이들에게 정말로 할인을 제공한다. (provide, do, a discount)

   = The amusement park ＿＿＿＿＿＿＿＿＿＿＿＿＿＿＿ to children.

2 내가 나의 사촌을 만난 때는 바로 지난 목요일이었다. (be, last Thursday, it, that)

   = ＿＿＿＿＿＿＿＿＿＿＿＿＿＿＿ I met my cousin.

3 나에게 유용한 조언을 주는 사람은 바로 나의 아버지이다. (who, it, my father, be)

   = ＿＿＿＿＿＿＿＿＿＿＿＿＿＿＿ gives me helpful advice.

4 George는 그의 에어컨을 정말로 수리하고 싶었다. (to repair, want, do)

   = George ＿＿＿＿＿＿＿＿＿＿＿＿＿＿＿ his air conditioner.

5 그 새로운 카페가 개업한 곳은 바로 길 건너편이었다. (across the street, be, it, that)

   = ＿＿＿＿＿＿＿＿＿＿＿＿＿＿＿ the new café opened.

[6-9] 다음 문장을 밑줄 친 부분을 강조하는 it-that 강조 구문으로 바꿔 쓰시오.

6 <u>A giant asteroid</u> caused the extinction of the dinosaurs.

   → ＿＿＿＿＿＿＿＿＿＿＿＿＿＿＿＿＿＿＿＿＿＿＿.

7 I saw <u>Larry</u> at the swimming pool yesterday.

   → ＿＿＿＿＿＿＿＿＿＿＿＿＿＿＿＿＿＿＿＿＿＿＿.

8 I submitted <u>my sales report</u> to Ms. Thompson.

   → ＿＿＿＿＿＿＿＿＿＿＿＿＿＿＿＿＿＿＿＿＿＿＿.

9 <u>The woman</u> joined the art class at the community center.

   → ＿＿＿＿＿＿＿＿＿＿＿＿＿＿＿＿＿＿＿＿＿＿＿.

POINT 2 부정

1. 부정의 의미를 가진 hardly/scarcely/rarely/barely/seldom/little 등은 not이나 never 등의 부정어와 함께 쓰지 않는다.

   Despite their reputation, great white sharks (~~don't hardly~~, **hardly**) attack people.

2. no/none/neither/never는 '아무것도/아무도/누구도/결코 ~않다'라는 의미로, 문장 전체를 부정할 때 쓴다.

   None of the stores near my apartment sell paper towels.

3. 「not + always/all/every/both」는 '항상/모두/둘 다 ~인 것은 아니다'라는 의미로, 문장 일부를 부정할 때 쓴다.

   Stress is **not always** as bad as you think. <수능>
   Not every resident of the building agrees with the parking policy.

[1-5] 다음 두 문장의 의미가 같도록 괄호 안에서 알맞은 것을 고르시오.

1 Some students didn't understand the explanation.
   → (No / Not all) students understood the explanation.

2 I use a late-night delivery service only once in a while.
   → I scarcely (use / don't use) a late-night delivery service. <학평 응용>

3 Both of my parents didn't drive me to school today.
   → (Neither / Not both) of my parents drove me to school today.

4 Every researcher is forbidden to use the laboratory this week.
   → (No / Not every) researcher is permitted to use the laboratory this week.

5 The shop will give customers either a T-shirt or a bag as a gift.
   → Customers will receive a T-shirt or a bag as a gift, but (neither / not both) will be given.

[6-10] 우리말과 같도록 괄호 안의 말을 알맞게 배열하시오.

6 좋은 시작이 항상 좋은 결말을 만드는 것은 아니다. (always, a good ending, does, a good beginning, make, not)
   = _____. <학평>

7 Brent는 요리하는 것을 즐기기 때문에 식당에 거의 가지 않는다. (goes, seldom, Brent, to restaurants)
   = _____ as he enjoys cooking.

8 우리 중 아무도 아직 자동차를 어떻게 운전하는지 배우지 않았다. (how to drive, has, of us, learned, none)
   = _____ a car yet.

9 그들은 최근의 지진에 관한 아무 정보도 받지 않았다. (no, received, information, have, they)
   = _____ about the recent earthquake.

10 모든 다이아몬드가 보석에 사용되기에 적합한 것은 아니다. (diamond, not, suitable, every, is)
   = _____ to be used in jewelry.

1. 장소나 방향의 부사(구)가 강조되어 문장 맨 앞으로 올 때는 「장소나 방향의 부사(구) + 동사 + 주어」의 형태로 쓴다.

On the platform **stood a man** holding a suitcase.
Into my head **popped the idea** of throwing a birthday party for Kyle.

> TIP ① 주어가 대명사인 경우 주어와 동사가 주로 도치되지 않는다.
> *Here* **he comes** into the mall.
> ② 「There + be동사」에서는 뒤에 오는 주어에 be동사를 수일치시키며, there는 해석하지 않는다.
> *There* **are** *more than 700 million cell phones* being used in the US today. <학평>

2. 보어가 강조되어 문장 맨 앞으로 올 때는 「보어 + 동사 + 주어」의 형태로 쓴다.

Too expensive **were the tickets** for the popular musical.

[1-3] 다음 두 문장의 의미가 같도록 문장을 완성하시오.

1 The singer walked onto the stage.

→ Onto the stage _____.

2 Daniel seemed very angry when he realized his bike had been stolen.

→ Very angry _____ when he realized his bike had been stolen.

3 She watched the scenery pass by out of the car window.

→ Out of the car window _____.

[4-7] 우리말과 같도록 괄호 안의 말을 활용하여 문장을 완성하시오.

4 곱슬머리를 가진 그 소년은 Lisa 옆에 앉았다. (the boy, sit)

= Next to Lisa _____ with curly hair.

5 그것은 그 포식자로부터 달아나기 위해 덤불 속으로 달렸다. (it, run)

= Into the bushes _____ to escape the predator.

6 네가 벌레에게 물리는 것을 예방하기 위해 할 수 있는 몇 가지 것들이 있다. (several things, be)

= There _____ you can do to prevent being bitten by insects. <학평 응용>

7 그 야구 선수권 대회를 보는 사람들은 신이 났었다. (the people, be)

= Excited _____ watching the championship baseball game.

---

8 다음 글에서 어법상 **틀린** 부분을 찾아 쓰고 바르게 고쳐 쓰시오.

> On Tuesday afternoon, Lewis took me for a picnic. Beautiful was the site he had selected for our meal. There was a lot of flowers growing in the meadow, and we had an excellent view.

_____ → _____

도치 II

1. 부정의 의미를 가진 말(not, never, hardly, rarely, little, only 등)이 강조되어 문장 맨 앞으로 올 때는 다음의 형태로 쓴다.

❶ be동사나 조동사가 있는 문장: 「부정어 + be동사/조동사 + 주어」
Rarely **is James** amused by his little brother's jokes.
Never **have I** eaten Indian food before.

❷ 일반동사가 있는 문장: 「부정어 + do/does/did + 주어 + 동사원형」
Seldom **does an owl hunt** for prey during the day.
Not until I called her **did Sophia wake** up.

2. '~도 그렇다/아니다'라는 의미로 so/neither를 쓸 때는 「so/neither + 동사 + 주어」의 형태로 쓴다.

Neil Armstrong walked on the Moon, and *so* **did Edwin Aldrin**.
In this temple, visitors shouldn't talk during the tour, and *neither* **should the tour guide**.

[1-4] 다음 두 문장의 의미가 같도록 문장을 완성하시오.

1 Nancy hardly met her friends last month.
→ Hardly _____.

2 Mr. Parker was never impressed by the presentation I gave.
→ Never _____.

3 The Grand Hotel has a pool, and the Palace Hotel has a pool, too.
→ The Grand Hotel has a pool, and so _____.

4 Drivers can no longer use Elm Street due to ongoing construction.
→ No longer _____.

[5-8] 밑줄 친 부분이 어법상 맞으면 O를 쓰고, 틀리면 바르게 고쳐 쓰시오.

5 Not often <u>Brenda is allowed</u> to use her brother's laptop.   → _____

6 Little <u>did he know</u> why Mary was angry with him.   → _____

7 Whales cannot breathe underwater, and neither <u>are dolphins</u>.   → _____

8 Barely <u>the baby had stopped</u> crying when his mom came.   → _____

9 우리말과 같도록 괄호 안의 말을 활용하여 문장을 완성하시오.

> 공상 과학 소설은 우리가 과학 원리를 이해하도록 도울 뿐만 아니라 우리의 창의력도 기른다. (help, science fiction)

= Not only _____ understand scientific principles, but it also builds our creativity. <학평 응용>

등위접속사나 상관접속사로 연결되는 말은 문법적으로 형태가 같아야 한다.

He **likes** going on a trip *but* **hates** traveling alone.
Your dog knows the way to make you feel **important** *and* **loved**. <학평 응용>
Neither **eating** *nor* **drinking** is permitted inside the art gallery.
After she finished college, she wanted **to go** abroad *and* **(to) study** medicine.
접속사로 to부정사가 연결될 때, 뒤에 오는 to부정사에서는 to를 생략할 수 있다. ↵

[1-7] 괄호 안에서 알맞은 것을 고르시오.

1 Emily not only exercises hard but also (eats / to eat) healthily.

2 Closing the curtains and (turn / turning) off the light enabled me to sleep.

3 The jacket Chloe purchased looks expensive and (style / stylish).

4 I went to the store to return the sweater and (buy / buying) a new skirt.

5 The documentary about rainforests was neither informative nor (interest / interesting).

6 My mother asked me not to take out the trash but (emptying / to empty) the dishwasher.

7 She teased me when I broke my arm and (needed / to need) to wear a cast. <학평 응용>

[8-14] 밑줄 친 부분이 어법상 맞으면 O를 쓰고, 틀리면 바르게 고쳐 쓰시오.

8 Henry plants some flowers or <u>watering</u> the lawn on weekends. → _____

9 The children were happy but <u>tired</u> after playing in the park all day. → _____

10 Jane enjoys neither listening to music nor <u>read</u> novels. → _____

11 Preparing a meal and <u>to clean</u> up afterward is a lot of work. → _____

12 I needed to provide my name and <u>show</u> my ticket at the entrance. → _____

13 Eric thought the roller coaster was exciting as well as <u>frighten</u>. → _____

14 Wolves howl either to communicate with the group or <u>warning</u> off enemies. → _____

15 (A), (B)의 각 네모 안에서 어법에 맞는 표현으로 가장 적절한 것을 고르시오.

> My grandmother is a strong woman who refuses to take medicine or (A) seek / seeking medical care.
> In fact, she criticizes my father for being weak and (B) go / going to the hospital frequently. <학평 응용>

1. **명사 뒤에 콤마(,), of, that을 써서 부연 설명을 덧붙일 수 있으며, 이를 동격이라고 한다.**

   King Kong, the imaginary giant ape, climbed the building in the movie. <명사 + 콤마(,) + 명사(구)>

   The boy fulfilled **his goal** *of* **learning to speak two languages.** <명사 + of + 명사(상당어구)>

   The news *that* **she got married** came as a surprise to me. <명사(fact, news 등) + that절>

2. **문장 안에서 반복되는 어구는 생략할 수 있다.**

   The eagle settled on a branch and (**the eagle**) watched the mouse.

   You can *borrow my book* if you want to (**borrow my book**).

3. **부사절의 주어가 주절의 주어와 같고 부사절의 동사가 be동사인 경우, 부사절에서 「주어 + be동사」를 생략할 수 있다.**

   When (**he was**) in high school, *he* edited his high school newspaper. <학평>

[1-6] 다음 밑줄 친 부분과 동격인 부분에 밑줄을 치시오.

1 Ludwig van Beethoven, the German composer, produced many masterpieces.

2 Her fear of flying prevents Cindy from taking planes.

3 Town residents received a warning that a powerful storm was approaching.

4 London, the capital of the United Kingdom, has a population of almost nine million.

5 I didn't believe his claim that he had visited 15 countries.

6 Some people are against the idea of allowing three-year-olds to use computers. <학평 응용>

[7-12] 다음 문장에서 생략할 수 있는 부분에 밑줄을 치시오.

7 We stopped for lunch while we were driving home.

8 My brother majored in economics and my brother now works at a bank.

9 He always snores loudly when he is asleep.

10 When you are in doubt, you should ask the teacher a question.

11 Julie is taking many pictures of the palace, but I'm not taking many pictures of the palace.

12 Please don't restart the machine until the technician tells you to restart the machine.

13 다음 글의 밑줄 친 ⓐ~ⓒ 중 어법상 틀린 것의 기호를 쓰고 바르게 고쳐 쓰시오.

> Sigmund Freud, ⓐthe famous Austrian neurologist, had a significant influence on the modern field of psychiatry. He developed the theory ⓑwhich an adult's mental problems resulted from negative childhood experiences. His idea was initially rejected ⓒbut is now widely accepted. *psychiatry: 정신 의학

_____ → _____

Review Test

[1-3] 다음 빈칸에 들어갈 알맞은 것을 고르시오.

1

> Rarely _____ the furniture in my apartment.

① my cat scratches   ② scratches my cat
③ does my cat scratch   ④ does scratch my cat
⑤ my cat does scratch

2

> Mandy loves going to a café, and _____ I.

① so am   ② so do   ③ so did
④ neither am   ⑤ neither do

3

> Across the street _____ as the light turned green.

① he walked   ② walked he   ③ he walking
④ walks he   ⑤ did walk he

[4-5] 다음 빈칸에 들어갈 알맞은 것을 모두 고르시오.

4

> It is our wedding anniversary _____ we will celebrate next week.

① who   ② whom   ③ which
④ where   ⑤ that

5

> Beth hopes to travel to Europe and _____ many historical castles next summer.

① tour   ② toured   ③ touring
④ to tour   ⑤ be toured

[6-7] 다음 중 어법상 틀린 것을 고르시오.

6

① Napoleon did conquer an extensive territory.
② On Jane's desk the large monitor sat.
③ Richard watches TV or climbs a mountain every Sunday.
④ People tend to smile or laugh if satisfied.
⑤ Hardly have I seen a room as clean as yours.

7

① There are a number of reasons for the bookstore's closure.
② It was lightning that started the forest fire.
③ Mr. Greer felt upset and annoy when he couldn't find a taxi.
④ Not often does it get cold in the southern parts of the country.
⑤ Hyperion, the tallest tree in the world, is located in California.

8 다음 중 어법상 틀린 것끼리 묶인 것은?

> ⓐ I don't scarcely see my brother these days because he is so busy.
> ⓑ Warren asked me to move some boxes or clean the floor.
> ⓒ They knew the fact which the painting was an authentic work.
> ⓓ The bird ran along the ground, flapped its wings, and then start flying.
> ⓔ He has never tried durian before, and neither have I.

① ⓐ, ⓑ, ⓒ   ② ⓐ, ⓒ, ⓓ   ③ ⓐ, ⓒ, ⓔ
④ ⓑ, ⓒ, ⓓ   ⑤ ⓒ, ⓓ, ⓔ

[9-10] 다음 문장에서 어법상 틀린 부분을 찾아 쓰고 바르게 고쳐 쓰시오.

9

Not until I got home I realized that I had left my purse at the bus stop. <학평 응용>

_____ → _____

10

Winning the fencing match and receive a gold medal made him feel proud.

_____ → _____

[11-14] 다음 문장을 밑줄 친 부분을 강조하는 문장으로 바꿔 쓰시오.

11

A large dog <u>needs</u> to be walked several times a day.
→ A large dog _____

_____.

12

<u>William</u> organized the workshop for the interns.
→ It _____

_____.

13

He waited <u>in front of the theater</u> to meet his friend.
→ In _____.

14

The restaurant is <u>no longer</u> offering discounts to students.
→ No _____

_____.

[15-17] 우리말과 같도록 괄호 안의 말을 알맞게 배열하시오.

15

성공적인 사람들의 자녀들이 모두 성공적이게 되는 것은 아니다. (all, become, of successful people, children, not)

= _____
successful. <수능>

16

Smith씨는 그녀의 휴가 동안 리조트에 가고 해변에서 휴식하기로 계획한다. (and, plans, relax, to a resort, go, on the beach, to)

= Ms. Smith _____

_____ during her vacation.

17

그 회관은 모든 회의 참석자를 위한 공간을 거의 가지고 있지 않다. (room, have, the hall, does)

= Barely _____ for every conference attendee.

18 우리말과 같도록 주어진 <조건>에 맞게 문장을 완성하시오.

> 그 국립공원은 봄과 가을 동안 캠프파이어를 거의 허용하지 않는다.

> <조건>
> 1. the national park, campfires, rarely, allow를 활용하시오.
> 2. 부정어를 강조하시오.
> 3. 7단어로 쓰시오.

= _____

during spring and autumn.

[19-20] 다음 글을 읽고 주어진 질문에 답하시오.

> Last Tuesday, Sarah went to the library and ⓐ do some research about Spain. There ⓑ was a new exchange student from Barcelona at her school, and Sarah wanted to make him feel welcome. However, she barely knew ⓒ nothing about Spanish customs. (A) 그녀는 그에게 그녀 자신을 소개하기 전에 더 많은 정보가 정말로 필요하다고 생각했다. (more information, need, do) While ⓓ doing some research, she noticed the exchange student, Max, coming to her. He saw Sarah ⓔ reading a book about Spain, so he thought they could be friends.

19 위 글의 밑줄 친 우리말 (A)와 같도록 괄호 안의 말을 활용하여 문장을 완성하시오.

= She thought that _____
before introducing herself to him.

20 위 글의 밑줄 친 ⓐ~ⓔ 중 어법상 틀린 것의 기호를 쓰고 바르게 고쳐 쓰시오.

(1) _____ → _____

(2) _____ → _____

21 (A), (B), (C)의 각 네모 안에서 어법에 맞는 표현으로 가장 적절한 것은?

> Never (A) Greg felt / did Greg feel like a success if he failed to get a score of 100 on an assignment. He eventually recognized that this attitude was causing him stress. So he came up with the creative idea (B) that / of posting notes everywhere with the simple message, "92 is still an A." Gradually, these simple reminder notes allowed Greg to have a different point of view and (C) realize / realized that he didn't have to be perfect at everything. <학평 응용>

	(A)	(B)	(C)
①	Greg felt	that	realized
②	Greg felt	of	realized
③	did Greg feel	of	realized
④	did Greg feel	of	realize
⑤	did Greg feel	that	realize

22 다음 글의 밑줄 친 부분 중, 어법상 틀린 것은?

> Some scientists have a belief ① that certain animals use a type of language. For example, vervet monkeys have different sounds for different predators. However, the monkeys aren't born ② knowing the meaning of each sound. Young monkeys learn the meaning of the sounds from listening to and ③ watching older monkeys. After young monkeys learn the alarm call for an eagle, they use it ④ whenever they see a large bird, even if the bird is harmless. Only after much trial and error ⑤ they can learn that the eagle call must be used only for eagles.
> <학평 응용>

기출에서 찾은 **점수 상승**의 기적!

기출로적중

해커스

고등영문법

초판 4쇄 발행 2024년 7월 8일
초판 1쇄 발행 2022년 5월 20일

지은이	해커스 어학연구소
펴낸곳	㈜해커스 어학연구소
펴낸이	해커스 어학연구소 출판팀
주소	서울특별시 서초구 강남대로61길 23 ㈜해커스 어학연구소
고객센터	02-537-5000
교재 관련 문의	publishing@hackers.com
	해커스북 사이트(HackersBook.com) 고객센터 Q&A 게시판
동영상강의	star.Hackers.com
ISBN	978-89-6542-478-9 (53740)
Serial Number	01-04-01

중고등영어 1위,
해커스북 HackersBook.com

해커스북 중·고등

· 깊은 이해로 이끄는 **예문/문제 해석 파일**
· 서술형 시험을 완벽하게 대비할 수 있는 **영작/해석 워크시트**
· 효과적인 단어 암기를 돕는 **어휘리스트 및 어휘테스트**

중·고등영어도 역시 1위 해커스

중·고등
해커스 young star°

중·고등영어의 압도적인 점수 상승,
해커스 영스타 중·고등에서 현실이 됩니다.

해커스 영스타 중·고등 강의 무료체험

내게 맞는 공부법 체크! 학습전략검사

해커스 중·고등교재 무료 학습자료

보카 강의 수강생 수
1위 박가은

기출로 적중
해커스
고등영문법

정답 및 해설

해커스 어학연구소

CHAPTER 1
문장의 형식

1 동사: is / 주격 보어: the biggest animal
2 동사: lived
3 동사: stay / 주격 보어: calm
4 동사: are
5 confident   6 bad
7 bitter   8 hopeful
9 comfortably → comfortable

POINT 2   3형식과 4형식   본책 p.15

1 will marry Rhonda
2 gave the driver her ticket
3 builds families in need homes
4 reached the surface of the moon
5 found an affordable apartment for me
6 brought a bunch of grapes to the prince
7 offered cold beverages to the passengers
8 asked many questions of the applicant
9 give more energy to us

POINT 3   5형식: 명사/형용사/to부정사를 목적격 보어로 쓰
는 동사   본책 p.16

1 to keep   2 competitive
3 to fall   4 allowed the students to read
5 consider polar bears extremely dangerous
6 wants the patient to report
7 kept their relationship a secret
8 causes global temperatures to rise
9 look → to look

POINT 4   5형식: 사역동사와 지각동사   본책 p.17

1 pick / to pick   2 sign
3 to think   4 take
5 fall / falling   6 locate
7 finished   8 practice
9 fixing   10 making / make
11 adopting → adopt

REVIEW TEST   본책 p.18

1 ①   2 ②   3 ⑤   4 ④   5 ②
6 ③   7 ④   8 developed → (to) develop
9 keeping → to keep
10 The tour guide got Carl a dance performance ticket
   The tour guide got a dance performance ticket for Carl
11 approached to → approached
12 There were many problems
13 Luke sold Brenda his old bicycle
14 Warren had a fried chicken delivered
15 She let me borrow her laptop computer
16 The hotel doesn't[does not] allow guests to smoke
17 The night sky helped past generations to keep
18 He made me clean the garage
19 (1) ⓐ → sad   (2) ⓑ → to be
20 ②   21 ⑤

1 · 동사 keep의 주격 보어 자리에는 명사나 형용사(quiet)가 온다.
  · 동사 make의 목적격 보어 자리에는 명사나 형용사(official)가 온다.

2 · 동사 resemble은 전치사 없이 바로 목적어를 가진다.
  · 4형식 문장은 「주어 + 동사 + 직접 목적어 + to/for/of + 간접 목적어」 형태의 3형식 문장으로 바꿔 쓸 수 있다.

3 · 동사 order의 목적격 보어 자리에는 to부정사(to advance)가 온다.
  · 사역동사(have)의 목적격 보어 자리에는 원형부정사(wear)가 온다.

4 · 준사역동사 get의 목적격 보어 자리에는 to부정사(to show)가 온다.
  · 동사 find의 목적격 보어 자리에는 명사나 형용사(comfortable)가 온다.

5 ② 지각동사(feel)의 목적격 보어 자리에는 원형부정사나 V-ing형이 오므로 to부정사 to drop을 drop[dropping]으로 고쳐야 한다.

6 ③ 동사 leave의 목적격 보어 자리에는 명사나 형용사가 오므로 부사 gloomily를 gloomy로 고쳐야 한다.

7 ⓐ 사역동사(let)의 목적격 보어 자리에는 원형부정사가 오므로 to부정사 to own을 own으로 고쳐야 한다.
  ⓓ 동사 advise의 목적격 보어 자리에는 to부정사가 오므로 원형부정사 save를 to save로 고쳐야 한다.

8 준사역동사 help의 목적격 보어 자리에는 to부정사와 원형부정사가 모두 올 수 있으므로 developed를 (to) develop으로 고쳐야 한다.

9 동사 tell의 목적격 보어 자리에는 to부정사가 오므로 V-ing형 keeping을 to keep으로 고쳐야 한다.

10 4형식 문장은 「주어 + 동사 + 간접 목적어(…에게) + 직접 목적어(~을)」의 형태이며, 「주어 + 동사 + 직접 목적어 + to/for/of + 간접 목적어」 형태의 3형식 문장으로 바꿔 쓸 수 있다.

11 동사 approach는 전치사 없이 바로 목적어를 가지므로 approached to를 approached로 고쳐야 한다.

12 「There + be동사」는 1형식 문장이며, be동사 뒤에 오는 명사가 주어이다.

13 4형식 문장은 「주어 + 동사 + 간접 목적어(…에게) + 직접 목적어(~을)」의 형태이다.

14 5형식 문장은 「주어 + 동사 + 목적어 + 목적격 보어」의 형태이다. 사역동사(have)의 목적어(a fried chicken)와 목적격 보어(deliver)의 관계가 수동이므로 목적격 보어 자리에 과거분사(delivered)가 왔다.

15 사역동사(let)의 목적격 보어 자리에는 원형부정사(borrow)가 온다.

16 동사 allow의 목적격 보어 자리에는 to부정사(to smoke)가 온다.

17 준사역동사 help의 목적격 보어 자리에는 to부정사와 원형부정사가 모두 올 수 있다. 단, 8단어로 써야 하므로 to부정사(to keep)를 쓴다.

18 사역동사(make)의 목적격 보어 자리에는 원형부정사(clean)가 온다.

19 ⓐ 감각동사(sound)의 주격 보어 자리에는 형용사가 오므로 부사 sadly를 sad로 고쳐야 한다.
ⓑ 동사 want의 목적격 보어 자리에는 to부정사가 오므로 V-ing형 being을 to be로 고쳐야 한다.

20 (A) 사역동사(make)의 목적격 보어 자리에는 원형부정사(work)가 온다.
(B) 동사 force의 목적격 보어 자리에는 to부정사(to change)가 온다.
(C) 동사 make의 목적격 보어 자리에는 명사나 형용사(difficult)가 온다.

21 ⑤ 감각동사(feel)의 주격 보어 자리에는 형용사가 오므로 부사 gratefully를 grateful로 고쳐야 한다.

CHAPTER 2
시제

POINT 1 현재시제와 과거시제
본책 p.22

1	rides	**2**	drank
3	ruled	**4**	covers
5	opened	**6**	feels
7	won	**8**	hosted
9	is	**10**	eats
11	completed	**12**	run
13	plays	**14**	painted
15	watched	**16**	elect
17	became		

POINT 2 미래시제
본책 p.23

1 The weather will be cold and rainy
2 Fans are going to wait in line to purchase the new album
3 My family members will gather
4 She is going to work as a swimming coach

5	O	**6**	receive
7	O	**8**	O
9	are going to[will]	**10**	O
11	get		

POINT 3 진행시제
본책 p.24

1	is treating	**2**	will be discussing
3	are polluting	**4**	was driving
5	hates	**6**	O
7	know	**8**	O
9	are liking → like		

POINT 4 현재완료시제
본책 p.25

1	has cared	**2**	slept
3	hasn't	**4**	gave up
5	has taken	**6**	has increased
7	has already become	**8**	walked
9	Have you ever tried	**10**	ⓑ → have used

POINT 5 과거완료시제
본책 p.26

1	had	**2**	had used
3	Had	**4**	have
5	hadn't	**6**	had known
7	had never seen	**8**	have bought
9	had wandered	**10**	had already woken
11	(A) had (B) had		

POINT 6 미래완료시제와 완료진행시제
본책 p.27

1	will have recovered	**2**	will have been
3	have been	**4**	had been
5	has been writing	**6**	had been crying
7	will have been taking	**8**	had been feeling
9	had been	**10**	O
11	will have invented	**12**	O

REVIEW TEST

본책 p.28

1 ②　　**2** ③　　**3** ⑤　　**4** ④　　**5** ③
6 ②　　**7** ③　　**8** attended → have attended
9 will become → becomes　　**10** has → had
11 is tasting → tastes　　**12** have → will have
13 had already memorized the alphabet
14 will have resolved the issues
15 has been saving money
16 had been reading a book
17 Karl had led the band for six years
18 had developed the mobile phone
19 (1) ⓐ → have carried　　(2) ⓔ → will have advanced
20 ③　　**21** ③

1 역사적 사실을 나타내는 과거시제를 쓴다.

2 현재완료시제와 자주 쓰이는 표현 'since ~'와 함께 과거(the beginning of society)에 발생하여 현재까지 영향을 미치는 일을 나타내는 현재완료시제를 쓴다.

3 특정 미래 시점(by ~ store)까지 완료될 일을 나타내는 미래완료시제를 쓴다.

4 특정 과거 시점(when ~ over) 이전에 발생하여 그 과거 시점까지 영향을 미치는 일이 진행 중임을 강조하는 과거완료진행시제를 쓴다.

5 ① 과거(At a younger age)에 진행되고 있는 동작을 나타내고 있으므로 과거진행시제(was working)로 고쳐야 한다.
② 현재완료시제와 자주 쓰이는 표현 'since ~'와 함께 과거(2018)에 발생하여 현재까지 영향을 미치는 일을 나타내고 있으므로 현재완료시제(has painted)로 고쳐야 한다.
④ 특정 과거 시점(when ~ home) 이전에 발생하여 그 과거 시점까지 영향을 미치는 일을 나타내고 있으므로 과거완료시제(had baked)로 고쳐야 한다.
⑤ 특정 미래 시점(next month)까지 계속될 일이 진행 중임을 강조하고 있으므로 미래완료진행시제(will have been serving)로 고쳐야 한다.

6 ② 시간을 나타내는 부사절(until ~ crown)에서는 미래의 일을 나타낼 때 미래시제가 아닌 현재시제를 쓰므로 will give up을 gives up으로 고쳐야 한다.

7 ⓐ 특정 과거 시점(When ~ news) 이전에 발생하여 그 과거 시점까지 영향을 미치는 일이 진행 중임을 강조하고 있으므로 현재완료진행시제(has been driving)를 과거완료진행시제(had been driving)로 고쳐야 한다.
ⓒ 상태를 나타내는 동사(love)는 진행형으로 쓸 수 없으므로 is loving을 loves로 고쳐야 한다.
ⓔ 현재완료시제와 자주 쓰이는 표현 'since ~'와 함께 과거(summer)에 발생하여 현재까지 영향을 미치는 일을 나타내고 있으므로 과거시제(stayed)를 현재완료시제(have stayed)로 고쳐야 한다.

8 현재완료시제와 자주 쓰이는 표현 'since ~'와 함께 과거(the day ~ school)에 발생하여 현재까지 영향을 미치는 일을 나타내고 있으므로 과거시제(attended)를 현재완료시제(have attended)로 고쳐야 한다.

9 조건을 나타내는 부사절(if ~ happy)에서는 미래의 일을 나타낼 때 미래시제가 아닌 현재시제를 쓰므로 will become을 becomes로 고쳐야 한다.

10 특정 과거 시점(until ~ there) 이전에 발생하여 그 과거 시점까지 영향을 미치는 일을 나타내고 있으므로 has를 had로 고쳐 과거완료시제를 써야 한다.

11 상태를 나타내는 동사(taste)는 진행형으로 쓸 수 없으므로 is tasting을 tastes로 고쳐야 한다.

12 특정 미래 시점(By ~ year)까지 계속될 일이 진행 중임을 강조하고 있으므로 have를 will have로 고쳐 미래완료진행시제를 써야 한다.

13 특정 과거 시점(before ~ classes) 이전에 발생하여 그 과거 시점까지 영향을 미치는 일을 나타내는 과거완료시제 문장이므로 「had + p.p.」를 쓴다.

14 특정 미래 시점(by ~ talking)까지 완료될 일을 나타내는 미래완료시제 문장이므로 「will have + p.p.」를 쓴다.

15 현재완료시제와 자주 쓰이는 표현 'since ~'와 함께 과거(January)에 발생하여 현재까지 영향을 미치는 일이 진행 중임을 강조하는 현재완료진행시제 문장이므로 「has been + V-ing」를 쓴다.

16 특정 과거 시점(when ~ home) 이전에 발생하여 그 과거 시점까지 영향을 미치는 일이 진행 중임을 강조하는 과거완료진행시제 문장이므로 「had been + V-ing」를 쓴다.

17 특정 과거 시점(when ~ album) 이전에 발생하여 그 과거 시점까지 영향을 미치는 일을 나타내는 과거완료시제 문장이므로 「had + p.p.」를 쓴다.

18 특정 과거 시점(Before ~ hit) 이전에 발생하여 그 과거 시점까지 영향을 미치는 일을 나타내는 과거완료시제 문장이므로 「had + p.p.」를 쓴다.

19 ⓐ 현재완료시제와 자주 쓰이는 표현 'since ~'와 함께 과거(the 1980s)에 발생하여 현재까지 영향을 미치는 일을 나타내고 있으므로 현재완료시제(have carried)로 고쳐야 한다.
ⓔ 특정 미래 시점(by ~ future)까지 완료될 일을 나타내고 있으므로 미래완료시제(will have advanced)로 고쳐야 한다.

20 (A) 특정 과거 시점(when ~ stopped) 이전에 발생하여 그 과거 시점까지 영향을 미치는 일을 나타내는 과거완료시제(had finished)를 쓴다.
(B) 현재완료시제와 자주 쓰이는 표현 'since ~'와 함께 과거(then)에 발생하여 현재까지 영향을 미치는 일을 나타내는 현재완료시제(have become)를 쓴다.
(C) 동사 expect의 목적격 보어 자리에는 to부정사(to run)가 온다.

21 ③ 현재완료시제와 자주 쓰이는 표현 'since ~'와 함께 과거(the change)에 발생하여 현재까지 영향을 미치는 일을 나타내고 있으므로 현재완료시제(haven't shown)로 고쳐야 한다.

CHAPTER 3
조동사

본책 p.32

POINT 1 can, may

1 be able to
2 Can
3 could
4 was able to
5 may
6 Can[Could] you wash
7 can make
8 could[may/might] benefit
9 can[may] share
10 can[are able to] communicate
11 will be able to concentrate

POINT 2 must, have to

1 must not
2 had to
3 must
4 can't
5 don't need to
6 doesn't have to
7 must not
8 must
9 will have to replace
10 don't have to visit[don't need to visit/need not visit]
11 must[has to] sign up

POINT 3 should, ought to

1 should
2 should
3 purchase
4 ought not to
5 should see
6 shouldn't focus
7 ought to ride
8 get
9 evacuates → (should) evacuate

POINT 4 used to, would

1 used to
2 cultivate
3 would
4 signing
5 used to have
6 are used to connect
7 was used to receiving
8 used to bury
9 helping → help

POINT 5 조동사 관용 표현

1 would rather
2 may as well
3 had better
4 would like to
5 may well
6 had better
7 would like to get
8 would rather go
9 had better admit
10 had better walk

11 may well earn
12 may as well review

POINT 6 조동사 + have + p.p.

1 must
2 may
3 can't
4 should
5 could
6 should have canceled
7 could have influenced
8 can't have slept
9 may[might] have met
10 must have forgotten
11 should have attached

REVIEW TEST

1 ④ 2 ③ 3 ⑤ 4 ① 5 ⑤
6 ③ 7 ③ 8 ③
9 were used to → used to[would]
10 taking → (should) take   11 can → be able to
12 You ought to know the national anthem
13 Windmills are used to produce renewable energy
14 You must have become
15 Staff members can[could/may] have a break
16 I would[I'd] rather stay home than go out
17 The flight attendant required that I (should) store hand luggage
18 The stranger can't have gone
19 My father recommended that I (should) learn
20 (1) ⓐ → used to[would] ask
   (2) ⓔ → ought to[should] read
21 ④   22 ②

1 능력을 나타내는 can은 be able to로 바꿔 쓸 수 있다.

2 의무를 나타내는 must는 have to로 바꿔 쓸 수 있다.

3 '전에는 그 공원에 큰 조각상이 있었다.'라는 의미이므로 과거의 상태를 나타내는 used to를 쓴다.

4 'Scott은 점심 식사 전에 그 퍼즐을 풀었을지도 모른다.'라는 의미이므로 「may + have + p.p.」의 may를 쓴다.

5 ⑤ ought to의 부정형은 ought not to이므로 ought to not을 ought not to로 고쳐야 한다.

6 ③ '자는 짧은 거리를 측정하는 데 사용된다(be used to + 동사원형).'라는 의미이므로 measuring을 measure로 고쳐야 한다.

7 ③ 의무를 나타내는 must의 미래형은 will have to를 쓰므로 will must를 will have to로 고쳐야 한다.

8 ⓑ '나에게 지하철역으로 가는 길을 말해주겠니?'라는 의미이므로 May를 요청을 나타내는 Can[Could]로 고쳐야 한다.
⑥ 필요를 나타내는 형용사(important) 뒤 that절의 동사 자리에는 「(should) + 동사원형」이 오므로 sets를 (should) set으로 고쳐야 한다.

9 '사람들은 지구가 태양계의 중심이라고 믿곤 했다.'라는 의미이므로 were used to를 과거의 반복적인 습관을 나타내는 used to[would]로 고쳐야 한다.

10 주장을 나타내는 동사(insist) 뒤 that절의 내용이 '~해야 한다'인 경우 동사 자리에 「(should) + 동사원형」이 오므로 taking을 (should) take로 고쳐야 한다.

11 조동사는 두 개를 연속해서 쓸 수 없으므로, 다른 조동사(might) 뒤에 있는 can을 be able to로 고쳐야 한다.

12 충고·의무(~해야 한다)를 나타내는 ought to를 쓴다.

13 '~하는 데 사용되다'라는 의미의 「be used to + 동사원형」을 쓴다.

14 '~했음이 틀림없다'라는 의미의 「must + have + p.p.」를 쓴다.

15 허가(~해도 된다)를 나타내는 can[could]나 may를 쓴다.

16 'B하느니 차라리 A하겠다'라는 의미의 「would rather A than B」를 쓴다.

17 요구를 나타내는 동사(require) 뒤 that절의 내용이 '~해야 한다'인 경우 동사 자리에 「(should) + 동사원형(store)」을 쓴다.

18 '~했을 리가 없다'라는 의미의 「can't + have + p.p.」를 쓴다.

19 제안을 나타내는 동사(recommend) 뒤 that절의 내용이 '~해야 한다'인 경우 동사 자리에 「(should) + 동사원형(learn)」을 쓴다.

20 ⓐ '나는 나의 부모님께 반려동물을 달라고 요청하곤 했다'라는 의미이므로 과거의 반복적인 습관을 나타내는 used to[would]를 써서 used to[would] ask로 고쳐야 한다.
ⓔ '나는 그 주제에 대한 책을 읽어야 한다'라는 의미이므로 의무를 나타내는 ought to[should]를 써서 ought to[should] read로 고쳐야 한다.

21 (A) 동사 cause의 목적격 보어 자리에는 to부정사(to die)가 온다.
(B) 조동사는 두 개를 연속해서 쓸 수 없으므로, 다른 조동사(must) 뒤에는 can 대신 be able to를 쓴다.
(C) '빨간 갓을 가진 버섯을 먹으면 안 된다'라는 의미이므로 강한 금지를 나타내는 must not을 쓴다.

22 ② '그 영업 부장은 판매원이 거래를 성사시킬 때마다 경적을 불곤 했다.'라는 의미이므로 과거의 반복적인 습관을 나타내는 used to[would]를 써서 used to[would] blow로 고쳐야 한다.

CHAPTER 4
수동태

POINT 1 능동태와 수동태
본책 p.42

1 The teacher was hurt
2 The champion was defeated

3 Many hikers are killed
4 A hair care product was invented
5 were discovered
6 appeared
7 was captured, spent
8 destroyed → was destroyed

POINT 2 다양한 형태의 수동태
본책 p.43

1 The suspect's voice is being recorded
2 Let the innocent people be released
3 Promising advances have been made
4 is being delivered
5 will be betrayed
6 should be included
7 have been documented
8 elect → be elected

POINT 3 4형식 문장의 수동태
본책 p.44

1 was cooked for the customers
2 were taught some English proverbs
were taught to us
3 was bought for my brother
4 were shown a sales performance
was shown to the team members
5 were asked of students
6 was offered billions of dollars
7 was made for his favorite actor

POINT 4 5형식 문장의 수동태
본책 p.45

1 The air was found scarce at the top of the mountain
2 The law is expected to benefit education in the country
3 A stranger was seen to enter[entering] a building sneakily
4 Citizens were persuaded to donate money for the poor
5 Rats are considered pests in much of Europe and North America
6 Some participants were made to think positively about themselves
7 An antelope was seen to run[running] through the trees
8 Chocolate is considered a tasty treat
9 going → to go

POINT 5 목적어가 that절인 문장의 수동태
본책 p.46

1 is said that wild animals ruined the agricultural land
2 are expected to undergo a counseling process after traumatic events

3 is known that big gifts are not necessarily the nicest ones

4 is considered to include unreliable information

5 is reported to have been the coldest day of the year

6 is supposed that the city will build

7 is reported to protect

8 is known that the company manipulated

9 is believed that Shakespeare didn't[did not] write

10 is estimated to have been

POINT 6 주의해야 할 수동태 본책 p.47

1 paid attention to
2 with
3 looked down on
4 composed
5 as
6 is interested in
7 was called off
8 was filled with
9 be caught up with

REVIEW TEST 본책 p.48

1 ③　　**2** ②　　**3** ④　　**4** ⑤　　**5** ④
6 ⑤　　**7** ③　　**8** ⑤
9 was disappeared → disappeared
10 leave → to leave[leaving]
11 preparing → prepared
12 Christmas carols are being played
13 We were told the truth about the rumor
　　The truth about the rumor was told to us
14 The sensitive issue was dealt with
15 is believed to have created the universe
16 The price of luxury items was raised
17 The food will be served
18 The seller was satisfied with
19 The landowner was given money by the real estate
20 is thought to have been a burial site
21 (1) ⓐ → is composed of　(2) ⓒ → might be proved
22 ⑤　　**23** ⑤

1 주어(Amy)가 행위(fire)의 대상이고 수동태는 「get + p.p.」의 형태로도 쓸 수 있으므로 fired를 쓴다.

2 your report가 행위(do)의 대상이고 명령문의 수동태는 「Let + 목적어 + be + p.p.」의 형태이므로 be done을 쓴다.

3 사역동사(make)가 쓰인 5형식 문장의 수동태에서 목적격 보어는 to부정사를 쓰므로 to cry를 쓴다.

4 주어(The reason for the old man's death)가 행위(believe)의 대상이므로 수동태 was believed를 쓴다.

5 ・직접 목적어가 주어인 수동태 문장에서 동사 teach는 간접 목적어 앞에 전치사 to를 쓴다.
　　・'~에 놀라다'라는 의미의 be surprised at을 쓴다.

6 ⑤ 상태를 나타내는 동사(resemble)는 수동태로 쓸 수 없으므로 is resembled를 능동태 resembles로 고쳐야 한다.

7 ③ 지각동사(hear)가 쓰인 5형식 문장의 수동태에서 목적격 보어는 to부정사나 V-ing형을 쓰므로 say를 to say[saying]으로 고쳐야 한다.

8 ⑤ 주어(The form)가 행위(fill)의 대상이고 조동사가 있는 수동태는 「조동사 + be + p.p.」의 형태이므로 fille을 filled로 고쳐야 한다.

9 목적어를 가지지 않는 동사(disappear)는 수동태로 쓸 수 없으므로 was disappeared를 능동태 disappeared로 고쳐야 한다.

10 지각동사(see)가 쓰인 5형식 문장의 수동태에서 목적격 보어는 to부정사나 V-ing형을 쓰므로 leave를 to leave[leaving]으로 고쳐야 한다.

11 주어(All the decorations in the living room)가 행위(prepare)의 대상이고 과거완료시제 수동태는 「had been + p.p.」의 형태이므로 preparing을 prepared로 고쳐야 한다.

12 진행시제 수동태는 「be동사 + being + p.p.」의 형태이다.

13 4형식 문장은 목적어가 두 개(us, the truth about the rumor)이므로 각 목적어를 주어로 하는 두 가지 형태의 수동태 문장을 만들 수 있다. 이때 직접 목적어가 주어인 수동태 문장에서 동사 tell은 간접 목적어 앞에 전치사 to를 쓴다.

14 구동사(deal with)를 수동태로 쓸 때, 동사만 「be동사 + p.p.」의 형태로 쓰고 나머지 부분은 그 뒤에 그대로 쓴다.

15 수동태 문장의 주어가 that절의 주어(The god Brahma)인 경우 that절의 시제(created)가 주절의 시제(believe)보다 앞서면 to부정사를 「to have + p.p.」의 형태로 쓴다.

16 주어(The price of luxury items)가 행위(raise)의 대상이므로 수동태 was raised를 쓴다.

17 미래시제 수동태는 「will be + p.p.」의 형태이다.

18 '~에 만족하다'라는 의미의 be satisfied with를 쓴다.

19 4형식 문장은 목적어가 두 개(the landowner, money)이므로 각 목적어를 주어로 하는 두 가지 형태의 수동태 문장을 만들 수 있다. 단, 9단어로 써야 하므로 간접 목적어(the landowner)를 주어로 쓴다.

20 수동태 문장의 주어가 that절의 주어인 경우 that절의 시제(was)가 주절의 시제(think)보다 앞서면 to부정사를 「to have + p.p.」의 형태로 쓴다.

21 ⓐ '~으로 구성되다'라는 의미의 be composed of를 써야 하므로 is composed of로 고쳐야 한다.
　　ⓒ 주어(This theory)가 행위(prove)의 대상이고 조동사(might)가 있으므로 might be proved로 고쳐야 한다.

22 (A) 주어(Our perception of food)가 행위(influence)의 대상이고 조동사(can)가 있으므로 be influenced를 쓴다.
　　(B) 주어(they)가 행위(give)의 대상이므로 수동태 were given을 쓴다.
　　(C) 주어(it)가 행위(color)의 대상이고 과거완료시제이므로 had been colored를 쓴다.

23 ⑤ 사역동사(make)가 쓰인 5형식 문장의 수동태에서 목적격 보어는 to부정사를 쓰므로 to get으로 고쳐야 한다.

CHAPTER 5
명사/관사/대명사

POINT 1 셀 수 있는 명사와 셀 수 없는 명사   본책 p.52

1 A lady	2 salt
3 are	4 air
5 owners	6 Canada, rivers
7 courage is	8 well-known historians were
9 committee is	10 police are

POINT 2 관사   본책 p.53

1 the	2 a
3 breakfast	4 the news
5 The	6 the
7 school	8 the universe
9 a	10 e-mail
11 O	12 the same place
13 The library	14 O

POINT 3 지시대명사   본책 p.54

1 That	2 that
3 Those	4 those
5 These	6 that of my shampoo
7 one of these flowers	
8 Those who need medical care	
9 that → those	

POINT 4 재귀대명사   본책 p.55

1 himself	2 mine
3 yourself	4 ourselves
5 her	6 myself
7 herself	8 him
9 themselves	10 yourself
11 them → themselves	

POINT 5 it의 다양한 쓰임   본책 p.56

1 ⓐ	2 ⓑ
3 ⓒ	4 ⓑ
5 ⓐ	6 ⓒ
7 The coach made it clear	
8 It has been three months	

9 It is important to help poor countries
10 It was dark
11 this → it

POINT 6 부정대명사: one, another, other   본책 p.57

1 ones	2 the others
3 it	4 the other
5 another	6 one
7 others	8 another → the other

POINT 7 부정대명사: all, each, none   본책 p.58

1 glass	2 are
3 was	4 was
5 None	6 Each ear helps
7 Every visitor is	8 Each of the answers is
9 None of the furniture has	
10 all of our brains contain	

POINT 8 부정대명사: both, either, neither   본책 p.59

1 sisters	2 has
3 recipe	4 want
5 Either	6 neither
7 Neither of the journalists apologized	
8 Either car is	
9 Both lakes were polluted	
10 neither is	

REVIEW TEST
본책 p.60

1 ⑤   2 ①   3 ③   4 ③   5 ②, ⑤
6 ①, ④   7 ④   8 same → the same
9 these → those   10 that → it
11 were → was   12 others → the others
13 Each of the components is critical
14 It was disappointing that neither athlete went
15 This convenience store, another store
16 her abilities rival those
17 I was proud of myself
18 Both pictures were taken by an unknown photographer
19 they express themselves
20 (1) ⓐ → information   (2) ⓑ → that
21 ⑤   22 ④

1 · 앞에서 언급된 복수명사(opinions)의 반복을 피하기 위해 those를 쓴다.

2 · 명사절(that ~ tonight)이 문장의 원래 주어이므로 주어 자리에 가주어 it을 쓴다.
· 날짜를 나타내는 비인칭 주어 it을 쓴다.

3 · '~마다(per)'를 나타내는 부정관사 an을 쓴다.
· only 앞에는 정관사 the를 쓴다.

4 · 앞에서 언급된 명사(fish)와 같은 종류의 불특정한 대상을 가리키고 있고, 빈칸 앞에 셀 수 있는 명사의 단수형 앞에 쓰는 부정관사 a가 있으므로 one을 쓴다.
· 「one ~, the other …」를 쓴다.

5 ② 셀 수 없는 명사는 복수형으로 쓸 수 없으므로 knowledge로 고쳐야 한다.
⑤ 동사(compare)의 목적어가 생략된 주어 You와 같은 대상이므로 재귀대명사 yourself[yourselves]로 고쳐야 한다.

6 ① 앞에서 언급된 특정한 단수명사(The computer)를 가리키고 있으므로 it으로 고쳐야 한다.
④ 「either of + 복수명사」의 형태로 쓰므로 teams로 고쳐야 한다.

7 ⓐ 「both (of) + 복수명사」는 복수 취급하므로 was를 were로 고쳐야 한다.
ⓒ every는 「every + 단수명사」의 형태로만 쓰고 단수 취급하므로 rooms are를 room is로 고쳐야 한다.

8 same 앞에는 정관사 the를 쓰므로 same을 the same으로 고쳐야 한다.

9 these를 '~한 사람들'이라는 의미의 those로 고쳐야 한다.

10 to부정사구(to put ~ words)가 동사(consider)의 원래 목적어이므로, 목적어 자리에 있는 that을 가목적어 it으로 고쳐야 한다.

11 none은 '셀 수 없는 명사(evidence)와 함께 쓸 때는 단수 취급하므로 were를 was로 고쳐야 한다.

12 「one ~, the others …」를 써야 하므로 others를 the others로 고쳐야 한다.

13 each는 '각각(의)'이라는 의미로 단수 취급하고, 「each of + 복수명사」의 형태로도 쓴다.

14 문장의 주어 자리에 명사절(that ~ final)이 와서 길어질 때는 주로 해당 자리에 가주어 it을 쓰고 원래 주어를 뒤로 보낸다.

15 첫 번째 빈칸에는 가까이 있는 단수명사(convenience store)를 가리키는 this를 쓰고, 두 번째 빈칸에는 '또 다른'이라는 의미의 another를 쓴다.

16 앞에서 언급된 복수명사(abilities)의 반복을 피하기 위해 those를 쓴다.

17 전치사(of)의 목적어가 주어(I)와 같은 대상이므로 재귀대명사 myself를 쓴다.

18 both는 '둘 다 (모두)'라는 의미로 복수 취급하고, 「both (of) + 복수명사」의 형태로도 쓴다. 단, 8단어로 써야 하므로 Both pictures로 쓴다.

19 동사(express)의 목적어가 주어(they)와 같은 대상이므로 재귀대명사

themselves를 쓴다.

20 ⓐ 셀 수 없는 명사는 명사 앞에 a(n)을 붙일 수 없으므로 information으로 고쳐야 한다.
ⓑ 앞에서 언급된 단수명사구(the collection ~ people)의 반복을 피하기 위해 쓰였으므로 that으로 고쳐야 한다.

21 (A) 명사절(that ~ well)이 문장의 원래 주어이므로 주어 자리에 가주어 it을 쓴다.
(B) 동사(ask)의 목적어가 생략된 주어 you와 같은 대상이므로 재귀대명사 yourself를 쓴다.
(C) '또 다른 이웃에게 당신이 그 문제를 해결하도록 돕는 것을 요청하는 것'이라는 의미이므로 '또 다른'이라는 의미의 another를 쓴다.

22 ④ to부정사구(to use the machine)가 동사(make)의 원래 목적어이므로, 목적어 자리에 있는 that을 가목적어 it으로 고쳐야 한다.

CHAPTER 6
형용사와 부사

POINT 1 형용사의 용법

1	moist	**2**	Someone brave
3	unfair	**4**	sleeping
5	competitive	**6**	frightened
7	brutal, extensive	**8**	O
9	accurate	**10**	important
11	O	**12**	bad
13	unreasonable	**14**	O
15	harmfully → harmful		

POINT 2 수량형용사
본책 p.65

1	much	**2**	few
3	plenty of	**4**	A little
5	some	**6**	many
7	any	**8**	some paint
9	little evidence	**10**	a few fierce hunting dogs
11	lots of women		

POINT 3 부사의 역할
본책 p.66

1	endlessly	**2**	late
3	severely	**4**	costly
5	Unfortunately	**6**	highly, simple
7	cautiously	**8**	O
9	O	**10**	hard

Chapter 6 형용사와 부사　**9**

11 absolutely   **12** closely

13 extreme → extremely

POINT 4   주의해야 할 부사의 위치   본책 p.67

1   seldom eat

2   soft enough

3   turn off the lights / turn the lights off

4   is usually

5   can hardly

6   picked it up

7   wake up her son / wake him up

8   you never use it

9   Watching a comedy cheers me up

10 Chad didn't sleep long enough

11 Irene will sometimes stop

12 The student wrote down the answers[The student wrote the answers down]

REVIEW TEST   본책 p.68

1 ⑤   **2** ③   **3** ④   **4** ①   **5** ①, ④

6 ②, ③ **7** ②, ⑤

8 frequent → frequently

9 positively → positive

10 ashamedly → ashamed

11 healthily → healthy

12 Ms. Miller turned it down

13 The dog is smart enough

14 The documentary made me aware

15 highly respected British writers

16 Her movie usually contains meaningful lessons

17 Obviously, children shouldn't eat too much junk food

18 will make you warm

19 (1) ⓒ → a few   (2) ⓓ → immediately

20 ③   **21** ③

1 · -one으로 끝나는 대명사는 형용사를 뒤에 쓰므로 Anyone scared 를 쓴다.

   · 부사로 쓰인 enough는 형용사를 뒤에서 수식하므로 rich enough 를 쓴다.

2 · 보어 자리에서 주어(The muffins)를 보충 설명하고 있으므로 형용 사 wonderful을 쓴다.

   · 동사(is increasing)를 수식하고 있으므로 부사 rapidly를 쓴다.

3 · 보어 자리에서 목적어(the babies)를 보충 설명하고 있으므로 형용 사 nervous를 쓴다.

   · people은 셀 수 있는 명사이므로 Few를 쓴다.

4 · '한 소행성이 우리 행성에 거의 부딪칠 뻔했다'라는 의미이므로 '거 의'라는 의미의 부사 nearly를 쓴다.

· 빈도부사는 조동사의 뒤에 위치하므로 will rarely를 쓴다.

5 ② 부정문이므로 any로 고쳐야 한다.

   ③ day는 셀 수 있는 명사이므로 a few로 고쳐야 한다.

   ⑤ information은 셀 수 없는 명사이므로 a little로 고쳐야 한다.

6 ① 보어 자리에서 주어(The national economy)를 보충 설명하고 있 으므로 형용사 stable로 고쳐야 한다.

   ④ 보어 자리에서 목적어(himself)를 보충 설명하고 있으므로 형용사 busy로 고쳐야 한다.

   ⑤ -thing으로 끝나는 대명사는 형용사를 뒤에 쓰므로 something important로 고쳐야 한다.

7 ① '그 매는 높이 날았다'라는 의미이므로 '높이, 높게'라는 의미의 부사 high로 고쳐야 한다. highly는 '매우, 대단히'라는 의미의 부사이다.

   ③ 동사(fell)를 수식하고 있으므로 부사 heavily로 고쳐야 한다.

   ④ 빈도부사는 be동사의 뒤에 위치하므로 is never로 고쳐야 한다.

8 동사(confuse)를 수식하고 있으므로 형용사 frequent를 부사 frequently로 고쳐야 한다.

9 명사(impact)를 수식하고 있으므로 부사 positively를 형용사 positive로 고쳐야 한다.

10 보어 자리에서 주어(Cameron)를 보충 설명하고 있으므로 부사 ashamedly를 형용사 ashamed로 고쳐야 한다.

11 보어 자리에서 목적어(your body)를 보충 설명하고 있으므로 부사 healthily를 형용사 healthy로 고쳐야 한다.

12 「타동사 + 부사」의 목적어가 대명사인 경우 「타동사 + 대명사 + 부사」 의 형태로 쓰므로 turned it down을 쓴다.

13 부사로 쓰인 enough는 형용사를 뒤에서 수식하므로 smart enough 를 쓴다.

14 형용사는 보어로 쓰여 목적어를 보충 설명하므로 made me aware를 쓴다.

15 '매우, 대단히'라는 의미의 부사 highly를 쓴다.

16 빈도부사는 일반동사의 앞에 위치하므로 usually contains를 쓴다.

17 부사는 문장 전체를 수식하므로 Obviously를 쓴다. junk food는 셀 수 없는 명사이고 8단어로 써야 하므로 '많은'이라는 의미의 much를 쓴다.

18 형용사는 보어로 쓰여 목적어를 보충 설명하므로 will make you warm을 쓴다.

19 ⓒ time이 '~ 번'이라는 의미의 셀 수 있는 명사로 쓰였으므로 a few로 고쳐야 한다.

   ⓓ 동사(can come)를 수식하고 있으므로 부사 immediately로 고쳐 야 한다.

20 (A) '보는 사람들에게 이미지를 이해하기 위해 열심히 노력할 것을 요청 하지 않는다'라는 의미이므로 '열심히'라는 의미의 부사 hard를 쓴 다. hardly는 '거의 ~않다'라는 의미의 부사이다.

   (B) 주어 it(화법의 새로운 방식)이 행위(make)의 대상이므로 수동태 was made를 쓴다.

   (C) 보어 자리에서 주어(these subjects)를 보충 설명하고 있으므로

형용사 appropriate을 쓴다.

21 ③ 보어 자리에서 주어(the girl)를 보충 설명하고 있으므로 형용사 cheerful로 고쳐야 한다.

CHAPTER 7
전치사

POINT 1 시간을 나타내는 전치사: at, on, in 본책 p.72

1 on	**2** in
3 at	**4** in
5 at	**6** in
7 in	**8** on
9 on	**10** on
11 in the morning	**12** on Christmas Eve
13 this Wednesday	**14** on Tuesdays

POINT 2 시간을 나타내는 기타 전치사 본책 p.73

1 from	**2** until
3 since	**4** by
5 During	**6** for
7 before the deadline	**8** until tomorrow
9 during the later years	**10** since middle school
11 after the game	

POINT 3 장소/위치를 나타내는 전치사 본책 p.74

1 below	**2** at
3 behind	**4** in
5 between	**6** next to
7 under	**8** in front of
9 among	

POINT 4 방향을 나타내는 전치사 본책 p.75

1 around	**2** for
3 along	**4** into
5 from	**6** across
7 to	**8** out of
9 toward	

POINT 5 기타 전치사 I 본책 p.76

1 by ferry	**2** without crews
3 for baking lessons	**4** with a mop
5 due to contamination	

POINT 6 기타 전치사 II 본책 p.77

1 with	**2** according to
3 about	**4** for
5 instead of	**6** except
7 on	**8** as
9 in spite of	**10** despite
11 of	**12** against
13 like	**14** such as

REVIEW TEST 본책 p.78

1 ③ **2** ④ **3** ⑤ **4** ① **5** ④
6 ③ **7** ⑤ **8** by → until **9** in → by
10 She stopped taking the medication because of the side effects
11 Instead of cutting other expenses
12 You can't focus on your exam without enough sleep
13 Despite[In spite of] his struggles, the old truck didn't[did not] work
14 Every classmate came to my birthday party except you
15 There is a dumpster behind the restaurant
16 They drove across the country during their road trip
17 I finished the practice by noon in spite of some pain
18 allows them to conserve energy for survival
19 ③ **20** ② **21** ④

1 · 표면(rocks)에 접촉한 상태를 나타낼 때는 전치사 on을 쓴다.
　 · 특정한 날의 오후(Friday afternoon)를 나타낼 때는 전치사 on을 쓴다.

2 · 어떤 행동이나 상황이 특정 시점(7 o'clock)까지 완료되는 것을 나타낼 때는 전치사 by를 쓴다.
　 · '~(교통수단)으로'라는 의미의 전치사 by를 쓴다.

3 · '~을 위해'라는 의미의 전치사 for를 쓴다.
　 · 빈칸 뒤에 숫자를 포함한 기간 표현(over four decades)이 있으므로 '~ 동안'이라는 의미의 전치사 for를 쓴다.

4 · 어떤 행동이나 상황이 특정 시점(next Thursday)까지 완료되는 것을 나타낼 때는 전치사 by를 쓴다.
　 · 빈칸 뒤에 특정 기간을 나타내는 명사(my stay)가 있으므로 '~ 동안'이라는 의미의 전치사 during을 쓴다.

5 · '~ (셋 이상) 사이에'라는 의미의 전치사 among을 쓴다.

・ 주로 완료시제와 함께 쓰여 어떤 행동이나 상황이 특정 시점(2009) 부터 계속되는 것을 나타낼 때는 전치사 since를 쓴다.

6 ① 시점(midnight)을 나타낼 때는 전치사 at을 쓴다.
② 비교적 좁은 장소나 하나의 지점(home)을 나타낼 때는 전치사 at을 쓴다.
③ 저녁(the evening)을 나타낼 때는 전치사 in을 쓴다.
④ 감정(surprised)의 원인(his team's enthusiasm and desire to win)을 나타낼 때는 '~에'라는 의미의 전치사 at을 쓴다.
⑤ 비교적 좁은 장소나 하나의 지점(the bus stop)을 나타낼 때는 전치사 at을 쓴다.

7 ① 세기(the 19th century)를 나타낼 때는 전치사 in을 쓴다.
② 비교적 넓은 장소(Berlin)를 나타낼 때는 전치사 in을 쓴다.
③ '~(언어)로'라는 의미의 전치사 in을 쓴다.
④ 비교적 넓은 장소(the universe)를 나타낼 때는 전치사 in을 쓴다.
⑤ 표면(the Moon)에 접촉한 상태를 나타낼 때는 전치사 on을 쓴다.

8 몇몇 나무들은 겨울 동안 휴면기이고 봄까지 다시 활동하지 않는다는 내용이므로, by를 어떤 행동이나 상황이 특정 시점(spring)까지 계속되는 것을 나타내는 전치사 until로 고쳐야 한다.

9 in을 '~(통신수단)으로'라는 의미의 전치사 by로 고쳐야 한다.

10 '~ 때문에'라는 의미의 전치사 because of를 쓴다.

11 '~ 대신'이라는 의미의 전치사 instead of를 쓴다.

12 '~ 없이'라는 의미의 전치사 without을 쓴다.

13 '~에도 불구하고'라는 의미의 전치사 despite[in spite of]를 쓴다.

14 '~에'라는 의미의 전치사 to와 '~을 제외하고'라는 의미의 전치사 except를 쓴다.

15 '~ 뒤에'라는 의미의 전치사 behind를 쓴다.

16 '~을 가로질러'라는 의미의 전치사 across를 쓴다. their road trip 은 특정 기간을 나타내는 명사이므로 '~ 동안'이라는 의미의 전치사 during을 쓴다.

17 어떤 행동이나 상황이 특정 시점(noon)까지 완료되는 것을 나타내는 전치사 by를 쓴다. 11단어로 써야 하므로 '~에도 불구하고'라는 의미의 전치사 in spite of를 쓴다.

18 동사 allow의 목적격 보어 자리에는 to부정사(to conserve)가 온다. '~을 위해'라는 의미의 전치사 for를 쓴다.

19 (A) '~ 때문에'라는 의미의 전치사 because of를 쓴다.
(B) '~(보다) 아래에'라는 의미의 전치사 below를 쓴다.
(C) '~처럼, 같이'라는 의미의 전치사 like를 쓴다.

20 (A) '~ 앞에'라는 의미의 전치사 in front of를 쓴다.
(B) dinner는 특정 기간을 나타내는 명사이므로 '~ 동안'이라는 의미의 전치사 during을 쓴다.
(C) 주어(her prayers)가 행위(answer)의 대상이므로 수동태 were answered를 쓴다.

21 ④ 최소한의 특징을 가진 고정 기어 자전거들은 추가되는 복잡성에 대한 비용 없이 단 하나의 일을 정말 잘 수행한다는 내용이므로 '~ 없이'라는 의미의 전치사 without으로 고쳐야 한다.

CHAPTER 8
부정사

POINT 1 명사적 용법 본책 p.82

1 to create **2** to pay
3 to judge **4** to post
5 to gather information **6** when to invest money
7 wise not to open **8** supply → to supply

POINT 2 형용사적 용법 본책 p.83

1 to read **2** not to access
3 to put on **4** to become
5 time to help **6** The games are to start
7 You are to arrive
8 Beautiful paintings are to be found
9 a chance to learn
10 friends to play with
11 It is necessary to pay, you are to avoid

POINT 3 부사적 용법 본책 p.84

1 우리는 당신을 우리의 연례 행사에 초대해서 기쁘다
2 그녀의 연설을 듣는다면, 너는 그녀에 의해 설득될 것이다
3 저 오래된 건물은 살기에 불안정해 보인다
4 몇몇 동물들은 그들 자신을 보호하기 위해 유용한 무기들을 개발했다
5 to say hurtful things
6 was surprised to win
7 is difficult to achieve
8 to become a famous musician
9 (in order[so as]) to express your ideas
10 To watch the sunrise

POINT 4 to부정사의 의미상 주어 본책 p.85

1 for me **2** of him
3 us **4** of her
5 for them **6** for plants to grow
7 to drive **8** the athlete to break
9 of the thief to confess **10** Mr. Williams to pay
11 to use
12 for some students to study
13 of the entrepreneur to launch

POINT 5 to부정사의 시제와 태
본책 p.86

1 be discouraged
2 have been infected
3 find
4 have encountered
5 to be remembered
6 to have exploited
7 to have been domesticated
8 to be repaired
9 to communicate
10 to be disturbed
11 to have ended

POINT 6 부정사를 목적격 보어로 쓰는 동사
본책 p.87

1 to touch
2 pay
3 play
4 to come
5 demonstrating
6 noticed the traffic light change[changing]
7 helps students (to) activate
8 asked the participants to divide
9 to realize → realize

POINT 7 to부정사 구문
본책 p.88

1 is strong enough to carry
2 took the man several weeks to recover
3 is so small that it can't[cannot] accommodate
4 was so various that it could satisfy
5 took firefighters two days to extinguish
6 performed well enough to move
7 was too poor to buy

POINT 8 독립부정사
본책 p.89

1 To tell (you) the truth
2 To make a long story short
3 so to speak
4 Strange to say
5 Needless to say
6 to say nothing of
7 To be frank (with you)
8 To begin[start] with
9 To make matters worse
10 To be sure

REVIEW TEST
본책 p.90

1 ③　2 ⑤　3 ②　4 ②　5 ④
6 ①　7 ⑤　8 avoid → to avoid
9 help → to help　10 saying → to say
11 was too shy to ask
12 seems to have been persuaded
13 was infectious enough to spread
14 The sailors were watching the shark come to the boat
15 It will take him at least an hour to decide what to eat
16 So to speak, inflation made living expenses increase
17 isn't[is not] desirable for adults to ignore
18 the decline in stock price seems to have been caused
19 it was too dark to find the cell phone
20 (1) ⓐ → ring[ringing]　(2) ⓒ → for me
21 ④　22 ③

1　동사 want는 to부정사를 목적격 보어로 쓰고, 목적어(you)가 행위(meet)의 주체이므로 「to + 동사원형」을 쓴다.

2　to부정사의 목적의 의미를 강조하기 위해 to 대신 so as to를 쓸 수 있고, 주어(You)가 행위(accept)의 대상이므로 「to be + p.p.」를 쓴다.

3　첫 번째 빈칸: 의미상 주어가 사람의 성격이나 성질을 나타내는 형용사(mature) 뒤에 쓰일 때는 「of + 목적격」의 형태로 쓴다.
　두 번째 빈칸: to부정사(구)가 주어로 쓰일 때는 주로 해당 자리에 가주어 it을 쓰고 to부정사(구)를 뒤로 보내므로 to를 쓴다.

4　② '~할, ~하는'의 의미로 명사(the opportunity)를 수식하는 형용사적 용법이다.
　①③④⑤ 판단의 근거, 감정의 원인, 목적, 조건을 나타내는 부사적 용법이다.

5　④ '~할, ~하는'의 의미로 명사(the capacity)를 수식하는 형용사적 용법이다.
　①②③⑤ 문장 안에서 목적어, 주어, 보어로 쓰이는 명사적 용법이다.

6　① 사역동사(have)는 원형부정사를 목적격 보어로 쓰므로 wrap으로 고쳐야 한다.

7　⑤ 동사(told)의 직접 목적어이므로 명사처럼 쓰이는 「의문사 + to부정사」 형태의 to leave로 고쳐야 한다.

8　to부정사의 목적의 의미를 강조하기 위해 to 대신 in order to를 쓸 수 있으므로 avoid를 to avoid로 고쳐야 한다.

9　준사역동사 get은 목적격 보어로 to부정사를 쓰므로 help를 to help로 고쳐야 한다.

10　'말할 필요도 없이'라는 의미의 독립부정사 needless to say를 써야 하므로 saying을 to say로 고쳐야 한다.

11　「so + 형용사/부사 + that + 주어 + can't + 동사원형」은 「too + 형용사/부사 + to부정사」로 바꿔 쓸 수 있다.

12　was persuaded가 수동태이고 주절의 시제(seems)보다 앞서므로 완료형 「to have been + p.p.」를 쓴다.

13 「so + 형용사/부사 + that + 주어 + can + 동사원형」은 「형용사/부사 + enough + to부정사」로 바꿔 쓸 수 있다.

14 지각동사(watch)는 원형부정사(come)나 V-ing형을 목적격 보어로 쓴다.

15 '…가 ~하는 데 (시간)이 걸리다'라는 의미의 「It takes + 목적어 + 시간 + to부정사」를 쓴다. 「의문사 + to부정사」가 동사(decide)의 목적어로 쓰였다.

16 '말하자면'이라는 의미의 독립부정사 so to speak을 쓴다. 사역동사(make)는 원형부정사(increase)를 목적격 보어로 쓴다.

17 to부정사(구)가 주어로 쓰일 때는 주로 해당 자리에 가주어 it을 쓰고 to부정사(구)(to ignore ~ opinions)를 뒤로 보낸다. to부정사가 나타내는 행위의 주체(adults)가 문장의 주어와 다르므로 의미상 주어 「for + 목적격」을 to부정사 앞에 쓴다.

18 주어(the decline in stock price)가 행위(cause)의 대상이고 주가의 하락이 야기됐던 것은 주절의 시제(seems)보다 앞서므로 완료형 「to have been + p.p.」를 쓴다.

19 '~하기에 너무 …한/하게'라는 의미의 「too + 형용사/부사 + to부정사」를 쓴다. it은 명암을 나타내는 비인칭 주어이다.

20 ⓐ 지각동사(hear)는 원형부정사나 V-ing형을 목적격 보어로 쓰므로 ring[ringing]으로 고쳐야 한다.
ⓒ to부정사가 나타내는 행위의 주체(me)가 문장의 주어(to forget ~ phone)와 다르므로 의미상 주어 「for + 목적격」 형태인 for me로 고쳐야 한다.

21 (A) 동사 ask는 to부정사(to act)를 목적격 보어로 쓴다.
(B) 주어(most of us)가 행위(know)의 주체이므로 능동태 know를 쓴다.
(C) 동사(know)를 수식하고 있으므로 부사 unconsciously를 쓴다.

22 ③ 사역동사(make)는 원형부정사를 목적격 보어로 쓰므로 cling으로 고쳐야 한다.

CHAPTER 9
동명사

POINT 1 동명사의 형태와 쓰임 본책 p.94

1 ⓓ **2** ⓒ
3 ⓑ **4** ⓐ
5 ⓒ
6 reducing the unemployment rate
7 Not arriving at the meeting on time was
8 reading books
9 achieving greater rewards
10 are → is

POINT 2 동명사의 의미상 주어 본책 p.95

1 you(r) inviting us to Korea
2 Luke('s) planning for the group project
3 my[me] coming home late
4 our[us] sitting at the same desk each class
5 firefighters(') sacrificing themselves to rescue people
6 don't[do not] like her pretending
7 was startled at a wolf('s) howling
8 were impressed by his[him] juggling
9 is tired of her husband('s) spending

POINT 3 동명사의 시제와 태 본책 p.96

1 being promoted **2** falling
3 having lost **4** having been awarded
5 being told **6** developing
7 having failed **8** having created
9 being determined **10** having been charged

POINT 4 동명사와 to부정사를 목적어로 쓰는 동사 Ⅰ 본책 p.97

1 to understand **2** putting
3 to make **4** visiting
5 accepting **6** refused to reveal
7 delayed moving **8** hopes to travel
9 gave up collecting **10** taking → to take

POINT 5 동명사와 to부정사를 목적어로 쓰는 동사 Ⅱ 본책 p.98

1 talking **2** fixing
3 growing **4** forgot to charge
5 will continue rising[to rise] **6** tried to be
7 to think → thinking

POINT 6 동명사 관용 표현 본책 p.99

1 was looking forward to going
2 are busy rehearsing
3 It is no use complaining
4 made a point of eating
5 kept[prevented] me from sleeping
6 is worth reading
7 spends most of his time writing
8 have difficulty[trouble] breathing
9 By increasing

10 On[Upon] learning

REVIEW TEST

본책 p.100

1 ④	**2** ②	**3** ②	**4** ⑤	**5** ④		

6 ③ **7** ② **8** persuade → persuading

9 staying → to stay

10 punishing → being punished

11 Mr. Brown('s) winning

12 having noticed

13 There is no solving the traffic problems

14 I do not mind you parking your car

15 kept calling his assistant

16 continue destroying[to destroy] natural habitats

17 was worried about not being treated

18 Controlling children's behaviors is difficult

19 By not turning off lights[By not turning lights off]

20 ③ **21** ④ **22** ④

1 '~한 것을 후회하다'라는 의미이므로 동사 regret 뒤에 동명사 yelling 을 쓴다.

2 동사 desire는 to부정사를 목적어로 쓰고 주어(The mayor)가 행위 (build)의 주체이므로 to build를 쓴다.

3 동명사는 전치사(of)의 목적어로 쓰이고, 주어(We)가 행위(form)의 주 체이므로 forming을 쓴다.

4 ⑤ 동사 need는 to부정사를 목적어로 쓰므로 evacuating을 to evacuate으로 고쳐야 한다.

5 ④ 주어로 쓰인 동명사구(Wearing seatbelts)는 항상 단수 취급하므 로 are를 is로 고쳐야 한다.

6 ③ 동사 quit은 동명사를 목적어로 쓰므로 to drink를 drinking으로 고 쳐야 한다.

7 ⓒ '(미래에) ~할 것을 잊다'라는 의미이므로 동사 forget 뒤의 동명사 bringing을 to부정사 to bring으로 고쳐야 한다.

　ⓓ '~하는 것에 관한 한'이라는 의미의 「when it comes to + V-ing」 가 쓰였으므로 bake를 baking으로 고쳐야 한다.

8 '~해도 소용없다'라는 의미의 「It is no use + V-ing」가 쓰였으므로 persuade를 persuading으로 고쳐야 한다.

9 동사 choose는 to부정사를 목적어로 쓰므로 staying을 to stay로 고 쳐야 한다.

10 주어(I)가 행위(punish)의 대상이고 처벌받는 것이 주절의 시제(was) 이후이므로 punishing을 「being + p.p.」 형태의 being punished 로 고쳐야 한다.

11 행위(win)의 주체(Mr. Brown)가 문장의 주어(The ruling party)와 다 르므로 소유격이나 목적격 형태의 의미상 주어 Mr. Brown('s)를 동명 사(winning) 앞에 쓴다.

12 had noticed가 주절의 시제(denied)보다 앞서므로 완료형 「having

+ p.p.」를 쓴다.

13 '~할 수 없다'라는 의미의 「There is no + V-ing」를 쓴다.

14 동사 mind는 동명사(parking)를 목적어로 쓴다. 목적격 형태의 의미상 주어(you)를 동명사 앞에 쓴다.

15 동사 keep은 동명사(calling)를 목적어로 쓴다.

16 동사 continue는 목적어로 동명사(destroying)를 쓸 때와 to부정사 (to destroy)를 쓸 때의 의미가 같다.

17 동명사는 전치사(about)의 목적어로 쓰인다. 주어(The student)가 행위(treat)의 대상이고 공정하게 대우받지 못하는 것이 주절의 시제 (was)와 같거나 그 이후이므로 「being + p.p.」를 쓴다. 동명사의 부 정형은 「not[never] + V-ing」이다.

18 주어로 쓰인 동명사구(Controlling children's behaviors)는 항상 단 수 취급하므로 is를 쓴다.

19 '~함으로써, ~해서'라는 의미의 「by + V-ing」를 쓴다. 동명사의 부정 형은 「not[never] + V-ing」이다.

20 (A) 목적의 의미를 나타내는 to부정사(to reduce)를 쓴다.
　(B) 주어로 쓰인 동명사구(being ~ sacrifices)는 항상 단수 취급하므 로 is를 쓴다.
　(C) 동사 avoid는 동명사(wasting)를 목적어로 쓴다.

21 (A) '~하는 데 어려움이 있다'라는 의미의 「have difficulty + V-ing」 가 쓰였으므로 giving을 쓴다.
　(B) '~할, ~하는'의 의미로 명사(a chance)를 수식하는 to부정사(to study)를 쓴다.
　(C) 주어(they)가 행위(ask)의 대상이므로 「being + p.p.」를 쓴다.

22 ④ 처음에 세탁기가 많은 소음을 냈고 나중에는 완전히 작동하는 것을 멈췄다는 내용이므로 동명사 operating으로 고쳐야 한다.

CHAPTER 10
분사

POINT 1 분사의 형태와 쓰임

본책 p.104

1 ⓑ		**2** ⓑ	
3 ⓐ		**4** ⓐ	
5 ⓑ		**6** ⓐ	

7 Everyone searching for a job

8 seemed disappointed at my report card

9 heard his name called by a bank teller

10 amazing talents of the chefs

11 language used in social media

12 keep the windows closed

13 shoppers buying Christmas gifts

POINT 2 현재분사와 과거분사 본책 p.105

1 involved	**2** encouraging
3 excited	**4** interesting
5 crawling	**6** was touching
7 accumulated result	**8** satisfying response
9 his car repaired	**10** are terrified
11 finding → found	

POINT 3 분사구문 만드는 법 본책 p.106

1 Feeling pain in my stomach
2 Trying to do too much at once
3 Cleaning her room
4 Retiring in 1952
5 Not[Never] understanding the instructions

6 Since being busy	**7** Greeting the guests
8 After changing his mind	**9** Not wearing glasses

10 Working as an editor

POINT 4 분사구문의 다양한 의미 본책 p.107

1 If	**2** As
3 and	**4** While

5 Although he was short
6 Since we arrived at the theater late
7 If you visit other countries
8 As soon as I heard a familiar voice behind me

POINT 5 분사구문의 시제와 태 본책 p.108

1 Having witnessed the car crash firsthand
2 (Being) Known to the public
3 Having heard the judge's solution
4 Baking a cake
5 (Being) Hurt by the economic recession
6 (Having been) Stored in the refrigerator
7 (Being) Used together with a pain reliever
8 knowing → being known

POINT 6 주의해야 할 분사구문 본책 p.109

1 The dress fitting nicely
2 His business succeeding
3 There being more work to complete
4 with tears running
5 with his head bandaged
6 Generally speaking

REVIEW TEST 본책 p.110

1 ④ **2** ③ **3** ⑤ **4** ② **5** ⑤
6 ③ **7** ④ **8** stealing → stolen
9 annoyed → annoying
10 (Having been) Hurt seriously
11 The shuttle bus arriving
12 thinking that Mom had hidden my new phone inside it
13 Many people use plastic products made from crude oil
14 Not wanting to upset him
15 This island remains isolated
16 with her baby crying
17 Having been exposed to the radiation
18 Inspired by the gravity railroads used in coal mines
19 (1) ⓐ → enjoyed (2) ⓔ → generating
20 ② **21** ④

1 목적어 air purifiers를 보충 설명하고 목적어와의 관계가 수동이므로 과거분사 installed를 쓴다.

2 Learning a foreign language는 감정을 일으키는 주체이므로 현재 분사 interesting을 쓴다.

3 주어(Julian)가 행위(betray)의 대상이고 그의 가장 친한 친구에 의해 배신당한 것이 주절의 시제(got)보다 앞서므로 완료형 「having been + p.p.」를 쓴다.

4 부사절과 주절의 주어가 같으므로 부사절의 접속사 While과 주어 she 를 생략하고 동사 read를 Reading으로 바꾼다.

5 분사구문에 완료형 「having + p.p.」가 쓰였으므로 주절의 시제 (became)보다 앞선 had waited를 쓴다.

6 ③ 명사 animals를 수식하고 명사와의 관계가 수동이므로 현재분사 endangering을 과거분사 endangered로 고쳐야 한다.

7 ④ 주어(they)가 행위(give)의 대상이므로, 앞에 Being이나 Having been을 생략하고 현재분사 Giving을 과거분사 Given으로 고쳐야 한다.

8 목적어 his wallet을 보충 설명하고 목적어와의 관계가 수동이므로 현재분사 stealing을 과거분사 stolen으로 고쳐야 한다.

9 The constant barking이 감정을 일으키는 주체이므로 과거분사 annoyed를 현재분사 annoying으로 고쳐야 한다.

10 부사절과 주절의 주어가 같으므로 부사절의 접속사 Since와 주어 she 를 생략하고, 부사절에 있는 수동태의 시제(had been hurt)가 주절의 시제(spent)보다 앞서므로 완료형 「having been + p.p.」를 쓴다. 이 때 having been은 생략할 수 있다.

11 부사절의 주어(the shuttle bus)와 주절의 주어(he)가 다르면 부사절 의 주어를 생략하지 않으므로 접속사 As만 생략하고 동사 arrived를 arriving으로 바꾼다.

12 부사절과 주절의 주어가 같으므로 부사절의 접속사 because와 주어 I 를 생략하고 동사 thought을 thinking으로 바꾼다.

13 분사가 명사를 수식할 때 구(made from crude oil)를 이루어 쓰이면 명사(plastic products) 뒤에 온다.

14 분사구문의 부정형은 「not[never] + 분사」이다.

15 주어 This island를 보충 설명하고 주어와의 관계가 수동이므로 과거분사 isolated를 쓴다.

16 '···이 ···한 채로/하면서'라는 의미의 「with + 명사 + 분사」에서 명사 her baby와 분사의 관계가 능동이므로 현재분사 crying을 쓴다.

17 주어(those vegetables)가 행위(expose)의 대상이고 방사능에 노출된 것이 주절의 시제(have)보다 앞서므로 완료형 「having been + p.p.」를 쓴다.

18 주어(Thompson)가 행위(inspire)의 대상이고 9단어로 써야 하므로 앞에 Being이나 Having been을 생략하고 과거분사 Inspired를 쓴다. 분사가 명사를 수식할 때 구(used in coal mines)를 이루어 쓰이면 명사(the gravity railroads) 뒤에 온다.

19 ⓐ 명사 the exciting rides를 수식하고 명사와의 관계가 수동이므로 과거분사 enjoyed로 고쳐야 한다.
ⓔ 주어 it(코니아일랜드에 있는 롤러코스터)이 행위(generate)의 주체이므로 현재분사 generating으로 고쳐야 한다

20 (A) 주어 it(비언어적인 의사소통)이 행위(serve)의 주체이므로 현재분사 serving을 쓴다.
(B) 준사역동사 help의 목적격 보어 자리에는 to부정사와 원형부정사(get)가 모두 올 수 있다.
(C) 「with + 명사 + 분사」에서 명사 your eyebrows와 분사의 관계가 수동이므로 과거분사 raised를 쓴다.

21 ④ He가 감정을 느끼는 대상이므로 과거분사 frightened로 고쳐야 한다.

CHAPTER 11
관계사

POINT 1 관계대명사의 역할과 종류
본책 p.114

1 ⓑ		**2** ⓑ	
3 ⓒ		**4** ⓐ	
5 ⓒ		**6** ⓐ	
7 which		**8** who	
9 whose		**10** who(m)	
11 whose		**12** which	

POINT 2 주격 관계대명사
본책 p.115

1 the one who came up with the idea
2 the astronauts who walked on the moon
3 a nice house which overlooked the whole city
4 a treatment which was effective for the patient
5 the thief who stole some jewelry
6 the film which was praised by both critics and audiences
7 which　　　　　**8** advertise
9 O　　　　　　**10** O
11 run → runs

POINT 3 목적격 관계대명사
본책 p.116

1 which I installed yesterday
2 who(m) Anna likes
3 which I dropped on the floor
4 which I watched every Friday night
5 who(m) I met at a conference many years ago
6 which scientists sometimes can't explain
7 who(m) we hired for the event
8 O　　　　　　**9** X
10 O　　　　　**11** O
12 X　　　　　**13** O

POINT 4 소유격 관계대명사
본책 p.117

1 whose drawing was the best
2 whose jobs include protecting the animals
3 whose grades were low
4 whose hearts have stopped beating
5 people whose houses were destroyed
6 a book the cover of which was blue[a book of which the cover was blue]
7 the person whose face is
8 a superhero whose superpower is teleportation
9 trees branches of which were covered[trees of which branches were covered]
10 a hotel the interior of which looked[a hotel of which the interior looked]
11 an economist whose study focused

POINT 5 관계대명사 that
본책 p.118

1 who, whom		**2** which	
3 who		**4** which	
5 which		**6** who, whom	
7 ⓑ		**8** ⓐ	
9 ⓒ		**10** ⓐ	
11 ⓒ		**12** ⓑ	

1　What they found in the box
2　what you have to consider first
3　what your doctor told you yesterday
4　what she does in her free time
5　What I admire about Frank
6　What　　　　　　　　7　that
8　that　　　　　　　　9　what
10　what　　　　　　　11　that
12　ⓑ → what

1　who(m)[that] I took yoga classes with
　　with whom I took yoga classes
2　which[that] they would soon work in
　　in which they would soon work
3　who(m)[that] I spoke about
　　about whom I spoke
4　O　　　　　　　　　5　from whom
6　O　　　　　　　　　7　from which
8　who(m)[that]
9　one central place to which television reporters submitted

1　when we got lost while hiking
2　why Steve and Charlie are no longer teammates
3　where you can learn foreign languages
4　how the artist drew such detailed pictures
5　when / on which
6　which
7　the way / how
8　the place / where / the place where
9　at which / where
10　(A) which　(B) where

1　who was sleeping
2　which I built
3　when they can wear
4　where a new airport will be constructed
5　who(m)　　　　　　6　which
7　who　　　　　　　　8　O
9　O　　　　　　　　　10　which
11　that means → which means

1　whoever visited his house
2　However hard she tried
3　whenever you want
4　whichever you choose to play
5　whatever was happening backstage
6　whomever / anyone whom
7　when
8　wherever / at any place where
9　whatever

REVIEW TEST　　　　본책 p.124

1　③　　2　⑤　　3　④　　4　②　　5　③
6　⑤　　7　②　　8　eats → eat
9　which → when　　10　in that → where[in which]
11　that → what
12　a playwright who[that] invented many new words and expressions
13　However[No matter how] busy I am
14　people whose research or actions benefit
15　when the construction of the Statue of Liberty
16　why the universe is expanding
17　which contributes to global warming
18　What the employees wanted
19　the place where[in which] they were
20　(1) ⓑ → which[that]　(2) ⓔ → What
21　④　　22　④

1　responsibilities는 선행사(a nurse)가 소유하는 대상이므로 소유격 관계대명사 whose를 쓴다.

2　장소 선행사(space)를 수식하는 관계사절에서 관계사가 부사 역할을 하므로 관계부사 where를 쓴다.

3　· 선행사(the safest city)에 최상급이 포함되어 있고 선행사를 수식하는 관계사절에서 관계사가 전치사(of)의 목적어 역할을 하므로 관계대명사 that을 쓴다.
　　· 동사(believes)의 목적어인 명사절을 이끄는 접속사 that을 쓴다.

4　· 사람 선행사(the suspect)를 수식하는 관계사절에서 관계사가 목적어 역할을 하므로 목적격 관계대명사 whom이나 that을 쓴다.
　　· 사람 선행사(The movie star)를 수식하는 관계사절에서 관계사가 목적어 역할을 하고 계속적 용법이 쓰였으므로 목적격 관계대명사 whom을 쓴다.

5　③ 동사 is 뒤에 선행사가 없으므로, that을 선행사를 포함하는 관계대명사 what으로 고쳐야 한다.

6　⑤ 선행사(two men)가 사람이고 콤마 뒤에 「부정대명사(both) + of + whom[which]」를 써서 선행사의 전체나 일부를 나타낼 수 있으므로, them을 계속적 용법의 관계대명사 whom으로 고쳐야 한다.

7 ⓐ face는 선행사(the old man)가 소유하는 대상이므로 whom을 소유격 관계대명사 whose로 고쳐야 한다.
ⓑ 선행사 the way와 관계부사 how는 둘 중 하나만 쓸 수 있으므로 the way how를 the way나 how로 고쳐야 한다.
ⓔ '사람들이 어디에 있더라도, 우리는 그들에게 즉시 연락할 수 있다' 라는 의미이므로 no matter wherever를 양보 부사절을 이끄는 no matter where나 복합관계부사 wherever로 고쳐야 한다.

8 선행사(cows)가 복수이므로 관계대명사절의 동사 eats를 eat으로 고쳐야 한다.

9 시간 선행사(a time)를 수식하는 관계사절에서 관계사가 부사 역할을 하므로 which를 관계부사 when으로 고쳐야 한다.

10 전치사(in)가 관계대명사 바로 앞에 올 때는 관계대명사 that을 쓸 수 없고, 장소 선행사(the context)를 수식하는 관계사절에서 관계사가 부사 역할을 한다. 따라서 in that을 관계부사 where 또는 「전치사 + 관계대명사」 in which로 고쳐야 한다.

11 동사 found 뒤에 선행사가 없으므로, that을 선행사를 포함하는 관계대명사 what으로 고쳐야 한다.

12 사람 선행사(a playwright)를 수식하는 관계사절에서 관계사가 주어 역할을 하므로 주격 관계대명사 who나 that을 쓴다.

13 '아무리 ~하더라도'라는 의미의 복합관계부사 however나 양보 부사절을 이끄는 no matter how를 쓴다.

14 research or actions는 선행사(people)가 소유하는 대상이므로 소유격 관계대명사 whose를 쓴다.

15 선행사(the year)가 시간을 나타내므로 in which를 관계부사 when으로 바꿔 쓴다.

16 선행사(the reason)가 이유를 나타내므로 for which를 관계부사 why로 바꿔 쓴다.

17 관계대명사는 계속적 용법에서 「접속사 + 대명사」의 의미이므로 it을 절(Carbon ~ air)을 선행사로 쓸 수 있는 관계대명사 which로 바꿔 쓴다.

18 선행사를 포함하고 있으며 '~한 것'이라는 의미의 관계대명사 what을 쓴다.

19 장소 선행사(the place)를 수식하는 관계사절에서 관계사가 부사 역할을 하므로 관계부사 where나 「전치사 + 관계대명사」 in which를 쓴다.

20 ⓑ 사물 선행사(a spot)를 수식하는 관계사절에서 관계사가 주어 역할을 하므로 주격 관계대명사 which나 that으로 고쳐야 한다.
ⓔ 동사 determines 앞에 선행사가 없으므로 선행사를 포함하는 관계대명사 What으로 고쳐야 한다.

21 (A) 전치사 of 뒤에 선행사가 없으므로 선행사를 포함하는 관계대명사 what을 쓴다.
(B) 선행사(the box)를 수식하는 관계사절에서 관계사가 목적어 역할을 하므로 목적격 관계대명사 which를 쓴다.
(C) 선행사(the next time)를 수식하는 관계사절에서 관계사가 부사 역할을 하므로 관계부사 when을 쓴다.

22 ④ 전치사 from 뒤에 선행사가 없으므로 선행사를 포함하는 관계대명사 what으로 고쳐야 한다.

CHAPTER 12
접속사

POINT 1 등위접속사

1 but **2** or
3 and **4** so
5 and **6** but
7 or **8** so
9 and
10 but he was too busy
11 and she is learning to play the piano
12 so the residents used the side door
13 or you will burn your fingers
14 so she left the party
15 and you will get an excellent score

POINT 2 상관접속사
본책 p.129

1 Not Owen but Jason is
2 ordered both pizza and French fries
3 Either Mr. Jensen or I will interview
4 is not only modern but also beautiful
5 neither watched a play nor attended a concert
6 O **7** have
8 neither **9** O
10 and

POINT 3 명사절을 이끄는 종속접속사: that
본책 p.130

1 ⓑ **2** ⓒ
3 ⓐ **4** ⓓ
5 ⓑ **6** ⓐ
7 that **8** O
9 O **10** (A) that (B) that

POINT 4 명사절을 이끄는 종속접속사: if/whether
본책 p.131

1 Whether **2** whether
3 if / whether **4** if / whether
5 whether **6** whether the fire started
7 Whether or not the event takes place
8 if she will wear a suit or not
9 whether they should book a room
10 if our flight time has changed
11 what → if[whether]

POINT 5 명사절을 이끄는 종속접속사: 의문사 본책 p.132

1 why he arrived
2 how effective this medicine is
3 Who should be our group leader
4 how laughing affects our bodies
5 where you buy it
6 When do you think we will be
7 how the weather gets colder
8 Who do you guess broke
9 what you want
10 why I failed　　　　11 O
12 O　　　　13 Why do you believe

POINT 6 부사절을 이끄는 종속접속사: 시간/조건 본책 p.133

1 when she was young
2 Unless you hurry up
3 in case an accident happens
4 until she died in 1906
5 as long as they are accompanied by an adult
6 while he was reading the letter
7 call　　　　8 O
9 while　　　　10 is

POINT 7 부사절을 이끄는 종속접속사: 원인/양보 본책 p.134

1 since　　　　2 Though
3 While　　　　4 because of
5 Although I got enough sleep
6 despite his many injuries
7 since I wasn't[was not] familiar
8 even if you stir the two liquids
9 because of their religion
10 While my sister likes to go

POINT 8 부사절을 이끄는 종속접속사: 목적/결과 본책 p.135

1 The room was so messy that
2 so that people can study
3 He is such a good teacher that
4 so that they can predict the weather
5 so old that
6 such a long journey that
7 so that
8 (1) ⓑ → so　(2) ⓒ → that

REVIEW TEST 본책 p.136

1 ④　2 ③　3 ②　4 ⑤　5 ③
6 ④　7 ②
8 Despite → Although[Though/Even though]
9 which → that
10 does she work → she works
11 that history always glorifies the winners
12 why Sam quit playing football
13 When do you suppose the economy will recover
14 Not only Sean but (also) Paul will compete
15 or the room will become too cold
16 Although[Though/Even though] humans have drunk,
  where coffee originated
17 as soon as it is exposed to oxygen
18 until[till] it becomes syrup
19 (1) ⓐ → begins　(2) ⓒ → so
20 ③　　21 ②

1 빈칸 뒤에 or가 있으므로 상관접속사 either A or B의 either를 쓴다.

2 that은 opinion 등의 명사를 부연 설명하는 동격절을 이끈다.

3 · '그녀는 실험실에 들어가면서 경비원에게 그녀의 신분증을 보여줬다.'라는 의미이므로 접속사 as(~하면서)를 쓴다.
  · '도시에서의 생활비가 비싸졌기 때문에, 사람들은 소도시로 이사하고 있다.'라는 의미이므로 접속사 as(~하기 때문에)를 쓴다.

4 · '나는 내가 정답을 골랐는지 기억할 수 없다.'라는 의미이므로 접속사 if[whether](~인지)를 쓴다.
  · '새로운 단어의 인기는 그것이 사전에 들어갈 수 있는지 없는지 결정한다.'라는 의미이고 빈칸 바로 뒤에 or not이 있으므로 접속사 whether(~인지)를 쓴다.

5 ③ 의문사(what)가 이끄는 명사절은 「의문사 + 주어 + 동사」의 형태로 쓰므로 did Carol cook을 Carol cooked로 고쳐야 한다.

6 ④ 시간을 나타내는 부사절에서는 미래의 일을 나타낼 때 미래시제가 아닌 현재시제를 쓰므로 will come을 comes로 고쳐야 한다.

7 ⓐ 상관접속사 neither A nor B로 연결된 주어 뒤에 오는 동사는 B에 수일치시키므로 want를 wants로 고쳐야 한다.
  ⓒ 'Brian이 방 안으로 너무 조용히 걸어 들어와서 나는 깜짝 놀랐다.'라는 의미이므로, such를 「so + 형용사/부사 + that ~」의 so로 고쳐야 한다.
  ⓔ 'it ~ outside'가 절이므로 전치사 because of를 접속사 because[since/as/now that]으로 고쳐야 한다.

8 'the war ended'가 절이므로 전치사 Despite를 접속사 Although[Though/Even though]로 고쳐야 한다.

9 that은 idea 등의 명사를 부연 설명하는 동격절을 이끄므로 which를 that으로 고쳐야 한다.

10 의문사(where)가 이끄는 명사절은 「의문사 + 주어 + 동사」의 형태로 쓰므로 does she work를 she works로 고쳐야 한다.

11 '역사가 항상 승자를 미화한다는 것은 흔하게 믿어진다.'라는 의미이고 명사절이 주어로 쓰일 때는 주로 주어 자리에 가주어 it을 쓰고 진주어 명사절을 뒤로 보내므로 접속사 that을 쓴다.

12 '나는 Sam이 축구하는 것을 왜 그만뒀는지 알지 못한다.'라는 의미이고, 의문사(why)가 이끄는 명사절은 「의문사 + 주어 + 동사」의 형태로 쓴다.

13 '너는 경제가 언제 회복할 것이라고 생각하니?'라는 의미이고, 주절이 do you suppose 등의 형태인 의문문에서는 의문사(when)를 문장 맨 앞에 쓴다.

14 'A뿐만 아니라 B도'라는 의미의 not only A but (also) B를 쓴다.

15 '…해라, 그렇지 않으면 ~'이라는 의미의 「명령문 + or ~」를 쓴다.

16 첫 번째 빈칸: '비록 ~이지만'이라는 의미의 접속사 Although[Though/Even though]를 쓴다.
두 번째 빈칸: 의문사(where)가 이끄는 명사절은 「의문사 + 주어 + 동사」의 형태로 쓴다.

17 '~하자마자'라는 의미의 접속사 as soon as를 쓴다.

18 '~할 때까지'라는 의미의 접속사 until[till]을 쓴다.

19 ⓐ 시간을 나타내는 부사절에서는 미래의 일을 나타낼 때 미래시제를 쓰지 않고 현재시제를 쓰므로 begins로 고쳐야 한다.
ⓒ '너무 작아서 어떤 피해도 일으키지 않는 구멍'이라는 의미이므로 「so + 형용사/부사 + that ~」의 so로 고쳐야 한다.

20 (A) '여행용 카라반은 네가 이곳저곳 여행하는 것을 즐길 수 있도록 너의 차의 뒤에 연결된 이동식 주택이다.'라는 의미이므로 「접속사 so that ~」(~할 수 있도록)을 쓴다.
(B) '만약 야영지나 이동식 주택 주차장이 있다면 많은 가족들은 그들이 원하는 어디든 갈 수 있다.'라는 의미이므로 접속사 if(만약 ~한다면)를 쓴다.
(C) 'they are staying'이 절이므로 접속사 while(~하는 동안)을 쓴다.

21 ② 동사(think)의 목적어인 명사절을 이끄는 접속사 that으로 고쳐야 한다.

CHAPTER 13
비교구문

POINT 1 비교급과 최상급 만드는 법 본책 p.140

1	deepest	**2**	better
3	easiest	**4**	worst
5	slowly	**6**	O
7	most loudly	**8**	bigger
9	O		

POINT 2 원급 비교와 원급 관련 표현 본책 p.141

1 as well as
2 nine times as strong as
3 not as[so] nervous as
4 not so much a hobby as an obsession
5 as many books as
6 as carefully as possible
7 ⓒ → twice as many as

POINT 3 비교급 비교 본책 p.142

1 more interesting than
2 superior to
3 much higher than
4 less crowded than
5 older than
6 to   **7** O
8 than   **9** fancier
10 very → much[even/still/far/a lot]

POINT 4 비교급 관련 표현 본책 p.143

1 12,000 times hotter than
2 The longer, the more fluent
3 more and more depressed
4 no less than 500 dollars
5 the more difficult of the two
6 The colder the weather becomes, the more reluctant I am

POINT 5 최상급 비교와 최상급 관련 표현 본책 p.144

1 the deadliest epidemic
2 one of the most common birds
3 (the) farthest
4 the most exciting activity (that) I have (ever) tried
5 Quite the best bread
6 the ninth most abundant metal
7 Frank Knight was one of the most influential economists

POINT 6 원급과 비교급을 이용한 최상급 비교 표현 본책 p.145

1 No (other) snake is as[so] venomous as
No (other) snake is more venomous than
more venomous than any other snake
more venomous than all the other snakes
2 No (other) restaurant is as[so] busy as

No (other) restaurant is busier than
busier than any other restaurant
busier than all the other restaurants

3 No (other) member was as[so] diligent as
No (other) member was more diligent than
more diligent than any other member
more diligent than all the other members

4 No (other) material is as[so] hard as
No (other) material is harder than
harder than any other material
harder than all the other materials

REVIEW TEST

본책 p.146

1 ④	**2** ⑤	**3** ①	**4** ①,③	**5** ②,③				

6 ④

7 as deeper than → as[so] deep as 또는 deeper than

8 very → much[even/still/far/a lot]

9 The biology teacher is the more experienced of the two

10 one of the best ways

11 not as[so] strict as

12 six times as heavy as my cat
six times heavier than my cat

13 The earlier we get, the longer we will wait

14 as great effort as possible
as great effort as I could

15 Picasso was more innovative than all the other painters

16 the more experience he got, the more skilled he would become

17 ⑤   **18** ④   **19** ③

---

1 · 빈칸 뒤에 than이 있으므로 비교급을 쓴다. '시베리아 횡단 철도는 다른 철도 노선들보다 더 멀리 운행한다.'라는 의미이므로 '거리가 먼'이라는 의미의 비교급 farther를 쓴다. further는 '정도가 더욱'이라는 의미의 비교급이다.
· 빈칸 앞에 the가 있으므로 최상급을 쓴다. ambitious는 2음절 이상인 형용사이므로 최상급은 most ambitious의 형태이다.

2 · '…보다 −배 더 ~한/하게'는 「배수사 + as + 원급 + as」의 형태로 쓰므로 as fast를 쓴다.
· 비교급 앞에 even을 써서 '훨씬'이라는 의미로 비교급을 강조할 수 있다.

3 · '다른 어떤 …보다 더 ~한'은 「비교급 + than any other + 단수명사」의 형태로 쓰므로 place를 쓴다.
· '가장 ~한 것들 중 하나'는 「one of the + 최상급 + 복수명사」의 형태로 쓰므로 ways를 쓴다.

4 ① '가능한 한 ~한/하게'는 「as + 원급 + as + possible」의 형태로 쓰므로 more를 much로 고쳐야 한다.
③ '…하면 할수록 더 ~하다'는 「the + 비교급, the + 비교급」의 형태로 쓰므로 wise를 wiser로 고쳐야 한다.

5 ② intelligent는 2음절 이상인 형용사로 비교급이 more intelligent의

형태이므로, intelligenter and intelligenter를 more and more intelligent로 고쳐야 한다.
③ as effective than을 원급 비교 as effective as 또는 비교급 비교 more effective than으로 고쳐야 한다.

6 ⓑ '가능한 한 ~한/하게'는 「as + 원급 + as + 주어 + can」의 형태로 쓸 수 있으므로 fewer를 few로 고쳐야 한다.
ⓔ '…번째로 가장 ~한'은 「the + 서수 + 최상급 + 명사」의 형태로 쓰므로 smaller를 smallest로 고쳐야 한다.

7 as deeper than을 「No (other) + 단수명사 ~ as[so] + 원급 + as」((다른) 어떤 −도 …만큼 ~하지 않은)의 as[so] deep as 또는 「No (other) + 단수명사 ~ 비교급 + than」((다른) 어떤 −도 …보다 더 ~하지 않은)의 deeper than으로 고쳐야 한다.

8 비교급 앞에 much, even, still, far, a lot을 써서 '훨씬'이라는 의미로 비교급을 강조할 수 있으므로 very를 much[even/still/far/a lot]으로 고쳐야 한다.

9 '둘 중 더 ~한/하게'라는 의미의 「the + 비교급 + of the two」를 쓴다.

10 '가장 ~한 것들 중 하나'라는 의미의 「one of the + 최상급 + 복수명사」를 쓴다.

11 '…만큼 ~하지 않은/않게'라는 의미의 「not + as[so] + 원급 + as」를 쓴다.

12 '…보다 −배 더 ~한/하게'라는 의미의 「배수사 + as + 원급 + as」와 「배수사 + 비교급 + than」을 쓴다.

13 '…하면 할수록 더 ~하다'라는 의미의 「the + 비교급, the + 비교급」을 쓴다.

14 '가능한 한 ~한/하게'라는 의미의 「as + 원급 + as + possible」과 「as + 원급 + as + 주어 + can」을 쓴다.

15 '다른 모든 …보다 더 ~한'이라는 의미의 「비교급 + than all the other + 복수명사」를 쓴다.

16 '…하면 할수록 더 ~하다'라는 의미의 「the + 비교급, the + 비교급」을 쓴다.

17 (A) '…만큼 ~하지 않은/않게'는 「not + as[so] + 원급 + as」의 형태로 쓰므로 not so를 쓴다.
(B) superior(우수한)는 than 대신 to를 쓰는 비교급이다.
(C) '가장 ~한 것들 중 하나'는 「one of the + 최상급 + 복수명사」의 형태로 쓰므로 entries를 쓴다.

18 (A) '…보다 −배 더 ~한/하게'는 「배수사 + 비교급 + than」의 형태로 쓰므로 more를 쓴다.
(B) 비교급 앞에 a lot을 써서 '훨씬'이라는 의미로 비교급을 강조할 수 있다.
(C) 명사절이 주어로 쓰일 때는 주로 주어 자리에 가주어 it을 쓰고 진주어 명사절을 뒤로 보내므로 접속사 that을 쓴다.

19 ③ 앞에 the가 있으므로 최상급 fastest로 고쳐야 한다.

22 영어 실력을 높여주는 다양한 학습 자료 제공 HackersBook.com

CHAPTER 14
가정법

POINT 1 가정법 과거   본책 p.150

1	could buy	2	ran
3	would be	4	were to
5	were	6	should meet

7 knew, would offer
8 would perform, weren't
9 studied, could get
10 were, would apologize
11 didn't have, would watch
12 could see, owned

POINT 2 가정법 과거완료   본책 p.151

1 had prepared, could have made
2 were, would buy
3 could have traveled, had become
4 hadn't driven, wouldn't have caused
5 the witness hadn't come forward, the criminal could have avoided jail
6 the boss hadn't acted rudely, the employee wouldn't have quit the job
7 the wait had been less than an hour, we would have stood in line
8 the tourist spoke the local language, she could ask for directions
9 ⓑ → hadn't stayed

POINT 3 혼합 가정법   본책 p.152

1 had followed, wouldn't need
2 had read, would love
3 hadn't worn, would have injured
4 had turned, wouldn't be
5 had reserved, could visit
6 the bank opened today, I would have cash now
7 the hikers had packed snacks, they wouldn't be hungry
8 you had taken the medicine, you would feel better now
9 we hadn't fought yesterday, my friend would talk to me
10 I had saved your cell phone number, I could have sent you a message
11 people had watched the news, they would know about the crisis

POINT 4 I wish 가정법   본책 p.153

1	lived	2	had known
3	cleaned	4	hadn't added
5	improved	6	she kept quiet

7 I had seen the eclipse of the moon
8 I wasted all my allowance
9 he doesn't cook pasta

POINT 5 as if[though] 가정법   본책 p.154

1	had pushed	2	were
3	learned	4	had used
5	looks, were	6	ate, hadn't had
7	screamed, saw	8	talk, had been

POINT 6 if를 생략한 가정법   본책 p.155

1 Were I stronger
2 Had I known the date
3 Were she honest
4 Were I free for the night
5 Had you called this morning
6 Had the firefighters been able to arrive on time
7 Were he more cooperative
8 Had Roy washed the dishes
9 Were this seat comfortable
10 Had she drunk enough water
11 Were it my birthday
12 Had you told me about your problem

POINT 7 Without[But for] 가정법   본책 p.156

1	would communicate	2	wouldn't have known
3	couldn't create	4	would have died

5 If it were not for a recycling program
6 If it had not been for such passion
7 If it were not for the explanation
8 If it had not been for the tornado warning
9 Without the influence of minorities, we wouldn't have

POINT 8 if절 대용어구   본책 p.157

1 Made by a famous director
2 To experience the river cruise
3 with my headphones
4 A strong leader could gather
5 visited her home

6 used the correct tools
7 had worked with him
8 had been a good instructor

REVIEW TEST

1 ③ **2** ⑤ **3** ④ **4** ③ **5** ③
6 ② **7** ③ **8** will → would
9 asked → had asked **10** are → were
11 would attend → would have attended
12 the city would experience more traffic congestion
13 It's time my little brother learned how to ride
14 if she had watered it every day
15 it had not been for sunscreen
16 I had watched the movie
17 he received a better grade
18 Without his planner, he would have forgotten his
schedule
19 you had visited, you would have seen
20 ④ **21** ② **22** ⑤

1 현재의 사실과 반대되거나 실현 가능성이 거의 없는 일을 가정하고 있으므로 가정법 과거를 쓰고, 가정법 과거에서 if절의 be동사는 주어에 상관없이 were를 쓰는 것이 원칙이다.

2 과거의 사실과 반대되는 일을 가정하고 있으므로 가정법 과거완료를 쓴다. 가정법에서 if절의 동사가 「had + p.p.」인 경우 if를 생략할 수 있고 이때 주어와 had의 위치가 바뀌므로 Had를 쓴다.

3 과거에 이루지 못한 일에 대한 아쉬움을 나타내는 「I wish + 가정법 과거완료」를 써야 하므로 had stopped를 쓴다.

4 과거의 사실과 반대되는 일이 현재까지 영향을 미치는 상황을 가정하는 혼합 가정법을 써야 하므로 wouldn't be를 쓴다.

5 ③ 과거의 사실과 반대되는 일을 가정하는 가정법 과거완료를 써야 하므로 trained를 had trained로 고쳐야 한다.

6 ② 과거의 사실과 반대되는 일을 가정하는 가정법 과거완료를 써야 하므로 We had brought을 If we had brought으로 고치거나, 가정법에서 if절의 동사가 「had + p.p.」인 경우 if를 생략할 수 있고 이때 주어와 had의 위치가 바뀌므로 Had we brought으로 고쳐야 한다.

7 ⓑ 현재의 사실과 반대되거나 실현 가능성이 거의 없는 일을 가정하는 가정법 과거를 써야 하므로 will have를 would have로 고쳐야 한다. if절이 '만약 ~한다면'이라는 의미의 조건을 나타내는 부사절이라면 didn't rain을 doesn't rain으로 고쳐야 한다.
ⓔ 과거의 사실과 반대되는 일을 가정하는 가정법 과거완료를 써야 하므로 were를 had been으로 고쳐야 한다.

8 현재의 사실과 반대되거나 실현 가능성이 거의 없는 일을 가정하는 가정법 과거를 써야 하므로 will을 would로 고쳐야 한다.

9 과거의 사실과 반대되는 일을 가정하는 가정법 과거완료를 써야 하므

로 asked를 had asked로 고쳐야 한다.

10 현재 이룰 수 없거나 실현 가능성이 거의 없는 일을 소망하는 「I wish + 가정법 과거」를 써야 하므로 are를 were로 고쳐야 한다.

11 과거의 사실과 반대되는 일을 가정하는 가정법 과거완료를 써야 하므로 would attend를 would have attended로 고쳐야 한다. if절에서 if를 생략하고 주어와 had의 위치가 바뀌어 있다.

12 현재의 사실과 반대되거나 실현 가능성이 거의 없는 일을 가정하는 가정법 과거를 써야 하고 「Without + 명사(구)」는 가정법의 if절을 대신할 수 있으므로, 주절은 「주어 + 조동사의 과거형 + 동사원형 …」의 형태로 쓴다.

13 했어야 하는 일을 하지 않은 것에 대한 유감을 나타내는 「It's (about) time + 주어 + 동사의 과거형」을 쓴다.

14 과거의 사실과 반대되는 일을 가정하는 가정법 과거완료를 써야 하므로 if절은 「if + 주어 + had + p.p. ~」의 형태로 쓴다.

15 과거의 사실과 반대되는 일을 가정하는 가정법 과거완료이므로 Without을 If it had not been for로 바꿔 쓴다.

16 과거에 이루지 못한 일에 대한 아쉬움을 나타내는 「I wish + 가정법 과거완료」를 써야 하므로 had watched를 쓴다.

17 가정법에서 if절의 동사가 「had + p.p.」인 경우 if를 생략할 수 있으며, 이때 주어와 had의 위치가 바뀐다.

18 과거의 사실과 반대되는 일을 가정하는 가정법 과거완료를 써야 한다. 「Without + 명사(구)」는 가정법의 if절을 대신할 수 있으며 주절은 「주어 + 조동사의 과거형 + have + p.p. …」의 형태로 쓴다.

19 과거의 사실과 반대되는 일을 가정하는 가정법 과거완료를 써야 하므로 「if + 주어 + had + p.p. ~, 주어 + 조동사의 과거형 + have + p.p. …」의 형태로 쓴다.

20 (A) 현재의 사실과 반대되거나 실현 가능성이 거의 없는 일을 가정하는 가정법 과거를 써야 하므로 wouldn't를 쓴다.
(B) 과거의 사실과 반대되는 일을 가정하는 가정법 과거완료를 써야 하므로 had traveled를 쓴다.
(C) 가정법에서 if절의 동사가 「had + p.p.」인 경우 if를 생략할 수 있으며, 이때 주어와 had의 위치가 바뀌므로 Had the English를 쓴다.

21 (A) 동사(told)의 목적어인 명사절을 이끄는 접속사 that을 쓴다.
(B) 현재의 사실과 반대되거나 실현 가능성이 거의 없는 일을 가정하는 가정법 과거를 써야 하므로 would를 쓴다.
(C) 과거에 이루지 못한 일에 대한 아쉬움을 나타내는 「I wish + 가정법 과거완료」를 써야 하므로 had received를 쓴다.

22 ⑤ 과거의 사실과 반대되는 일을 가정하는 가정법 과거완료를 써야 하므로 hadn't helped로 고쳐야 한다.

24 영어 실력을 높여주는 다양한 학습 자료 제공 HackersBook.com

CHAPTER 15
일치와 화법

본책 p.162
POINT 1 수 일치 I

1 is	2 takes
3 find	4 was
5 remain	6 O
7 is	8 O
9 perform	10 was
11 ⓒ → develop	

POINT 2 수 일치 II
본책 p.163

1 are	2 were
3 prefer	4 drive
5 was	6 is
7 lives	8 exist
9 grow	10 is
11 are	12 ⓑ → comes

POINT 3 시제 일치
본책 p.164

1 thought, had completed
2 hoped, would depart
3 said, had to provide
4 suggested, had failed
5 implied, would live
6 complained, the shop sold
7 explains, the equipment needs
8 promised, he would be
9 remember, the community center provided
10 said, the fairies had given

POINT 4 시제 일치의 예외
본책 p.165

1 wakes	2 are
3 became	4 speak
5 take	6 humans began
7 blood is	8 the Nile River passes
9 O	10 has
11 achieved	12 O

POINT 5 화법 전환: 평서문
본책 p.166

1 said, those cookies were quite tasty
2 told, we would review the chapter that day
3 said to, The street was closed yesterday
4 told, he had lost his wallet in the park two hours before
5 said, I saw the woman stealing the car last Sunday
6 said to, I will introduce my guest now
7 tells, I need to be humble
8 said, My family lived here ten years ago
9 told, she was planning on meeting her friend the next[the following] day

POINT 6 화법 전환: 의문문/명령문
본책 p.167

1 the zookeeper if[whether] there were any lions there
2 Jenny to wear comfortable shoes
3 me when I was going to clean up my room
4 Bill to return the books by the following Monday
5 me who had called me the previous night
6 how he could install the program
7 to pay a fine
8 why I hadn't[had not] turned my report
9 if[whether] their safety helmets fit

REVIEW TEST
본책 p.168

1 ② 　 2 ⑤ 　 3 ③ 　 4 ④ 　 5 ①, ④
6 ②, ⑤ 　7 ③ 　 8 is → are
9 could she → she could 　 10 lived → live
11 Not only apples but (also) peaches are on sale
12 told, rolling stones gather no moss
13 Much of my time was spent
14 told, had to run several tests on me that day
15 asked, when she had signed that contract
16 asked, if[whether] he could borrow my textbook the next[the following] day
17 told[asked/ordered/advised], to build a wall
18 Half of the houses in the neighborhood were damaged
19 funding the construction of new bike lanes is
20 ③ 　 21 ④ 　 22 ②

1 · 주어(About 165 kilometers)가 거리의 단위인 경우 항상 단수동사를 쓰므로 is를 쓴다.
· 주어(The socks)가 분사구(lying ~ floor)의 수식을 받을 때는 수식받는 주어에 동사를 수일치시키므로 belong을 쓴다.

2 · 「some of + 명사」 형태의 주어는 of 뒤 명사(the dishes)에 동사를 수일치시키므로 are를 쓴다.
· 「the + 형용사」(The rich)는 '~한 사람들'이라는 의미로 복수명사처

럼 쓰여 복수 취급하므로 pay를 쓴다.

3 종속절이 역사적 사실을 나타낼 때는 주절의 시제(heard)와 상관없이 항상 과거시제를 쓰므로 caused를 쓴다.

4 의문사가 없는 의문문의 간접 화법은 「ask (+ 목적어) + if[whether] + 주어 + 동사」의 형태로 쓰므로 whether를 쓴다.

5 ① every가 포함된 주어(Every patient)는 항상 단수동사를 쓰므로 are를 is로 고쳐야 한다.
④ 주어가 동명사구(Ordering some sandwiches)인 경우 항상 단수동사를 쓰므로 were를 was로 고쳐야 한다.

6 ② 의문사가 있는 의문문의 간접 화법은 「ask (+ 목적어) + 의문사 + 주어 + 동사」의 형태로 쓰므로 had he를 he had로 고쳐야 한다.
⑤ 「a number of + 명사」 형태의 주어는 항상 복수동사를 쓰므로 was를 were로 고쳐야 한다.

7 ⓑ 명령문의 간접 화법은 「tell[ask, order, advise 등] + 목적어 + to 부정사」의 형태로 쓰므로 choosing을 to choose로 고쳐야 한다.
ⓔ 「neither A nor B」 형태의 주어는 B(Serbia)에 동사를 수일치시키므로 are를 is로 고쳐야 한다.

8 주어(The passengers)가 전치사구(on the ferry)의 수식을 받을 때는 수식 받는 주어에 동사를 수일치시키므로 is를 are로 고쳐야 한다.

9 의문사가 있는 의문문의 간접 화법은 「ask (+ 목적어) + 의문사 + 주어 + 동사」의 형태로 쓰므로 could she를 she could로 고쳐야 한다.

10 종속절이 일반적인 사실을 나타낼 때는 주절의 시제(heard)와 상관없이 항상 현재시제를 쓰므로 lived를 live로 고쳐야 한다.

11 「not only A but (also) B」 형태의 주어는 B(peaches)에 동사를 수일치시키므로 are를 쓴다.

12 종속절이 속담을 나타낼 때는 주절의 시제(told)와 상관없이 항상 현재시제를 쓰므로 gather를 쓴다.

13 「much of + 명사」 형태의 주어는 항상 단수동사를 쓰므로 was를 쓴다.

14 전달동사 say to는 tell로 바꾸고, 전달동사가 과거시제이므로 종속절의 have를 had로 바꾼다. 전달하는 사람의 입장에 맞게 인칭대명사 you를 me로 바꾸고 부사 today를 that day로 바꾼다.

15 의문사가 있는 의문문의 간접 화법은 「ask (+ 목적어) + 의문사 + 주어 + 동사」의 형태로 쓴다. 전달동사가 과거시제이므로 종속절의 did ~ sign을 had signed로 바꾼다. 전달하는 사람의 입장에 맞게 인칭대명사 you를 she로 바꾸고 this를 that으로 바꾼다.

16 의문사가 없는 의문문의 간접 화법은 「ask (+ 목적어) + if[whether] + 주어 + 동사」의 형태로 쓴다. 전달동사가 과거시제이므로 종속절의 Can을 could로 바꾼다. 전달하는 사람의 입장에 맞게 인칭대명사 I를 he로, your를 my로 바꾸고 부사 tomorrow를 the next[the following] day로 바꾼다.

17 명령문의 간접 화법은 「tell[ask, order, advise 등] + 목적어 + to부정사」의 형태로 쓴다.

18 「half of + 명사」 형태의 주어는 of 뒤 명사(the houses)에 동사를 수일치시키므로 were damaged를 쓴다.

19 주어가 동명사구(funding ~ lanes)인 경우 항상 단수동사를 쓰므로 is를 쓴다.

20 (A) 의문사가 없는 의문문의 간접 화법은 「ask (+ 목적어) + if[whether] + 주어 + 동사」의 형태로 쓰므로 if를 쓴다.
(B) 「B as well as A」 형태의 주어는 B(A lack of bike lanes)에 동사를 수일치시키므로 was를 쓴다.
(C) each가 포함된 주어(each person)는 항상 단수동사를 쓰고, 주어가 관계절(who ~ work)의 수식을 받을 때는 수식 받는 주어에 동사를 수일치시키므로 represents를 쓴다.

21 (A) 명령문의 간접 화법은 「tell[ask, order, advise 등] + 목적어 + to 부정사」의 형태로 쓰므로 to clean을 쓴다.
(B) 주어가 명사절(Whether ~ not)인 경우 항상 단수동사를 쓰므로 was를 쓴다.
(C) 동명사 doing 뒤에 선행사가 없으므로 선행사를 포함한 관계대명사 what을 쓴다.

22 ② 주어(places)가 전치사구(like ~ Koreatown)의 수식을 받을 때는 수식 받는 주어에 동사를 수일치시키므로 exist로 고쳐야 한다.

CHAPTER 16
특수구문

POINT 1 강조

1 does provide a discount
2 It was last Thursday that
3 It is my father who
4 did want to repair
5 It was across the street that
6 It was a giant asteroid that[which] caused the extinction of the dinosaurs
7 It was Larry that[who(m)] I saw at the swimming pool yesterday
8 It was my sales report that[which] I submitted to Ms. Thompson
9 It was the woman that[who] joined the art class at the community center

POINT 2 부정
본책 p.173

1 Not all | **2** use
3 Neither | **4** No
5 not both
6 A good beginning does not always make a good ending
7 Brent seldom goes to restaurants
8 None of us has learned how to drive

9 They have received no information
10 Not every diamond is suitable

POINT 3 도치 I
본책 p.174

1 walked the singer
2 seemed Daniel
3 she watched the scenery pass by
4 sat the boy
5 it ran
6 are several things
7 were the people
8 There was → There were

POINT 4 도치 II
본책 p.175

1 did Nancy meet her friends last month
2 was Mr. Parker impressed by the presentation I gave
3 does the Palace Hotel
4 can drivers use Elm Street due to ongoing construction
5 is Brenda allowed
6 O
7 can dolphins
8 had the baby stopped
9 does science fiction help us

POINT 5 병렬
본책 p.176

1 eats	2 turning
3 stylish	4 buy
5 interesting	6 to empty
7 needed	8 waters
9 O	10 reading
11 cleaning	12 O
13 frightening	14 (to) warn
15 (A) seek (B) going	

POINT 6 동격, 생략
본책 p.177

1 the German composer
2 flying
3 a powerful storm was approaching
4 the capital of the United Kingdom
5 he had visited 15 countries
6 allowing three-year-olds to use computers
7 we were
8 my brother
9 he is
10 you are

11 taking many pictures of the palace
12 restart the machine
13 ⓑ → that

REVIEW TEST
본책 p.178

1 ③ **2** ② **3** ① **4** ③, ⑤ **5** ①, ④
6 ② **7** ③ **8** ②
9 I realized → did I realize
10 receive → receiving
11 does need to be walked several times a day
12 was William that[who] organized the workshop for the interns
13 front of the theater he waited to meet his friend
14 longer is the restaurant offering discounts to students
15 Not all children of successful people become
16 plans to go to a resort and relax on the beach
17 does the hall have room
18 Rarely does the national park allow campfires
19 she did need more information
20 (1) ⓐ → did   (2) ⓒ → anything
21 ④   **22** ⑤

1 일반동사가 있는 문장에서 부정의 의미를 가진 말(Rarely)이 강조되어 문장 맨 앞으로 올 때는 「부정어 + do/does/did + 주어 + 동사원형」의 형태로 쓴다.

2 '~도 그렇다'라는 의미로 so를 쓸 때는 「so + 동사 + 주어」의 형태로 쓰고 앞 절의 동사(loves)가 일반동사의 현재형이므로 do를 쓴다.

3 방향의 부사구(Across the street)가 강조되어 문장 맨 앞으로 올 때 주어가 대명사(he)인 경우 주어와 동사가 주로 도치되지 않는다.

4 목적어(our wedding anniversary)를 it과 that 사이에 써서 강조할 수 있고, 강조하는 대상이 사물이므로 that 대신 which를 쓸 수 있다.

5 to travel과 등위접속사(and)로 연결되는 말은 문법적으로 형태가 같아야 하며 접속사로 to부정사가 연결될 때 뒤에 오는 to부정사에서는 to를 생략할 수 있으므로 to tour와 tour를 쓴다.

6 ② 장소의 부사구(On Jane's desk)가 강조되어 문장 맨 앞으로 올 때는 「장소의 부사(구) + 동사 + 주어」의 형태로 쓰므로 the large monitor sat을 sat the large monitor로 고쳐야 한다.

7 ③ upset과 등위접속사(and)로 연결되는 말은 문법적으로 형태가 같아야 하며 접속사로 형용사와 분사를 연결할 수 있으므로 annoy를 annoyed로 고쳐야 한다.

8 ⓐ 부정의 의미를 가진 scarcely 등은 not 등의 부정어와 함께 쓰지 않으므로 don't scarcely를 scarcely나 don't로 고쳐야 한다.
ⓒ 명사 뒤에 that절을 써서 부연 설명을 덧붙일 수 있으므로 which를 that으로 고쳐야 한다.
ⓓ ran, flapped와 등위접속사(and)로 연결되는 말은 문법적으로 형태가 같아야 하므로 start를 started로 고쳐야 한다.

9 일반동사가 있는 문장에서 부정의 의미를 가진 말(Not until I got home)이 강조되어 문장 맨 앞으로 올 때는 「부정어 + do/does/did + 주어 + 동사원형」의 형태로 쓰므로 I realized를 did I realize로 고쳐야 한다.

10 Winning과 등위접속사(and)로 연결되는 말은 문법적으로 형태가 같아야 하므로 receive를 receiving으로 고쳐야 한다.

11 일반동사(needs)를 강조할 때는 「do동사(do/does/did) + 동사원형」의 형태로 쓴다.

12 주어(William)를 it과 that 사이에 써서 강조할 수 있고, 강조하는 대상이 사람이므로 that 대신 who를 쓸 수 있다.

13 장소의 부사구(In front of the theater)가 강조되어 문장 맨 앞으로 올 때 주어가 대명사(he)인 경우 주어와 동사가 주로 도치되지 않는다.

14 be동사가 있는 문장에서 부정의 의미를 가진 말(No longer)이 강조되어 문장 맨 앞으로 올 때는 「부정어 + be동사 + 주어」의 형태로 쓴다.

15 '모두 ~인 것은 아니다'라는 의미로 문장 일부를 부정하는 not all을 쓴다.

16 to go와 등위접속사(and)로 연결되는 말은 문법적으로 형태가 같아야 하며 접속사로 to부정사가 연결될 때 뒤에 오는 to부정사에서는 to를 생략할 수 있으므로 relax를 쓴다.

17 일반동사가 있는 문장에서 부정의 의미를 가진 말(Barely)이 강조되어 문장 맨 앞으로 올 때는 「부정어 + do/does/did + 주어 + 동사원형」의 형태로 쓴다.

18 일반동사가 있는 문장에서 부정의 의미를 가진 말(Rarely)이 강조되어 문장 맨 앞으로 올 때는 「부정어 + do/does/did + 주어 + 동사원형」의 형태로 쓴다.

19 일반동사(need)를 강조할 때는 「do동사(do/does/did) + 동사원형」의 형태로 쓴다.

20 ⓐ went와 등위접속사(and)로 연결되는 말은 문법적으로 형태가 같아야 하므로 did로 고쳐야 한다.
ⓒ 부정의 의미를 가진 barely 등은 not이나 never 등의 부정어와 함께 쓰지 않으므로 anything으로 고쳐야 한다.

21 (A) 일반동사가 있는 문장에서 부정의 의미를 가진 말(Never)이 강조되어 문장 맨 앞으로 올 때는 「부정어 + do/does/did + 주어 + 동사원형」의 형태로 쓰므로 did Greg feel을 쓴다.
(B) 명사 뒤에 「of + 명사(상당어구)」를 써서 부연 설명을 덧붙일 수 있으므로 of를 쓴다.
(C) to have와 등위접속사(and)로 연결되는 말은 문법적으로 형태가 같아야 하며 접속사로 to부정사가 연결될 때 뒤에 오는 to부정사에서는 to를 생략할 수 있으므로 realize를 쓴다.

22 ⑤ 조동사가 있는 문장에서 부정의 의미를 가진 말(Only after much trial and error)이 강조되어 문장 맨 앞으로 올 때는 「부정어 + 조동사 + 주어」의 형태로 쓰므로 can they learn으로 고쳐야 한다.

수능·내신 한 번에 잡는
해커스 불변의 패턴 시리즈

해커스 수능 어법 불변의 패턴

[기본서]
필수편 [고1]

· 역대 수능·모의고사 기출에서 뽑아낸
  55개의 불변의 패턴
· 출제포인트와 함정까지 빈틈없이 대비하는
  기출 예문 및 기출 문제

[훈련서]
실력편 [고2]

· 역대 수능·모의고사 기출 분석으로
  실전에 바로 적용하는 **37개의 불패 전략**
· 핵심 문법 설명부터 실전 어법까지
  제대로 실력을 쌓는 **단계별 학습 구성**

해커스 수능 독해 불변의 패턴

[기본서]
유형편 [예비고~고1]

· 역대 수능·모평·학평에서 뽑아낸
  32개의 불변의 패턴
· 끊어 읽기와 구문 풀이로
  독해 기본기 강화

[실전서]
실전편 [고2~고3]

· 최신 수능·모평·학평 출제경향과 패턴을
  그대로 반영한 **실전모의고사 15회**
· 고난도 실전모의고사 3회분으로
  어려운 수능에 철저히 대비

해커스 중고등 교재 MAP | 나에게 맞는 교재 선택!

	초5	초6	예비중	중1	중2
문법			Hackers Grammar Smart Starter	Hackers Grammar Smart Level 1 기출로 적중 해커스 중학영문법 1학년	Hackers Grammar Smart Level 2 기출로 적중 해커스 중학영문법 2학년
서술형				해커스 쓰기 자신감 Level 1	해커스 쓰기 자신감 Level 2
구문					
독해	Hackers Reading Smart Starter Level 1	Hackers Reading Smart Starter Level 2	Hackers Reading Smart Level 1	Hackers Reading Smart Level 2 Hackers Reading Path Level 1	Hackers Reading Smart Level 3 Hackers Reading Path Level 2 해커스 첫수능 영어 기초독해
듣기				해커스 중학영어듣기 모의고사 24회 Level 1	해커스 중학영어듣기 모의고사 24회 Level 2
어휘				해커스 3연타 중학영단어 해커스 보카 중학 기초	해커스 보카 중학 필수 해커스 보카 중학 숙어

	READING	LISTENING	VOCA
토플	HACKERS APEX READING for the TOEFL iBT Basic/Intermediate/Advanced/Expert	HACKERS APEX LISTENING for the TOEFL iBT Basic/Intermediate/Advanced/Expert	HACKERS APEX VOCA for the TOEFL iBT HACKERS VOCABULARY

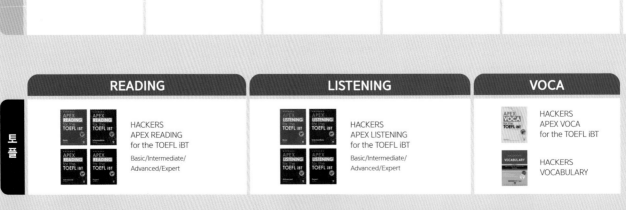